# The Human Tradition in Modern China

# The Human Tradition around the World Series
## Editors: William H. Beezley and Colin M. MacLachlan

# The Human Tradition in Modern China

Edited by
Kenneth J. Hammond and Kristin Stapleton

ROWMAN & LITTLEFIELD PUBLISHERS, INC.
Lanham • Boulder • New York • Toronto • Plymouth, UK

ROWMAN & LITTLEFIELD PUBLISHERS, INC.

Published in the United States of America
by Rowman & Littlefield Publishers, Inc.
A wholly owned subsidary of The Rowman & Littlefield Publishing Group, Inc.
4501 Forbes Boulevard, Suite 200, Lanham, Maryland 20706
www.rowmanlittlefield.com

Estover Road, Plymouth PL6 7PY, United Kingdom

Cover image: 1927 poster produced by the Political Department of the Military
Commission of the Guomindang National Government. The caption reads
"The National Revolutionary Army is the Army of the Nation's People!" Courtesy of
the Hoover Institution Archives at Stanford University.

British Library Cataloguing in Publication Information Available

**Library of Congress Cataloging-in-Publication Data**
The human tradition in modern China / edited by Kenneth J. Hammond and
Kristin Stapleton.
    p. cm. — (Human tradition around the world)
  Includes bibliographic references and index.
  ISBN-13: 978-0-7425-5465-8 (cloth : alk. paper)
  ISBN-10: 0-7425-5465-1 (cloth : alk. paper)
  ISBN-13: 978-0-7425-5466-5 (pbk. : alk. paper)
  ISBN-10: 0-7425-5466-X (pbk. : alk. paper)
  1. China—Biography. I. Hammond, Kenneth James. II. Stapleton, Kristin Eileen.
  CT1826.H855 2008
  920.051—dc22

                                                              2007028437

Printed in the United States of America

♾™ The paper used in this publication meets the minimum requirements of American
National Standard for Information Sciences—Permanence of Paper for Printed Library
Materials, ANSI/NISO Z39.48-1992.

~

# Contents

~

# Introduction

This volume picks up where its predecessor, *The Human Tradition in Premodern China*, left off. The transition to modernity in China was a complex historical process, one that has been the subject of much recent scholarship. There are many characteristics that are proposed as marking the onset of the modern period and defining modernity itself. Many of these have been derived from the experience of Europe and North America, and have reflected the historical trajectory from the Renaissance through the industrial era and into the latest age of globalization. The development of science and technology, the increasing bureaucratization of the state, the spread of industrial capitalism, and the effects of these on social and cultural life have all been seen as representative features of the early modern and modern periods. Some of these developments, such as technological innovation and bureaucracy, already had long histories in China.

Recent histories of the Ming (1368–1644) and Qing (1644–1912) dynasties, such as Timothy Brook's *The Confusions of Pleasure*, William Rowe's *Saving the World*, and Ken Pomeranz's *The Great Divergence*, have pointed to the extent to which consumer culture and other aspects of the Chinese socioeconomic order resembled the early modern culture taking shape in western Europe. Industrialization in China began in the latter half of the nineteenth century under the influence of interactions with Euro-Americans and Japanese, and its pace quickened after a political revolution led to the collapse of the imperial system in 1911–1912. The twentieth century witnessed a wide variety of political, social, and economic transformations. The Republic of China, established in 1912, was centralized under the control of the Nationalist Party after 1927. Eight years of war with Japan (1937–1945) was barely over when civil war forced the Nationalists to withdraw to the island of Taiwan, while the victorious Communist Party established the People's Republic of China (PRC) on the mainland in 1949. After a period of radical social experimentation under the leadership of Chairman Mao Zedong (1893–1976), the Communist Party opened the PRC to the rest of the world and carried out decentralizing reforms in the 1980s and 1990s, leading to rapid economic growth and cultural change.

The essays in this volume do not attempt a comprehensive analysis of the characteristics of early modern China or provide a detailed time line for the transition to modernity. On the contrary, we invite readers to use the life stories presented here to arrive at their own conclusions about what modernity means in a Chinese setting. One aspect of modernity that does have particular relevance for our project in the *Human Tradition* is the significant expansion of historical materials about ordinary people, individuals who were not the great leaders or wielders of power in their times but whose stories tell us a great deal about the history of human societies. The stories we have been able to tell in this volume include those of people whose lives were not prominent or exceptional, along with some who were. The closer we get to the present day the more we can retrieve from the historical record about ordinary lives, and the more these stories can tell us about the feel of daily life and the challenges faced by a variety of men and women.

The development of scientific thinking and practice has been widely seen as an attribute of modernity, and Ken Hammond's chapter on the Ming dynasty scholar and medical practitioner Li Shizhen shows that early modern China was the site of important activities in this area. Li's use of direct empirical investigation and systematic analysis of his materials highlight the scientific world of sixteenth-century China, and his interactions with a circle of intellectual colleagues shows that he was not an isolated or unique figure.

The position of women in society was also changing in the late Ming period. Daria Berg's chapter on the early seventeenth-century woman Xue Susu introduces a fascinating individual who not only practiced the traditional artistic skills of painting and writing poetry but also was a horsewoman and archer, a much more physically active and dynamic woman than the stereotype of the Chinese courtesan. The late Ming was a time of great social fluidity, and the roles of men and women, and of different classes in Chinese society, were in flux. Xue was able to make the most of opportunities in this environment to maximize her own interests as a cultural entrepreneur.

From the sixteenth century on China was increasingly drawn into direct interactions with the Western world. From the first ongoing European presence established at Macao in 1533 through the end of the eighteenth century this was mostly a matter of Westerners coming to China to seek their fortunes or to spread the ideas of Christianity. Western ideas and products found some niches in China, but the Chinese remained largely self-contained culturally. By the beginning of the nineteenth century this relationship began to change rapidly. The industrial revolution gave the leading Western powers a military advantage over the Chinese, and the sale of opium in China reversed the flow of silver from one that had greatly enriched China to one that drained wealth from the country at a hectic pace. British victory in the Opium War of 1839–1842 forced China to open itself to the Western world in many ways. Yet China also continued to develop on its own, carrying on rich intellectual and cultural dynamics inherited from earlier eras.

Oliver Moore's chapter on Zou Boqi shows how educated Chinese participated in the development of science and technology, not only in partnership with the West, but often on their own as well. Zou's explorations in the field of photography built on Chinese precedents and advanced the knowledge of this new mode of reproducing images among his contemporaries in mid-nineteenth-century China. As Moore notes, Zou's work on photography and the production of images indicates that China was not a passive recipient of modern technology from the West but was a place of dynamic investigation and creation in its own right.

The rise of Chinese nationalism is an important phenomenon of the last years of the nineteenth century, when many intellectuals began warning their countrymen (and women) that China seemed likely to be "carved up like a melon" by the imperialist powers. Several of the most articulate of these intellectuals lived or had spent time in Hong Kong, which had developed as a British colony populated primarily by Chinese immigrants following the 1842 Treaty of Nanjing that ended the Opium War. John Carroll introduces us to one of these men, Ho Kai, whose essays inspired many Chinese political activists. Carroll shows that Ho Kai's Chinese identity coexisted with a strong sense of allegiance to his local community in Hong Kong, which he saw as a good model for a future China. Ho Kai hoped China would develop into a constitutional monarchy, along the lines of Great Britain. He and his fellow members of the new Hong Kong bourgeoisie established trading networks across Southeast Asia and ensured the Chinese merchants based in Hong Kong had a place at the heart of global commerce.

During the lifetimes of Zou Boqi and Ho Kai, the people at the apex of the government of China were the descendants of the founders of the Qing dynasty, who considered themselves a separate people from the majority of Chinese. They called themselves the "Man" (Manchu) or banner people, and called the majority of Chinese the "Han," after one of the most illustrious dynasties of Chinese antiquity. Shuo Wang's essay provides a glimpse of life among the Manchus inside the Qing court at the end of the dynasty. The dynasty, beset by internal unrest and foreign aggression, had fallen on very hard times. To learn more about the Europeans who threatened her rule, the powerful Empress Dowager Cixi invited a young Manchu girl, who had lived in Europe because of her father's career as a diplomat, to serve as her lady-in-waiting. Der Ling's experience at court illustrates the complexity of the political situation in Beijing in the first decade of the twentieth century, and the inability of the Qing court to handle the challenges facing it. The 1911 Revolution ended the period of imperial rule in China.

Our volume next looks at people who grew up during the last years of the Qing but forged careers for themselves in the new Republic of China. Li Chenggan, as Joshua Howard shows, was influenced by a Nationalist message that identified modern industry as the way to save China. After a traditional education in the Confucian classics, Li turned to engineering and ended up as director of some of China's modern arsenals. His management techniques were heavily influenced by his neo-Confucian training, but his career illustrates the new state-centered development projects launched by the Nationalist government after 1927. In Howard's words, Li Chenggan dedicated himself to "China's struggle to modernize, resist imperialist invasion, and become self-reliant."

Students have played critical roles at several points in modern China's history. In the 1890s young examination candidates helped spark protests over China's defeat in the Sino-Japanese War of 1894–1895 and later contributed to the agitation surrounding the Hundred Days' Reform movement in 1898, when progressive officials and a modernizing emperor sought to salvage the Qing dynasty by adopting new institutions and political ideas. In the twentieth century, students were central to the emergence of new and radical movements seeking to fundamentally change China's society. Fabio Lanza presents a collective biography of students in the May Fourth Era, the mass movement beginning in 1919 that ushered in the era of revolutionary struggle that ultimately led to the rise of the Chinese Communist Party.

The collapse of the old imperial order and the conflicts that ensued plunged China into a prolonged period of tremendous stress and insecurity, which took its toll not only on institutions and public life but also on individuals. At the same time there was an increasing convergence between Western and Chinese medical practices, at least in China's great cities, which created new ways of perceiving and treating people who were suffering in various ways from the effects, physical and psychological, of China's crises. Hugh Shapiro's chapter uses medical records to take us deep into the troubled life of Jin Daming and reveals deep interconnections between one man's personal suffering and breakdown and the larger deterioration of material and mental life in Republican China.

Hu Lanqi's response to the national crisis during the first half of the twentieth century was as life shaping as Li Chenggan's or Jin Daming's but very different from each of theirs. As Kristin Stapleton writes, Hu was inspired by the activists of the New Culture Movement to reject an arranged marriage and assert her identity as an autonomous woman. When the Whampoa Military Academy started recruiting women, she joined up and found herself in the middle of the complicated Nationalist Revolution of the 1920s. Over the decades of the 1930s and 1940s she worked with both Nationalist and Communist organizations. Although she welcomed the Communist victory in 1949, her earlier involvement with non-Communist groups was held against her, and she suffered in many of the Maoist campaigns to stamp out "Rightist" thought. The story of Hu's ups and downs shows the treacherousness of Chinese politics as well as the extent to which daily life changed over the twentieth century.

Our final chapter looks at how the post-Mao economic transformation has affected the life of Zhao Ruiqin, an illiterate rural woman who traveled to the big city to work. Yihong Pan describes the huge gap in material conditions between Zhao's home village in Gansu and the national capital, Beijing, in the 1980s and 1990s. Zhao's story calls attention to the fact that much of the modern transformation that occurred in Chinese cities in the nineteenth and twentieth centuries had little impact on village life. Nevertheless, the Communist state did affect some village matters—strict birth control regulations meant that Zhao was finished with childbearing by the time she was twenty-four years old and had two living children. Thus, she was able to join the millions of other young women seeking employment opportunities in the booming cities in the 1990s. Local agencies of the state helped recruit rural laborers and introduced them to urban jobs. It is appropriate that we end this book with a chapter that shows how the great divide between rural and urban China that was in part a product of the modern period is being narrowed somewhat in recent decades by increased migration and economic development.

# CHAPTER ONE

~

# Li Shizhen: Early Modern Scientist

### Kenneth J. Hammond

One of the most characteristic features of modernity, as it has generally been understood in the history of Europe and the Western world, has been the rise of science as a system of thought and a prominent cultural paradigm. Indeed, for many people the "scientific revolution" is one of the most salient markers of the arrival of the modern era, and figures like Galileo or Francis Bacon are seen as the harbingers of the new age. By contrast, other cultures outside the West, from Africa to India or the lands of East Asia, have often been seen as in some ways also outside the rise of modernity, and the supposed absence of a "scientific revolution" in these lands has been part of their assumed "otherness." There has been no widely recognized historical personage from outside the West who has been seen as a scientist or scientific thinker.

Recent scholarship has begun, however, to modify this view. Both in terms of Western history and the history of other parts of the world, there has been a good deal of discussion of new kinds of periodization and new understandings of the processes by which the world has become "modern." Modernity has come to be seen as having deep roots, extending back several centuries at least. And a period increasingly referred to as the early modern is now seen as having preceded the development of a fully modern age, often associated with the rise of industrial society in Europe and North America. These new discussions of modernity have also extended to reexamining the history of other parts of the world, and this has led to new insights and understandings.

1

It is increasingly apparent that in at least some places, such as India, the Middle East, and China, many of the features of early modernity were present in the centuries before the rise of Western industrialism and colonialism. Indeed, in some ways early modernity in these regions might have preceded similar developments in Europe.

The position of science and scientific thought in areas outside Europe is one area where our understanding of early modern history has been changing. It is increasingly clear that there were comparable, sometimes parallel, developments taking place in Asia or the Islamic world and that the history of science needs to be reconsidered in a more globally balanced way. This has in some instances been a matter of the discovery of new knowledge or information, while in other cases it has been more a process of rethinking material that has been known for a long time.

One such instance is the subject of this chapter. In the sixteenth century in China, Li Shizhen was a medical practitioner and a researcher of materia medica, the various herbs, drugs or other substances that were used to prepare medications. Over a long span of years, Li traveled around China studying local plants, animals, minerals, and other kinds of things used for medical purposes. He visited libraries at local academies or the private collections of scholars. He met with colleagues. He kept careful notes and eventually wrote up his work as a compendium of pharmaceutical knowledge called the *Bencao gangmu*, the *Systematic Materia Medica*, which was published in 1596, after Li's death. Li was not an isolated individual but rather a participant in a vibrant intellectual culture in which he shared his ideas and results with others and took part in an ongoing conversation about understanding the world and how it works. In both his own work and through this dynamic intellectual community, Li represents the early modern development of scientific thought in China.

Li Shizhen was born in 1518 in the village of Waxiaopa, near the city of Qizhou, located in the Yangzi River valley in central China, in what is today Hubei province. This was a fairly prosperous region, enriched by the growing trade along the river that was part of an overall expansion of the commercial economy in the Ming dynasty. The Ming had been established in 1368 as the previous rule of the Mongol Yuan dynasty collapsed. After a period of stabilization and political consolidation through the end of the fourteenth century and into the early decades of the fifteenth, China's economy began a long period of growth, which featured an especially rapid expansion of commercial activity. Localized centers of commodity production developed in several regions of China, and these were increasingly linked through long-distance trading mechanisms. The Yangzi River was one of the most important east-west routes for trade goods, linking the rich interior region of the Sichuan Basin and the tea-growing areas of modern Hunan province to the Jiangnan area, the richest and most advanced part of the empire, which was a major center for both silk and cotton textile production. Qizhou was not far southeast of Wuchang, the provincial capital, where north-south overland routes crossed the east-west artery of the Yangzi. This was also a region where plants such as wormwood and other medicinal herbs grew and that had a strong local tradition of medical knowledge.

Li Shizhen's family had been engaged in the practice of medicine for several generations by the time of his birth. The practice of medicine was a respected profession in Ming China. Since the Song dynasty (960–1279) there had been a growing level of specialization and professional qualification among medical men. Indeed, this was period when the practice of medicine became increasingly dominated by educated men from the ranks of the elite, the *shidafu* or literati. Healing had long been associated with shamanism and midwifery, generally the realm of female practitioners. In the early modern period there was a gender shift in which women were increasingly marginalized and stigmatized as witches or dismissed as "grannies," while men came to be seen as serious doctors and scholars of medicine. The highest calling of the literati was to serve as officials in the imperial government. But the number of available positions fell far short of the number of educated men competing for them, and elite gentlemen increasingly found themselves seeking careers in other fields. Teaching and medicine were respectable livelihoods with an appropriate intellectual cachet.

Li Shizhen's grandfather was probably an itinerant peddler of medical preparations. These men were called "bell doctors" because they rang a kind of bell to let people know they were passing in the street or setting up a stall in a marketplace. Although he died when Li Shizhen was only a small boy, and thus had little direct influence on Li's development, it seems likely that it was his success in this field that allowed the family to accumulate sufficient wealth to educate his son, Li Shizhen's father, to sit for the imperial civil service examination. The examinations were the main means of recruiting talented young men into service in the imperial administration. A complex system of local, provincial, and national exams had developed since they began to be widely used in the Song dynasty, though some recruitment through examinations went much further back in Chinese history. In the Ming, examinations took place over a three-year cycle, with only about 10 percent of candidates passing at each level. Only around three hundred men passed the highest level exams every three years. This was a very narrow path to the top of the imperial system, but even to pass the lower exams brought prestige and often career advancement.

Preparing a young man for the challenge of undertaking the civil examinations was a major investment for a family to make. The examinations relied heavily on the reproduction of the classical texts of the Confucian tradition, which had to be memorized for immediate recall by the examinee. The ability to compose poetry in certain prescribed forms was also important. To learn the requisite texts and master the correct forms and styles, a young man would have to study full-time for many years. It was quite rare for a man to pass the examinations at an age younger than twenty. Boys began preparing for the exams at around three years of age. Full preparation thus often took eighteen or more years. During this time a boy would not be available to his family for productive labor, so a family had to have a certain level of economic security and disposable resources to be able to afford to educate a son for the exams. Li Shizhen's grandfather had to have accumulated sufficient wealth to be able to spare his son from gainful employment and spend his youth studying.

Li Shizhen's father, Li Yanwen, passed the lowest level exam but, like the great majority of examination takers, seems not to have advanced any further in the system. He remained in Qizhou and pursued a medical career. Later in his life, in 1549 when his son Shizhen was already thirty-one years old, he received an appointment to the Imperial Medical Academy in Beijing, the capital, where he studied further and had access to the important medical library there. After a period of life in the capital, though, Li Yanwen returned to Qizhou and resumed his role as a respected doctor in the local community. He not only practiced medicine but also wrote books about diagnosis, on certain medicinal plants, and on the disease smallpox. He was widely known as an authority on the use of the measurement of the pulse as a diagnostic technique, though he was careful to note that this could not be used in isolation from other means of assessment. He was also the author of a famous book, one of the first of its kind, on the ginseng root and its medicinal properties.

Li Yanwen was the father of two sons and a daughter and seems to have early on sensed in his son Shizhen the potential for outstanding intellectual achievement. He supported the boy in studying for the imperial examinations, perhaps hoping like his father before him that success in the higher examinations would lead to a career in government and with that an overall rise in the family's fortunes. This was the greatest ambition of most educated men in early modern China, and Li Yanwen might have hoped that success in the exams for Shizhen would erase his own memories of having failed to rise above the first level.

Li Shizhen would have spent many hours each day in his studies, and this might account for the fact that he was not a robust child. He was frequently ill, and not surprisingly this gave rise in him to a strong interest in medicine. He was a bright and articulate boy, and discussed medical questions with his father. Nonetheless it was the family's hope that he would rise in the civil examination system and bring prestige and prosperity to the household, rather than taking up his father's and grandfather's profession.

In 1531, when he was only thirteen years old, Li Shizhen passed the county-level examination, which entitled him to enroll in the county school in preparation for the next level of the exams. He failed, however, to pass the provincial examinations in three successive tries, and after 1538 he abandoned further efforts. Whether or not his father was disappointed in him, he turned his attention to medicine and science and in the end became a much more important figure than most civil officials. He took up his practice in Qizhou, alongside his father, first retreating to his parents' home to read and study the medical classics, then beginning to work with his father, learning through observation and practical experience.

In the course of the 1540s, Li Shizhen's career took off, and he began to develop a reputation in his own right for the effective diagnosis and treatment of diseases. He became frustrated, however, with the state of knowledge about medicines and the materials used to produce them. The study of pharmacology had ancient roots in China. Much of the knowledge about the effects of various substances on the human body came from the spiritual discipline known as Daoism. This was a mystical set of doctrines emphasizing harmony with natural order, tracing its origins back to the ideas of the sage Laozi, a perhaps semimythical figure from the Warring States Period (481–221 BCE). Around the third century of the present era, Daoism developed an intense interest in the quest for immortality, a process that often involved ingesting magical elixirs that allowed the spiritual seeker to enter into communication with the realm of the Immortals. While some of these elixirs contained toxins like mercury, other components included a variety of hallucinogenic compounds. Daoist masters often undertook systematic investigation of the properties of plant and animal materials to evaluate their potential efficacy as agents of the transcendent experience. In this they were not unlike medieval alchemists in Western history who made great contributions to the development of chemical knowledge. As Daoist masters learned more and more about the properties and uses of various substances, they learned not only which were effective in enhancing spiritual encounters with the hidden realm of the Immortals but also many things that were useful in more mundane applications. Over the centuries this knowledge came to be recorded and organized in books and manuals of pharmacology.

During the Song dynasty, as the first stirrings of early modern commercial development took place in China, changes in the field of medicine, along with the rise of commercial printing and publishing, led to the proliferation of books dedicated to spreading knowledge of the pharmacopoeia, the whole range of materials used in making medicines. Song publishers produced great compendia in many areas of knowledge, not only medicine. But the demand for such information led to the compilation of works with the term *bencao*, literally trees and grasses, in their titles. These provided a model for Li Shizhen's later efforts.

During the following Yuan dynasty, from 1272 to 1368, medical scholars began to critique some of these collections, and in the first two centuries of the Ming period this process continued. Many of the criticisms focused on the absence of solid practical evidence of the use or effectiveness of substances discussed, or in some cases the mythical nature of materials described, which were not in fact real plants or animals but exotic fantasies handed down from ancient times.

As he developed his own medical practice in Qizhou during the 1540s, Li Shizhen came to share in the critical view of many received texts about medicinal materials. He began to conduct his own investigations into the properties and efficacies of various prescriptions contained in the classical medical texts and more recent compendia. Initially, he could only engage in these activities as a sideline. He was still learning much about medicine from his father and gaining direct experience diagnosing and treating patients. He was apparently talented and industrious in this work, and as noted he began to develop a very positive reputation in the central Yangzi region. He came to the attention of the household of the Prince of Chu around 1550, when he was called in to diagnose and treat the son of Zhu Xian, the prince at that time. Chu was an ancient name for the central Yangzi area, and it was the practice of the Ming dynasty to appoint the sons of emperors to hereditary fiefs in important regions around the empire. In 1551 a new prince succeeded to the local throne, Zhu Yingxian, who occupied the princely court at Wuchang until he died in 1571. Imperial princes maintained their own courtly establishments, and Li Shizhen was appointed to a ceremonial post that included responsibilities for medical care at the court. The exact date of his appointment is not known, nor is it clear if the youth he had treated was the heir to the princely throne, but the ascension of the new prince in 1551 would certainly have provided a fitting occasion to reward Li's service with such a prestigious position.

His appointment to a princely court further enhanced Li's reputation. After serving in Wuchang for a short period he was further honored with appointment to the Imperial Medical Academy in Beijing, following closely on his father's service there in 1549. Li Yanwen provided introductions to prominent medical men in the capital who could aid Li Shizhen in his studies.

Like his father, Li Shizhen did not stay at the capital for a very long time and returned to Qizhou to carry on his private medical practice and research. Nonetheless, his time in the capital was of great significance in providing him the opportunity to read rare books in the medical library, and to examine a range of medical materials in the imperial pharmacy, at least some of which would not have been available to him in his native region. Despite having access to the imperial library and the medical collection in the capital, however, Li remained unsatisfied with the state of pharmacological knowledge.

It was after his return to Qizhou by the end of 1552 that Li Shizhen seems to have embarked on what would become his life's work and his greatest scientific legacy. From 1552 to 1578, with some revisions and additions continuing even after that date, Li devoted himself to the empirical investigation of plants, animals, minerals, and other substances used in making medicines, and written about in the received medical literature. He combined practices of textual criticism and comparison that were deeply rooted in the Confucian exegetical tradition with more practical examination of materials and their effects. He observed the administration of many different kinds of medicinal preparations and noted both what they seemed to do and how this compared with qualities and effects attributed to them.

For the first few years of this project Li worked mostly at home. He read many texts available in the libraries of local wealthy families and gathered and examined herbs and other materials from the local area. But before long he came to feel that to make a truly serious analysis and correction of the state of pharmaceutical knowledge he would have to broaden his geographic base. He simply could not find all the extant writings on the subject in his region, nor could he find samples of many of the materials discussed. Beginning in 1556 he undertook a series of journeys around the empire, visiting other scholars, reading widely in both private libraries and in the collections of academies and schools in many places, and seeking out any opportunity to directly study medical materials and their effects. From his writings we know he traveled in the modern central Chinese provinces of Jiangxi, Jiangsu, Anhui, Hebei, and Hunan, and he might well have visited other areas as well, possibly including the large southwestern province Sichuan. Jiangsu includes many of the wealthiest towns and cities of early modern China and was the region with the highest concentration of literati families, the educated elite that dominated the cultural and intellectual life of the empire. Travel along the great waterway of the Yangzi River would have been relatively easy and convenient, and this seems to have formed the main axis of his journeys.

These travels brought Li into contact with other scholars and allowed him to develop his ideas through conversation and sharing time during visits to their homes, as well as through ongoing correspondence before or after actual meetings. Some of the most prominent intellectual figures of mid-sixteenth-century China were among Li's circle of friends, including Gu Wen, a prominent official who was also noted as a philosophical thinker, and his brother Gu Que, also an official; Luo Hongxian, a geographer; and Chu Jiusi, who was an official scholar at the Hanlin Academy in Beijing, the most prominent scholarly institution in the empire. Another important friend was also an imperial prince, Zhu Houkun, though Li does not seem to have ever held office under this branch of the imperial family. These men shared Li's commitment to solid research and the investigation of things, and the circulation and refining of ideas among such correspondents was an important part of the development of scientific thought in China in the early modern period. The relationship with the Gu brothers was especially close, and indeed the Li and Gu families remained closely linked over several generations, with Gu Que's grandson writing a biographical study of the Li family.

One other individual needs to be mentioned in relation to Li Shizhen and his work. This is Wang Shizhen, perhaps the most prominent intellectual and cultural figure of the later sixteenth century in China. He belonged to a wealthy family in the Jiangnan town of Taicang and had a dramatic career in government service that brought him into conflict with some of the most powerful political leaders of the time. This resulted in Wang spending several periods in enforced retirement at his home, during which he pursued his own literary and other studies and became famous as a patron of the arts and scholarship, as well as a builder of gardens. Late in his career Li Shizhen sought out Wang Shizhen and asked him to write a preface to the book Li had produced as a result of his researches. Wang did so, and his preface became a lasting testimony to the importance of Li's work in the development of Chinese scientific thought and practice. We will return to the encounter between Li and Wang shortly, but first we need to consider the outcome of Li Shizhen's travels and research.

In the course of his career Li Shizhen wrote perhaps a dozen books. Most of these dealt with medical topics such as diagnosis and symptomology, and included one devoted to the study of a type of snake found in his native region that was known for its healing properties. He also, in the manner of most educated gentleman in imperial China, produced a collection of poetry. Most of these writings are no longer to be found.

The crowning work of Li's life, though, was the *Bencao gangmu*. It was in this book that Li brought together the results of his textual criticism and his empirical investigations. To understand Li's role as an early modern scientist we must understand this work in some detail. In the course of his travels, and during his time at the Imperial Medical Academy, Li had been able to read a wide range of materials. These included some 40 previous studies of the pharmacopoeia, 361 other medical texts, and an additional 591 books, some of them historical or literary in nature, others compilations of information about natural phenomena or other subjects. Of the medical texts cited, 277 were used by Li Shizhen for the first time, thus considerably expanding the base of references in his research. A considerable portion of the other works used by Li had not been previously cited in the study of medical materials, some three-quarters of the total number.

Li not only expanded the inventory of sources used in his study but also incorporated information about new plants and other materials that had not been studied earlier. Among these were new plants introduced into China in the sixteenth century as a result of contact with Europeans, notably the Spanish through their trade in the Philippines. These included sweet potatoes and maize, which began to be used as food crops and also were used in some medical applications. Li also took note of the appearance of syphilis in China, also brought by the Spanish from the New World. The appearance of these newly introduced foods and diseases in Li's book remind us of how much in flux the world of the sixteenth century was and how this unsettled existing fields of knowledge as well as ways of life.

Li's methods of observation, and his way of thinking about the plants and animals he observed in particular, foreshadow, and to some extent directly influenced, later developments in the scientific understanding of biology and ecology. He noted ways in which particular organisms seemed to have adapted themselves to particular ecological niches. He described, without necessarily being able to explain, what we understand as genetic characteristics, and the way traits are passed down in generations. He was also aware of intentional manipulation of traits and the practices of selective breeding. Indeed, as knowledge of Li Shizhen's work entered into Western scientific circles through the writings of Jesuit missionaries that circulated back in Europe, they ultimately came to be part of the source materials used by Charles Darwin in developing his theories about evolution and natural selection. Li's study of materia medica was both a textual and an empirical enterprise.

Having worked his way through this vast array of source material, and having spent many years in the direct study of a wide range of substances and their uses, Li then undertook to revise the traditional ways in which knowledge about medical materials was organized and to present the results of his investigations in a new and more systematic way. This was the main task of the *Bencao gangmu*. Li based his system of organization on the morphology, or appearance, of plants, animals, mineral, and other substances, with a total of 1,892 individual entries. He devoted seven chapters to inanimate things like water, fire, earth, metals, and stones. Twenty-five chapters dealt with plants, and another fifteen with animals, including humans. One chapter was concerned with things like clothing and utensils to be used by medical practitioners. There were two sections of illustrations, showing some 1,100 images of minerals, plants, and animals to be used in identifying materials. Li also included a bibliography of the works he had consulted, an important aspect of his efforts to contribute to the ongoing study of materia medica.

One of Li's main concerns in writing his book was the concept of the "rectification of names." This is an idea that goes back to the origins of Confucian philosophy. Confucius is reported to have said that to establish good government he would take the "rectification of names" as his first task. By this he meant specifically the return to proper ritual terminology, which had been abandoned in the period of political disarray known as the Spring and Autumn Period, beginning in about 771 BCE. But the idea became more generalized and came to be seen as underlying the proper organization of knowledge as well. Li wished to ensure that items included in the *Bencao* were properly identified and referred to in a consistent and standardized way. He endeavored to use the earliest recorded name used for a particular substance as the proper one, while noting the many synonyms that might have occurred over time. This kind of approach to the problem of standardization has become the accepted scientific norm in modern times.

The *Bencao gangmu* was more than just a compendium of information. It was also to be used as a guide to medical practice. Li included some 11,096 prescriptions in the text and outlined the principles he believed should be used in prescribing medications for particular diseases or conditions. In this he sought to apply the knowledge he had developed through his own empirical investigations and to set the stage for the further testing of his results in actual practice.

Li worked on the *Bencao* for more than twenty years before putting it into an initial form for circulation. By 1578 he was preparing the first edition of the text in manuscript. As this work came together he decided to approach Wang Shizhen and ask him to write a preface to the book. It was a common practice in early modern China for prefaces by prominent scholars to be solicited in order to enhance the commercial appeal of a book, and this might have been part of Li Shizhen's motivation in approaching Wang. Wang Shizhen was widely known and admired for his literary views and writings, and as an arbiter of good taste and quality in cultural and intellectual life. Having his name associated with the *Bencao gangmu* would have been a commercially valuable move.

But it seems likely that Li Shizhen was seeking more than a marketing boost in establishing a connection with Wang Shizhen. Wang was also engaged in historical studies that were part of the intellectual current in China that would later develop into the school of evidential studies, a method of careful, critical analysis of texts and other kinds of historical materials like paintings that attempted to rationally understand their significance and meaning. This kind of critical scholarship was related to the scientific studies of Li Shizhen, and Li might have hoped that Wang would embrace his work as that of a kindred spirit. In this he was not to be disappointed.

Li Shizhen went to Wang Shizhen's home in the fall of 1580. Wang agreed to write a preface for the *Bencao gangmu*, and the two men seem to have spent a pleasant time visiting and getting to know one another. Wang wrote a poem to commemorate the occasion and recorded his pleasure at making Li's acquaintance in some occasional notes written at the time. It appears, however, that Wang did not immediately set about writing the actual preface. Indeed, it was not until ten years later that Wang finally sent the completed preface to Li. The preface refers to some new materials added to the *Bencao* between 1580 and 1587, when the final version of the text seems to have seen settled.

In the preface he ultimately produced for the book, Wang highly praised Li's project and particularly noted the careful rationality of the research Li had carried out to produce the text. He used the terminology of science then current in China, referring to Li's work as an exercise in the investigation of things, and noting Li's delineation of natural principles. He emphasizes the role of the rectification of names in Li's organization of his information. Wang's preface to the *Bencao gangmu* situates the work in the early modern development of scientific thought and singles out Li Shizhen as an exemplar of the ideals of scholarship and empirical research. Li himself presented his work as an exercise in the investigation of things and the elaboration of natural patterns and principles, and Wang's endorsement of this underlines the fact that Li's conception of natural science was not isolated or unique.

Obtaining this preface might, in the end, have played a useful role in getting the *Bencao gangmu* published. Li Shizhen was able to get Hu Chenglong, a commercial publisher in Nanjing, the secondary capital of the Ming dynasty, to agree to bring out the book, and the process of carving the wooden printing blocks got under way early in the 1590s. Sadly, however, Li Shizhen died in 1593, before the book was actually in print. The first edition of the text did not come out until 1596. A second edition was produced in 1603, and it was this slightly revised and expanded version that became the model for the many subsequent printings through later centuries. Li's work was rapidly recognized as an important contribution to the scientific study of medical materials. Its fame soon spread to other countries as well. Translations of parts of the book appeared in Japanese by 1637 and in Western languages including Latin in 1656, French in 1735, and English in 1736.

Li Shizhen's life, of course, encompassed more than his masterwork of pharmacology. Although he had not succeeded in rising up the ladder of success in the imperial examination system, his medical career, and his fame as a scholar of early modern medicine, gave him the means to not only pursue his research and writing but also advance his family's fortunes. Though Li was married and had four sons, we do not know his wife's name. His sons, however, were all able to receive good educations, indicating the level of economic prosperity the family had attained. The eldest son, Li Jianzhong, succeeded where his grandfather and father had not, and passed the second, provincial level of the civil examinations, receiving the *juren* degree in 1564. He went on to have a modest career in local administration in southwest China. The other three sons were also successes in their own ways. The second, Li Jianyuan, became a student at the provincial academy, while the fourth, Li Jianmu, studied at the local school in Qizhou. Li's third son, Li Jianfang, followed both his father and grandfather to the Imperial College of Medicine in Beijing, though he seems to have stayed there for a longer career than either of his predecessors.

The prosperity built up in Li's lifetime carried on to one more generation. Three of Li's grandsons achieved at least some success, with Li Shuben becoming known as a calligrapher and Li Shuzhong having a modest literary career. But it was Li Shuchu who brought the fortunes of Li Shizhen's family to their height, passing the highest level of the civil examinations and winning the *jinshi* degree in 1619. He pursued an official career, which included military posts. In 1627 he had a memorial arch built to honor his family, recording great achievements by his ancestors, including of course Li Shizhen. The good fortune of the Li family, however, seems to have come to an end in the chaos that brought the Ming dynasty to an end in the middle of the seventeenth century. Li Shuchu was killed in 1643, the year before the final fall of the dynasty, by rebels while defending his hometown of Qizhou.

In the wars that engulfed central China with the transition from the Ming to the Qing dynasty, the Li family sank into obscurity.

The fame of Li Shizhen, however, was assured by the success of the *Bencao gangmu*. The full development of the early modern scientific thought and practical activities of Li Shizhen and his circle of intellectual correspondents did not take place in China until the twentieth century. The Qing conquest in the mid-seventeenth century, and the troubled history of China's interactions with the Western world through the final centuries of imperial rule, led the course of China's intellectual history in somewhat different directions, which eventually led to a convergence with Western science in the last century. Li Shizhen has been reclaimed in modern China as an exemplar of China's own scientific culture and has been widely studied. His book has been reprinted in modern editions, in both Taiwan and the People's Republic.

## Further Reading

Elman, Benjamin. *On Their Own Terms: Science in China, 1550–1900*. Cambridge, Mass.: Harvard University Press, 2005.

Lloyd, Geoffrey, and Nathan Sivin. *The Way and the Word: Science and Medicine in Early China and Greece*. New Haven, Conn.: Yale University Press, 2002.

CHAPTER TWO

~

# Amazon, Artist, and Adventurer: A Courtesan in Late Imperial China

*Daria Berg*

## The Pleasure Quarters of Late Imperial China

A seventeenth-century Chinese eyewitness called the Qinhuai, the pleasure quarters of old Nanjing, the "Capital of the Immortals in the World of Lust."[1] In late imperial China this corner of the world exerted a considerable impact on its visitors, observers, and chroniclers, who fell prey to its charms and attractions. The Qinhuai River divided Nanjing in a curious way: to the north there was the traditional examination compound, the site of China's examination hell, where scholars competed for entry into the civil service, China's imperial administration. Passing the examinations would open doors into the charmed circle of the elite and would provide membership of the ruling class in a meritocratic system. It was a world enticingly open to all: anyone could compete, apart from women, slaves, and the offspring of prostitutes. To the south of the river, nestled within the city walls, you would find the pleasure quarters that exercised the imagination of the literati, China's intellectual and political elite, and have continued to fascinate modern-day students of China's past.

The Qinhuai existed as a place of song, dance, and entertainment for centuries. When Nanjing was the capital of China in the fourteenth century, the first Ming emperor (r. 1368–1398) officially established its pleasure quarters. They flourished until the end of the Ming dynasty (1368–1644) in the mid-seventeenth century. The place was situated within the cultural heartland of late imperial China, the Yangzi Delta region. The economic prosperity of this area in the late Ming era was mainly due to its salt monopoly, the port cities that fueled trade with Japan, the influx of silver from Japan and Peru during a time of worldwide economic growth, and the fact that the highest-ranking officials in the imperial administration tended to choose it as a place to settle and retire.

The fall of the Ming dynasty in 1644 reduced the Qinhuai pleasure quarters to ruins. The Qing dynasty (1644–1911) took control over China, and the new Manchu government declared prostitution to be no longer official. The profession continued in the private sector but never regained its former glory. Later literati looked back with nostalgia to the days when the Qinhuai had flourished. Many poets and writers imagined and recreated its past glamour in their writings. The famous scholar-official Wang Shizhen (1634–1711), for example, recalled the atmosphere as a place of bittersweet romance and tragedy:

Throughout the ages the boats of Nanjing witnessed the breaking of many hearts,
The pavilions on the banks of the Qinhuai river are filled with dreams.[2]

## The Chinese Courtesan

The inhabitants of the Qinhuai were the courtesans, although the place also housed a large number of artists and their families. The Chinese term for prostitute (jinü) refers to both the common lowly prostitute and the high-class courtesan. Modern scholars have used the term geisha for the Chinese courtesan. Geisha is a suitable term as it literally means "artist," but it remains peculiar to the Japanese context, referring to a strict training process and hierarchy. The Chinese system for training courtesans, however, did not draw such clear-cut boundaries or distinctions.

The Chinese courtesan differed from a prostitute by virtue of her fame and artistic talent. She acquired the status of mingji (literally, famous prostitute) or courtesan, a term better suited for those jinü (prostitutes) who were literate, highly trained, and specialized entertainers, performers, and artists and not primarily paid for sexual services. The late imperial Chinese courtesan participated in and belonged to the world of letters, the domain of the literati, China's male elite. She was not only a well-known woman who became public property by virtue of being written about but also a writing woman who usually distinguished herself by means of her poetry and whose literary works, calligraphy, or paintings circulated in public.

The history of the courtesan in China dates back to the institution of singing girls at the court of the Zhou dynasty (eleventh century BCE–256 BCE) when princes kept troupes of trained female entertainers (*nüyue*) who later became attributes of social prominence. Private troupes remained exclusive to ruling-class families due to economic constraints, while professional entertainers became available in commercial brothels. Courtesans began to share in literati culture only in the days of the Tang dynasty (618–907) when court entertainers became part of the Office of Music Instruction in 714.

In late Ming times courtesans appeared at the center of elite culture, featuring as prominent protagonists in poetry, plays, and prose pieces. Simultaneously they also gained fame as poetesses, calligraphers, and painters in their own right. Famous courtesans formed intellectual companionships with elite men, sharing their interest in learning and helping out in the scholars' studios, composing poetry, compiling, collating, editing, proofreading, and annotating literary works. Courtesans of outstanding literary talent would also acquire the semihonorific title of female "collator" or "book reviser" (*jiaoshu*).

In contrast to gentry women, courtesans were even able to own property in their own right. Some courtesans invested their savings in town mansions, country villas, and gardens. They used these sites to entertain elite men, often with a view to making a good match in marriage before their fame declined or old age put an end to their careers.

The Manchu rulers ended state patronage of official courtesans and restored orthodoxy during the Qing dynasty. As a consequence courtesan culture declined, while gentlewomen from ruling-class families began to take part in elite culture instead. This process entailed the vulgarization of the courtesan as her caliber plummeted and the economic basis of courtesan culture dissipated.

## Girls in Gaily Painted Boats

The girls of Qinhuai lived in "gaily painted boats," as male connoisseurs described their vision of the establishments on the river. The male observers conjured up images of banquets, song, and dance on the floating brothels. One poem tells us that the music never ended in the realm of mist and flowers. Another writer evoked the profusion of lanterns and boats on the Qinhuai River and depicted the scene thus: "When dusk fell, it did not take long until the lantern boats accumulated like the wriggling of a fire-spitting dragon and their lights glowed so bright that they lit up both the land and the sky."[3] The resonance of the drumbeats shook the waves, and the noise of gaudy celebration continued until dawn. This is how male observers perceived the sights of the Qinhuai.

However, the girls on the gaily painted boats lived a life of servitude, not much different from slavery. Some of them had been sold into prostitution, while others came as war trophies or Mongol captives. They spent their days in subservience and often ended them in poverty, even if they had enjoyed fame and fortune in their prime. Others committed suicide in desperation. These aspects of their lives do not feature prominently in the writings about courtesans, nor in the courtesans' own works. Feelings of pity and the awareness of the link between sex, bondage, and shame came to the literati only later, across the distance of time, when the world of Qinhuai had vanished. Looking back in time, they suddenly perceived the waters of the Qinhuai to be "soaked in tears." The courtesans by contrast would express their anger, if they did so at all, only through wit and sarcasm.

Modern scholars who write about female entertainers in China have reminded us of the more prosaic sides of the courtesans' lives. The exchange of sex work for money finds mention only in the accounts of modern historians. This choice of vocabulary would not have occurred in the late imperial Chinese discourse, neither in the words of the literati nor in those of the women writers. The concept of exchange, however, played an important role on another level, as we shall see below.

In the view of the law, the girls on the boats counted among the social outcasts. Traditional opinion relegated actresses, artists, and prostitutes to the bottom of the social scale, and as we have noted, imperial Chinese law excluded their offspring from the civil service in perpetuity.

## Bohemian Beauty

Listen to the voice of one of the beauties of Qinhuai, the courtesan Xue Susu (ca. 1565–ca. 1650),[4] inviting the scholar-official Censor He to drink on an autumn day:

> Inside the city walls of stone in the pleasure quarters,
> I feel deeply mortified that my talents outshine all the others.
> The river glitters, the waters clear, and seagulls swim in pairs,
> The sky looks hollow, the clouds serene, and wild geese fly in rows.
> My embroidered dress partly borrows the hue of hibiscus,
> The emerald wine shares the scent of lotus.
> If I did not reciprocate your feelings,
> Would I dare feast with you, Master He?[5]

Xue Susu counted among the most accomplished artists and entertainers in late imperial China. A bohemian free spirit so full of paradoxes and complexities, she merits a closer look to see what her story can tell us about women, life, and culture in late imperial China. Xue Susu stands at the center of a social network of negotiations and exchange that revolves around not only seduction and money but also poetry, paintings, emotions, elegance, luxury, and dreams of gentility.

The sources are divided about the details of Xue Susu's place and date of birth, background, career, and death. She was probably born in either Suzhou or Jiaxing sometime between 1565 and 1573: she must have been at least fifteen years of age when a famous art critic admired her painting sometime prior to 1588. She gained fame as a courtesan and artist in the Yangzi Delta region and spent a number of years in Nanjing.

One of Xue Susu's admirers, Hu Yinglin, composed an erotic poem for Susu when she was living in Nanjing in her teens:

Who transplanted this flower of a renowned species to the imperial garden?
Hers is a smile worth a thousand pieces of gold.
She lives near the mooring like Taoye [Peach Leaf], under the wind.
She resembles rushes, standing in the water, embracing the moon and humming.
The red phoenix (shoe) is half raised because of her mate.
Her eye-brows are slightly frowning, expecting a heart to share.
This is the moment to read "Eternal regret," the poem of Bo Juyi . . .
Beside the bed, she is awaiting the lute of jade.[6]

This poem gives evidence that Xue Susu did live in the Qinhuai pleasure quarters during her time in Nanjing, or at least that she was associated with the place in the literati's minds. The Peach Leaf Ford (Taoye du) near the Bridge of Convenient Fording was a well-known tourist attraction in the Qinhuai. Its name reminded visitors of the Jin dynasty calligrapher, painter, and scholar Wang Xianzhi (344–386) who wrote a poem about the place where he parted from his lover and concubine, the courtesan Peach Leaf, who then crossed the canal at this point.

Susu thus appears as one of the many bohemian beauties, artists, and entertainers that populated the Qinhuai, a place that boasted the most talented and high-ranking courtesans of late imperial China. Perhaps she lived there only for a few years, not long enough to make it into the diaries and notes of Qinhuai visitors such as Yu Huai (1616–1696) who depicted the delights of the place and recorded the names and details of its most famous inhabitants, or Pan Zhiheng (1556–1622). Perhaps there were simply too many celebrated courtesans to list and catalog them all. Or perhaps, at least in Yu Huai's case, the omission is simply due to the fact that she lived in Qinhuai over half a century before his time.

In the literati's eyes Xue Susu, too, belonged to the Qinhuai and its world of pleasure and seduction. It is likely that she only became truly famous later on, after she had left the Qinhuai. She seems to have established her reputation as a celebrity in literati circles only during her stay in Beijing in the 1590s where she hosted poetry parties and literary soirees for poets, scholars, officials, and military officers. She would entertain her patrons with her poetry and play a jade lute at banquets. Her martial spirit earned her a reputation as an archer, a horsewoman, and a knight-errant, and she would display her Amazonian skills on horseback in public. She even became involved in political campaigns and adventures. And yet, despite her public prominence, she almost disappeared from sight for nearly half a century when her career as a courtesan in the public eye appears to have ended.

After 1600 her traces become blurred. At around that time she probably married and left courtesan life behind. It is possible that she lived into the 1650s, as she seems to have joined a circle of prominent women writers and artists with whom she exchanged poems and paintings in mid-seventeenth-century Hangzhou. Her invisibility over the decades between her time as a celebrated courtesan and her death might be connected to her marital history during those decades. As a wife and concubine, she seems to have become a much-prized and jealously guarded commodity.

## Flowers and Flute: The Courtesan Painter

As an artist, Xue Susu's reputation soared beyond that of many other courtesans, and in the minds of later generations she acquired a place among the "Eight Great Courtesans of the Ming Dynasty." Xue Susu's paintings can be dated from 1598 to 1637, although other undated works also exist.

Like many courtesans, she excelled at depicting orchids. This flower symbolized purity and seclusion and was perceived as a secluded, hidden rarity, just like the courtesan herself. One scholar wrote with admiration of Dong Xiaowan (1624–1651), another renowned Qinhuai courtesan: "I found her again like a fragrant orchid flower growing in a secluded valley."[7] The orchid was also associated with a young girl's chamber or a marital chamber, symbolizing love and beauty. A union of golden orchids denoted the bond of friendship or love. In the ancient classic Yijing (Book of Changes), the orchid refers to harmony. In the late imperial Chinese imagination the orchid was

seen as a symbol of gentlemanly and scholarly ideals. In all its different connotations, it aptly epitomizes the courtesan's situation in the social no-man's-
land between feminine eroticism and masculine erudition.

Susu also painted bamboo, plum blossoms, chrysanthemums, and other
flowers, as did other courtesan painters. One painted fan by Xue Susu shows
a cicada on a leaf. The cicada was thought of as an emblem of resurrection
because of the insect's life cycle. The imagery of the cicada also evoked associations of beautiful women.

Xue Susu also displayed her skills in figure painting—a subject less commonly tackled by courtesan painters. The leading painter and art critic of the
day, Dong Qichang (1555–1636), is said to have fallen in love with her
painting in ink of the bodhisattva Guanyin the moment he saw it. Full of enthusiasm for her work, he copied out the Heart Sutra to accompany the
painting and affixed it with a colophon.

She also produced a portrait of a girl on a garden terrace, playing a flute.
The figure is seated in the midst of a rock garden, framed by flowers and a
bamboo tree. Modern art critics surmise that it might be a stylized self-
portrait. Like the girl in the painting, Susu would play the flute at parties.
On an allegorical level, representations of flute-playing women also had
erotic connotations; a picture by the Yuan dynasty painter Qian Xian, for
example, shows the archetypal lover, the Tang dynasty emperor Xuanzong
(r. 712–756), teaching his favorite concubine Yang Guifei (700–755),
China's most famous femme fatale, to play the flute.

## Amazon and Archer

Legends also ranked around the reputation of Xue Susu as an archer and
horsewoman. Her Amazon style inspired artistic and literary representations
not only in the late Ming era but also in later times, as a woodblock carving
of Susu on horseback practicing archery shows. In her childhood she spent
some time in Beijing and practiced archery on horseback outside the city
walls on the open fields. Hu Yinglin describes her skills in vivid detail:

> She also excels at horse riding and archery. She is able to shoot two balls from
> her crossbow one after another and make the second ball strike the first ball
> and break it in mid-air. Another trick she can do is to place a ball on the
> ground and, by pulling the bow backwards with her left hand, while her right
> hand draws the bow from behind her back, hit it. Out of a hundred shots, she
> does not miss a single one.[8]

Susu was not too shy to display her skills in public. Her performances on horseback attracted large crowds, and she also entertained the guests at her parties with her archery. The poet Lu Bi composed a poem entitled "The Song of Observing Susu Perform Archery":

Tipsy on wine we request her to perform a game of archery,
She ties a thin shirt around her waist and nonchalantly gives it a trial shot.
Her red sleeves wrapped up slightly half expose her archer's armguard,
Her hair tied like a cloud in a knot, she tilts her head to estimate the distance
and stretches her arms [to guide the crossbow and arrow].
When the servant girl takes a ball in her hand and places it on top of her head,
She turns around, hits it with another ball, and both balls fall to the ground.
She is ready much faster than it takes to recount,
And while we still wish she would carry on a bit longer, she is done.[9]

## In the Literati's Eyes

Xue Susu primarily appears in the historical sources through the filter of male-authored discourse. In her earlier years, the poet, scholar, and bibliophile Hu Yinglin (1551–1602) was smitten with Susu's skills as an artist and archer. Here he describes her beauty and talent: "Xue Wu [Susu] has a lovely and elegant appearance. She talks in a sophisticated way and her comportment is graceful. She excels at regular style calligraphy and surpasses anyone in painting bamboo and orchids. She employs swift strokes of the brush and her paintings testify to her liveliness."[10]

By the time Hu Yinglin's notes on Xue Susu were published in 1581, she must have been at least a young teenager. This would also suggest that she was born between 1565 and 1570. Hu Yinglin recalled that, on their first meeting, she had called him the "most outstanding scholar of his time." He in turn addressed her with the gender-neutral honorific "Master Xue" and enthused, "Even those famous painters with excellent skills cannot surpass her."[11]

Hu also exchanged poetry with Susu. His poems describe the parties she hosted; praise her prowess as a poet, artist, and horsewoman; and reminisce about mutual faraway friends.

The scholar-official, painter, and art critic Li Rihua (1565–1635) was another of her admirers and lovers who became her husband for some time. He commented with sarcasm on Susu having become a Buddhist and a vegetarian in later life. In his note on her portrait of the "Bodhisattva Guanyin in Flower" he wrote,

Xue [Susu] was good at playing the zither and lute, styling her eyebrows, and curling the hair on her temples. This made her so lovely and delightful that she would seduce men one after another. However, when she advanced in age, men would be tempted elsewhere and there was little she could do about it. Here again she has painted a delicate image of the Bodhisattva to pray for all couples in love in this world to have offspring. As she makes up for a great deficiency in this way, I am delighted to express my praise for her.[12]

This is one of the few surviving comments on Xue Susu from the first decades of the seventeenth century, written sometime before 1635.

After her death another scholar remembered her glamour and charm:

In spite of her long life, ingenious Xue retained her glamorous reputation. After she passed away, legends grew around her saying that she had possessed witchcraft by means of which she attached younger men to her. But this is fiction only. Studying her portrait, one sees a fastidious but unpretentious woman. It is more likely that, as Daoist tradition has it, her high spiritual power preserved her charm.[13]

## Culture and Commerce

Xue Susu's native Yangzi Delta region in late Ming China appears as a hotbed of cultural activities. The era witnessed a flourishing of the creative arts and new developments in literature, painting, and color printing. But it was also an era characterized by the literati's inward turn as many scholar-officials withdrew from public life, frustrated with corruption at court and at all levels of the civil service. Many of them began to devote more time to the arts and became obsessed with elegant living, religious events, and unorthodox cults.

A period of worldwide economic growth at the turn of the seventeenth century fanned the economic boom in China. As silver dollars rolled into China from as far as Japan and Peru, the coastal cities in particular, those centers of trade close to ports and canals, saw the arts flourish on an unprecedented scale. One Qinhuai visitor described the opulence and conspicuous consumption of the place at that time:

The markets and shops in the pleasure quarters looked neat, tidy and rather unusual. They only sold luxury goods of the highest quality such as perfume sachets, embroidered slippers, well-known wines, delicious teas, malt-sugar candies, pickled savouries, pan pipes, flutes, strings and lutes. The male buyers from the outside world did not mind the exorbitant prices and thus the girls never received vulgar or ordinary gifts.[14]

New developments in print technology and book distribution let the publishing industry boom. Commercial publishers produced not only textbooks for the rising numbers of examination candidates and aspiring scholars but also literature for entertainment, catering to a new audience of urban dwellers, newly rich merchant families, and educated women. The publishing industry responded to an increasing demand for fictional narratives; poetry; anthologies; guidebooks on style, elegance, and gentility; erotic handbooks; pornography; and a flood of romantic literature, including works of prose, poetry, and drama on love and emotions.

In the late Ming women appeared in ever-increasing numbers as the authors of works of poetry and drama and as the editors of literary anthologies. Changes in the perceptions of women led to the formation of a new beauty ideal. The literati began to celebrate women who combined talent, beauty, and virtue and showed a particular fascination with female child prodigies and talented teenage girls who often tragically died young. In the literati's perception these young females appeared to embody purity, simplicity, and sincerity in a way no man could.

In the late Ming intellectual climate, the cult of emotions played an important part in the lives of the literati. They celebrated love and romance in the creative arts and valorized the courtesan in their prose, poetry, and drama. In the eyes of the connoisseurs, the courtesan would enact the drama of emotions in her life and give her literati lovers a part to play in the spectacle. Mixing myth, fantasy, and memory, the elite men would perceive the courtesan as the emblem of literati culture, embodying aestheticism, talent, and beauty. The tragic fate of many a courtesan—bondage, servitude, subordination, and even premature death or suicide—appeared to the literati as an apt allegory for their own political situation at the end of the Ming dynasty and also later on when the foreign Manchu rulers had forced China into submission. The courtesan acquired an aura of glamour and fame in the minds of her audience.

## The Gentlewomen's Gaze

We see Xue Susu not only through male eyes but also from the female perspective, depicted through the gentlewomen's (guixiu) gaze. In late Ming times gentlewomen, or gentry women from literati or scholar-official families, members of the ruling class and intellectual elite, did have some contact with high-class courtesans and shared with them the same literary culture. They even composed poems for courtesans.

Xu Yuan (1560–1620) was an unconventional poetess from Suzhou and the wife of a high-ranking scholar-official, the secretary in the Ministry of War Fan Yunlin (1558–1641), another admirer of Xue Susu and her paintings. Xu Yuan wrote a series of five poems for Susu in which she goes into raptures about the beauty of the courtesan's body:

> Beneath the curves of your soles and the delicate petticoats lotus grows,
> Your waist so willowy and feather-light you could dance on a palm.[15]

Xu Yuan might have overstepped social boundaries in forging friendships with courtesans, but her readers did not criticize her for it, and she enjoyed literary fame.

Lu Qingzi (fl. 1590), another gentry poetess from Suzhou who shared Xu Yuan's literary circle, also composed verse for the courtesans she counted among her friends and visitors. Here she depicts the beauty of one of them:

> Poem for a Courtesan
> In a frock the hue of halcyon and a gown purple as peony,
> You arrive deep in a meadow dotted with flowers on your ornamental carriage.
> Picking a red leaf to inscribe some impromptu verse,
> You have no need to envy Collator Xue [the courtesan poetess], of bygone days.[16]

It is not clear whether Lu Qingzi, a close friend of Xu Yuan's, also knew or met Xue Susu. Her reference to Collator Xue, the Tang dynasty courtesan and poetess Xue Tao (768–ca. 832) could be read as an allusion to Xue Susu, as in Xu Yuan's poems for Susu. Hu Yinglin confirms that people referred to Susu as "collator" when she was only a teenager living in the Qinhuai. Xue Susu herself used the term "female collator" as her sobriquet in the seal on one of her paintings in 1633. Hence it is possible that the above poem by the gentlewoman Lu Qingzi addresses none other than Xue Susu.

Lu Qingzi celebrates in her poetry the emotions she shares with female friends, both other gentry wives and female entertainers. She does not refrain from expressing her feelings of love and longing for these women. In the poem quoted above she highlights both the courtesan's physical beauty and her literary ability.

Huang Yuanjie (ca. 1620–ca. 1669), a professional artist and writer from an impoverished literati family in Jiaxing, Zhejiang province, exchanged calligraphy and paintings with Xue Susu. She was known as a Ming loyalist who, after losing her husband, supported herself by selling her paintings and poetry. She lived with some famous gentry women poets and also the courtesan Liu Rushi (1618–1664). After the fall of the Ming dynasty, Xue Susu became Huang Yuanjie's neighbor in Hangzhou on the shores of the West Lake, and the gentry woman and the courtesan began to entertain each other. During the late 1640s, Susu must have already been in her eighties. These examples show how courtesans and gentry ladies occasionally shared the same literary culture in late imperial China.

## Emancipation, Power, and Politics

Courtesans reached male-level proficiency in literature and the arts. Calligraphy, painting, and poetry traditionally counted as male-gentry arts. In Xue Susu's earlier days, a few gentry women followed in the courtesans' footsteps and distinguished themselves in these domains, too. Talented courtesans often literally earned their reputation as "collators" or "book revisers" as they participated in their literati partners' literary activities in the studio, helping to collate, edit, discuss, and compose poetry.

The literati removed the courtesans from cultural constraints by gentrifying and masculinizing them. They amused themselves by cross-dressing courtesans as members of the elite, a pastime made possible by the luxury trades in fashions in late Ming times. Such events took place at a time when gentry wives only gradually and slowly began to push gender boundaries in literacy and the arts.

Another favorite literati pastime in the pleasure quarters was to play the flower register game. The literati ranked and crowned courtesans as examination candidates. They performed a kind of cross-dressing in status terms, making the courtesans parade as degree holders. They entered the girls' names in a mock honor roll, pretending they equaled the highest degree holders, or "advanced scholars." The game contained double irony as not only women but in particular the prostitutes and their offspring counted among the few social groups barred from participating in the public examinations. In this ironic and bizarre way the entertainment quarters reflected the competition and rat race for success in the official world, as if holding up a grotesque mirror to the examination system and power politics that were being played out in the triennial provincial examination compound across the river. By way of punning on the word *ye*—meaning to melt, fuse metal; to seduce; and also used to refer to Nanjing—the Qinhuai became the melting pot of power politics as well as a place of temptation and seduction.

Xue Susu enjoyed autonomy over her life to a certain extent and exerted authority in her world as she was in the position to choose her lovers. Her contemporaries depict her as rejecting generous and extravagant offers by love-struck suitors who would lavish thousands of taels in gold on her. One observer tells us that she held herself in high esteem and refused to receive common people, accepting only learned and intelligent men. Rumors circulated that the Pacification Commissioner Peng of Youyang in Sichuan spent a fortune on her, but to no avail. The same fate befell a Mr. Feng from Suzhou who falsely boasted he could possess Xue Susu and lavished an enormous amount of gold on her without getting anywhere.

Seventeenth-century sources inform us that Xue Susu was married several times, but none of the unions lasted. This is a curious statement in the context of late imperial Chinese society with its Confucian hierarchy and male-dominated lifestyle, raising questions about a courtesan's emancipation and autonomy. It is conceivable that she outlived her husbands, as courtesans often married older men. Another possibility is that her husbands terminated the marriage as men often did with courtesan concubines who were then passed on from one to another. Or perhaps the courtesan herself decided to end the relationships. We know that Xue Susu terminated at least one of her affairs, and other courtesans also managed to escape from unsatisfactory or disappointing unions.

Xue Susu's husbands or long-term partners included high-ranking and influential men from various walks of life: a military officer, called Li the Subduer of Barbarians; famous literati such as the scholar and painter Li Rihua and the dramatist and essayist Shen Defu (1578–1642); and finally a wealthy merchant from Suzhou who was her last husband as she was growing older.

It was not unusual for a celebrated courtesan to propose marriage to men, as Xue Susu did when she sought a relationship with her military officer. Another prominent example is that of the courtesan Liu Rushi, who visited the distinguished and elderly scholar-official Qian Qianyi (1608–1664) to propose marriage to him. Other courtesans acted in similar ways: the Qinhuai courtesan and painter Bian Sai proposed to the poet Wu Weiye (1609–1671), and another star of Qinhuai, the courtesan Dong Xiaowan, proposed to the poet Mao Xiang (1611–1693).

Xue Susu's Amazon spirit showed in her prowess not only as a horsewoman and archer but also as a political activist on the national stage. During her stay in Beijing she met the National University student Yuan Baode (d. 1604) who became her lover. In 1592 she urged him to suppress a rebellion and later encouraged him to lead an expedition against the Japanese in

Korea and offered to provide the necessary funding. When he failed to comply Xue Susu left in a huff and ended the relationship:

> With great composure she said to him: "Although you have elderly parents, you still linger here in idle recreation. Is this because of me? As I cannot emulate the Duchess of Qian and assist you in bringing glory to your family, I certainly cannot bear to let you offend against propriety. Even if some day you were to consume my flesh, that would still not be adequate as an expiation for my offence. I should leave." Weizhi [Yuan Baode] was too attached to her to go along with this, so Susu without warning mounted her quick steed and set off for the south. Only after three days had passed did Weizhi learn of her departure. En route she dispatched a servant with a packet of one hundred taels to deliver to Weizhi, accompanied by a letter bidding him farewell and declaring that she would no longer be his lover.[17]

This episode as recounted by Song Maocheng (1569–ca. 1620), an unconventional scholar and classical storyteller from Songjiang, casts Xue Susu in the shape of a female knight-errant (*nüxia*).

## The Female Knight-Errant

The concept of chivalry (*xia*), a powerful force guiding human behavior, appears as even more important than love and passion (*qing*) in the late Ming era. The concern with chivalry reflects the literati's attempts to restore a martial spirit to late Ming culture. As an Amazon, artist, and adventurer, Xue Susu became the symbol of such aspirations.

Xue Susu chose "Fifth Boy," as one of her sobriquets, and considered herself a bold, generous, and chivalrous heroine.[18] She described herself as a knight-errant. Hu Yinglin confirmed that her spirit was "heroic" and called her a knight-errant. Xu Yuan's husband Fan Yunlin, who acquired one of her ink orchid fans and treasured it like a piece of precious jade, praised this quality in Susu, too. He commented in his colophon on her painting of flowers dated 1615,

> Once during the time when Sujun [Xue Susu] was in the "blue building" [brothel], from even a Tiger Hill [excursion] boat did I espy half her face, and then I realized that she was not just another pretty powdered [face]. . . . As for the other [stories] about Sujun, such as the account of downing birds with pellets, of not sparing a thousand pieces of gold to rescue someone from the most desperate circumstances, they testify truly to her reputation as a female knight-errant of all ages—deserving far more praise than a mere mention on a page of discourse from a treatise on painting.[19]

Other courtesans portrayed as knights-errant include the famous Ming loyalist Liu Rushi; the Qinhuai poet, painter, and dramatist Ma Shouzhen (1548–1604); and the Nanjing courtesan Yang Wan (ca. 1600–ca. 1647). Another Qinhuai beauty, Kou Baimen (fl. mid-seventeenth century), also claimed the status of a knight-errant after buying herself out of an unsatisfactory marriage to a wealthy military commander; she then lived her life as she pleased, received poets and statesmen at her garden studio, and later ended a union with a scholar when she lost interest in him.

The courtesans themselves echoed the male discourse that endowed them with this martial and chivalrous spirit. This phenomenon resonates through the late Ming discourse: the Suzhou courtesan Du Wei, who like Susu selected her partners herself, called herself a "knight among women."[20] The anthology Qingshi leilüe (Anatomy of Love) compiled sometime after 1628 by the master storyteller Feng Menglong (1574–1646)—a contemporary of Xue Susu—also features a story about a courtesan knight-errant called Zhang.

## Paradoxes

In the stories and lives of late imperial China's courtesans, paradoxes abound: despite their lowly status, they gained recognition as artists and poetesses ahead of ruling-class women. Despite their condition of servitude, they enjoyed autonomy of body and spirit as no elite lady did. The courtesans also found themselves free to travel, in contrast to the cloistered gentlewomen.

Xue Susu, like many other courtesans and gentlewomen of her time, became devoted to Buddhism and began to prefer the life of a recluse. In 1633 she inscribed the following poem about her life as a recluse on a painted fan depicting chrysanthemums and bamboo:

> After the frost the twig turned pale gold,
> Its blossoms by the wattle fence in the mellow twilight of dusk about to unfold.
> Why should I bother to drink again with another in the hills of the South?
> Dwelling in seclusion I have plenty of dry provisions in my house.[21]

Another seventeenth-century courtesan painter from Qinhuai who was known as Fan Jue appeared to her male observers as even more extreme:

> She discarded all her clothes and ornaments, musical instruments, and all other items that looked gay, luxurious or extravagant. The only thing she did was to shut her doors, burn incense, make tea and sit down with nothing but a stove for brewing medicines and several volumes of sutras.[22]

The theme of the courtesan's hermit lifestyle and withdrawal from the world also echoes the late Ming literati's frustration with official life and their desire to leave the world of politics. In their depictions of courtesans these male writers constructed these women as mirror images of their own fantasies and desires. Xue Susu imagined herself as a hermit in another poem entitled "Painting Orchids":

> In a deserted dale there is a beauty who surpasses all the others,
> Her belt sports kingfisher-blue gauze, her body is made of jade.
> But I regret to say that she gets confused with the common grasses,
> Her secret scent remains her own unknown surprise.[23]

Another paradox of the discourse on courtesans lies in the conflation of the concepts of chivalry and chastity. The scholar and artist Chen Jiru (1558–1639) defined the term knight-errant (xia) in the late Ming as follows: "A chivalrous official is a man who is loyal, a chivalrous lady is a woman who is chaste, and a chivalrous companion is someone who is reliable."[24] This shows that in late Ming perceptions the courtesan who is described as chivalrous takes on a male or androgynous role—that of the official or friend—rather than that of a woman. Or perhaps she embodies a masculine version of chastity on an allegorical level, as a mirror image of a loyal official or a reliable companion. In depicting the courtesan as combining chivalry and chastity the literati yet again envisaged her as crossing and transcending traditional gender boundaries.

The extraordinary story of Xue Susu might leave us wondering whether a woman artist and adventurer like her was perhaps above all a Bohemian, a figure of free-and-easy habits, an eccentric lady in an almost modern sense who defied convention but for whom her contemporaries had no other classification than that of a courtesan. In her lyrical imagination, she does not always appear as a performer and entertainer but also as a solitary poet and artist who has found fulfillment in life. Let her have the last word, as the woman of pleasure portrays herself as a woman whose pleasure is hers alone:

> Drinking in Solitude
> Full of aroma is the taste of wine beneath the bloom,
> Tinged in azure the gate surrounded by bamboo.
> In solitude I watch the seagulls sail across the sky,
> Carefree and content, I feel fully satisfied.[25]

## Further Reading

Cass, Victoria Baldwin. *Dangerous Women: Warriors, Grannies, and Geishas of the Ming* (Lanham, Md.: Rowman and Littlefield, 1999).

Levy, Howard. *A Feast of Mist and Flowers: The Gay Quarters of Nanking at the End of the Ming* (Yokohama, Japan: no pub., 1966).

## Notes

1. I am indebted to Professor Alan Barr for his insightful comments on an earlier version of this chapter.

2. Wang Shizhen, "Qinhuai zashi," in *Yuyang shanren jinghualu xunzuan*, comp. Hui Dong (*SBBY* edition), 5A.29a-32a, poem 1.

3. Yu Huai, *Banqiao zaji* (Shanghai: Shanghai zhengqi shuju, 1949), A.2.

4. Xue Susu had many names. Apart from Susu, her personal names include Wu, Suju, Suqing, Runniang, Runqing, Qiaoqiao, and Su.

5. Xue Susu, "Qiuri you He shiyu yin de hangzi," in Zhang Mengzheng, *Qinglou yunyu* (1616, repr. Shanghai: Guji, 1994), 1.78–79.

6. Tseng Yu-ho, "Hsüeh Wu and Her Orchids in the Collection of the Honolulu Academy of Arts," *Arts Asiatiques* 2, no. 3 (1955): 197–208, 203. Transcription adapted by the author.

7. Mao Pijiang, *The Reminiscences of Tung Hsiao-wan*, trans. Pan Tze-yen (Shanghai: Commercial Press, 1931), 12.

8. Hu Yinglin, *Jiayi shengyan* (1581), repr. in *Shuoku*, ed. Wang Wenru (Hangzhou, China: Zhejiang guji chubanshe, 1986), 5a.

9. Qian Qianyi, *Liechao shiji xiaozhuan* (Shanghai: Gudian wenxue chubanshe, 1957), 770.

10. Hu Yinglin, *Jiayi shengyan*, 5a.

11. Hu Yinglin, *Jiayi shengyan*, 5a.

12. Li Rihua, "Xue Su huali Guanyin xiang," in Bian Yongyu, *Shigutang shuhua huikao* (1682, repr. n.p., 1921), 30.28b–29a.

13. Kang-i Sun Chang and Haun Saussy, eds., *Women Writers of Traditional China: An Anthology of Poetry and Criticism* (Stanford, Calif.: Stanford University Press, 1999), 228.

14. Yu Huai, *Banqiao zaji*, A.3–4.

15. Xu Yuan, "Zeng Xue Susu wushou," *Luoweiyin* (1613, microfilm Taipei, China: Guoli zhongyang tushuguan, 1986), 8.23a.

16. Lu Qingzi, "Zeng ji," in Zhong Xing, *Mingyuan shigui*, repr. *Siku quanshu cunmu congshu, jibu* 339 (Jinan, China: Qilu shushe chuban, 1997), 32.20b.

17. Allan Barr, "The Wanli Context of the 'Courtesan's Jewel Box' Story," *Harvard Journal of Asiatic Studies* 57, no. 1 (1997): 107–41, 122.

18. This term appears on one of her painted fans. See Tang Shuyu, *Yutai huashi*, *Meishu Congshu* edition (Shanghai: Shenzhou guoguangshe, 1928–1936).

19. Marsha Weidner et al., *Views from Jade Terrace: Chinese Women Artists, 1300–1912* (New York: Rizzoli, 1988), 85.

20. Barr, "The Wanli Context," 127.

21. Xue Susu, "Zhuju tushan mian," repr. in Weidner et al., *Views from Jade Terrace*, 86, 225.

22. Yu Huai, *Banqiao zaji*, B.11.

23. Xue Susu, "Hua lan," in Zhong Xing, *Mingyuan shigui*, repr. *Siku quanshu cunmu congshu, jibu* 339 (Jinan, China: Qilu shushe chuban, 1997), 31.13a.

24. Chen Jiru, *Chen Meigong xiansheng quanji* (Ming edition; microfilm in National Central Library, Taiwan), 4.37a.

25. Xue Susu, "Du zhuo," in Zhong Xing, *Mingyuan shigui*, repr. *Siku quanshu cunmu congshu, jibu* 339 (Jinan, China: Qilu shushe chuban, 1997), 31.12b–13a.

# CHAPTER THREE

Zou Boqi on Vision and Photography
in Nineteenth-Century China

*Oliver Moore*

In 1869, on an unrecorded day in late June or early July, Zou Boqi (1819–1869), a well-known member of the gentry in Guangdong province died prematurely and unexpectedly at fifty. His death followed several years of apparently deliberate attempts to avoid notice from the political establishment and to not court too much attention within late Qing scholarship. Only a few years earlier, Zou Boqi had turned down two separate job offers from the leading actors in national politics inviting him to work in the newly established and most forward-looking academic colleges of the day. Aside from his contribution to a topographical work on Guangzhou, he had published none of the writings that he bequeathed to his relatives and admirers. They at least saw fit to edit and print a portion of them. The remaining facts of Zou Boqi's life are few, so that he is unlikely to gain the same lengthy attention that biographers devote to more richly documented subjects of his period. Certainly, he is by no means a household name on a par with the famous Ming savant Li Shizhen, also featured in this volume, but, as a scholar and a member of China's ruling class, his life attracted considerably more of his contemporaries' notice than those discussed in most other chapters.

More valuable than the scant biographical record, however, is what concerns Zou Boqi's scientific interests. These provide the means to relate the man and his ideas to some of the major intellectual and social changes of the nineteenth century. Zou Boqi was one of a number of men and women who advanced the century's growing interest in mechanics and technology and, above all, its application to new forms of vision. He was also a cardinal figure in the earliest Chinese history of photography. Finally, the manner in which he expressed his interests permits a rewarding view of a Qing scholar facing the advent of China's modernization, a man fully conscious of his intellectual obligations to China's intellectual heritage and, at the same time, receptive to new views of a changing world.

To look at Zou Boqi is more than just a metaphor for academic inquiry, for Zou might have been the author of his own self-portraits taken with a plate camera that he constructed himself. One of these slightly theatrical enigmas is reproduced as figure 3.1. The image represents one of the earliest surviving photographic expressions of a Chinese biographical subject. However, Zou was engaged in more than just reflexive acts of looking, for he was a paradigmatic figure in the Chinese educated classes' broader awareness of new technologies that China needed to assimilate in its efforts to modernize. Thus, to call Zou Boqi a photographer is to isolate only one of his many activities, but it provides a useful thread for the larger story of his interests and their context in China. The photographic camera and its antecedent, the camera obscura, are the mechanisms of visual media, and Zou's interest in them was at the base of his concerns to define physical surroundings and astronomical patterns as well as to record human portraits through a means of visualization that symbolized a radical break with the past.

The nineteenth century was a period when the visual assumed ever-growing importance in both Eastern and Western cultures' engagement with nearly all branches of knowledge. Processes such as photography, new forms of printing (e.g., lithography—printing from stone plates), and three-dimensional molding (seldom recalled or even used outside highly specialist agencies today) were crucial to many societies' various experiences of modernization. Historians of Western culture generally acknowledge that the nineteenth century witnessed the culmination of several centuries' shift from aural to visual modes of interpreting experience.[1] Arguably, in China, this shift occurred over an even longer period —especially given China's much earlier discovery of printing texts and images —but the nineteenth century was equally a period of rapid advance in developing and using new technologies of vision and observation. Zou Boqi was only one participant, and a minor one at that, in the long process of China's modernization. However, his scientific interventions are an especially interesting example of how mid-nineteenth-century intellectuals reviewed Chinese traditions in order to fit them with the intense process of epistemological renewal that accompanied China's efforts to close ranks with the most rapidly modernizing nations of the West.

## Zou Boqi's Life and Intellectual Outlook

Typical of many Chinese life stories drafted in the elegant prose of formal biographies and edited by the subject's contemporaries or relatives, the documents of Zou Boqi's life provide at best a series of fleeting glimpses. The longest biographical account, published three years after his death in the county gazetteer of Nanhai, relates that much of his scholarship had already been lost. Nevertheless, a collection of some of his writings does survive, and some of his possessions with a few of his descendants' recollections provide extra evidence of his life and thought.

Zou Boqi was from Nanhai, a garrison county on the right bank of the Pearl River, immediately west of Guangzhou, the great port city and provincial capital of Guangdong in China's subtropical south. His membership in the Guangdong gentry and his rise to some prominence during his final years fits the common social and intellectual trends of China in the 1860s. Once the Qing government had suppressed the Taiping rebellion and the state of the same name (1851–1864), the deaths of probably more than thirty million people and an unmitigated catastrophe of material destruction had forever weakened what was once the cultural and intellectual preeminence of the Lower Yangzi valley. This degeneration—by no means absolute, given the coeval rise of a new metropolitan culture in Shanghai—did at least provide avenues for a number of scholars from Guangdong and other regions of China to step more prominently into their country's political life and cultural engagements.[2] Zou Boqi was eminently qualified to act as one of the new men from the South, but as subsequent events proved, he seems to have remained unwilling to avail himself of the career opportunities that postrebellion conditions offered.

Zou lived mostly on his small family estate at a village called Michong (Mi brook). He married twice, and some of his descendants still live in Michong today. He received a standard Confucian education as a student at the Nanhai government college, which would have prepared him for entrance to the lower tiers of the nationwide imperial examination system. It seems that he gained none of the degree titles offered by the successive stages of this system. Perhaps any such career ambitions were thwarted during the course of his thirties when the government suspended examinations and instead concentrated on controlling the Taiping crisis, which convulsed huge areas of central and eastern China in protracted and violent campaigns. Like most men of his class, Zou created his own private study at home, and he named it the "Study like a boat," an overt reference to the following aphorism: "Across an ocean of study moves a boat; if it does not move ahead it drifts back." But Zou's intellectual engagement was not simply a constant perusal of books. The abruptly rising slopes of the Aofenggang (Turtle Peak Hill), near Michong, provided an excellent vantage point to which he often climbed to indulge his lifelong passion for observing and recording the night sky. His daytime involvements, by contrast, were sometimes nearer the center of village life. In 1857 he appears prominently in local affairs, successfully proposing and overseeing the erection of a new bridge over the Mi.

Albeit only vaguely discerned, Zou was also a figure in city life. He worked in Guangzhou's celebrated Xuehai College, becoming its director in 1857. Late in his life, major tributes to his intellectual gifts came from senior statesmen who sought to employ him in the new colleges established as part of the sporadic modernization effort that began during the postrebellion restoration. In 1864, Guo Songtao (1818–1891), governor of Guangdong—and later China's first leader of an embassy to England and then France—urged Zou Boqi to accept a post teaching mathematics at Guangzhou's Tongwen Academy. This famous training school for interpreters was founded first in Beijing in 1862 in response to perceptions of Western technological—particularly naval—superiority. A branch school was also established in Guangzhou. The principal subjects of the early Tongwen syllabus were European languages, Japanese, and mathematics. Later, Zeng Guofan, chief architect of the Taiping suppression, offered Zou Boqi another teaching post at the Jiangnan Ironworks, founded one year later in Shanghai. Zou turned down both offers. He claimed in the first instance that he was ill, and he insisted later that he must stay close to home in order to look after his mother. The Jiangnan Ironworks' launch of China's first steamship in 1868, a founding cultural moment in China's modernization, would happen the year before Zou Boqi died.

Considerably more can be gleaned for a picture of Zou Boqi's intellectual outlook during these years of midcentury change. From early on, his biographers tell us, Zou Boqi was interested in accounts of China's geography whenever they surfaced in the Confucian classical texts that were de rigueur in the Qing school syllabus. Likewise, he collected all the mathematical problems to be found in ancient Chinese books. Aside from proving his interests in particular subjects, these recollections signal two crucial elements in his thinking: he pursued knowledge that offered ultimately practical applications and he sought empirical data in the Confucian scriptural canon as well as other ancient Chinese texts. This approach is also evident in his work concerning optics and photography. Even though he paid close attention to Western science, his reliance on predominantly Chinese systems of knowledge to explain subjects of an increasingly universalistic scientific discourse remained rooted in tradition.

Zou's identification with the Chinese intellectual past was typical of attitudes current in China since the Chinese eighteenth century. It stood in stark contrast to the considerably more radical Chinese adoptions of Western science and technology that prevailed only a few years after his death. According to another recollection from his biography, Zou once viewed a world map drawn with the most up-to-date instruments, but nothing in this recollection suggests that he demurred for a moment with the cartographer's decision to place the Chinese imperial capital at the center of this two-dimensional rendition of the earth's surface. In stark comparison, in 1890 Liang Qichao (1873–1929), another Cantonese scholar, experienced a profound shock upon seeing a map in which China appeared as merely one geographical zone among others, one nation *beside* (at the extreme right) a cluster of others (at the European center).[3] Liang Qichao's observation stimulated him to rethink entirely—ultimately to unthink—his relationship to Qing imperial rule.

This suggestion of a certain conservatism on Zou Boqi's part, highlighted by comparison of two generations' worldviews, is not entirely fair. Zou Boqi also anticipated future generations with his strikingly modern views of China's development. Unfailingly practical as ever, he advocated high standards in the manufacture and use of instruments and machines. His consideration of universal standards even looked to the future in more traditional fields of Chinese study. For instance, his interest in Chinese regional phonetics was motivated partly by his desire to find a unifying solution to the divisive predicament that China faced in its huge speech variations (variations that written Chinese to this day continues to disguise). Sound, in fact, was another modern concern, which, beside light, chemistry, and electricity, soon emerged as a dominant field of late Qing technological inquiry.

New standards also supported Zou Boqi's willingness to discard traditional explanations in favor of new. For instance, he advocated reducing observable phenomena to optical and mathematical terms even at the expense of debunking solutions in which most members of his social class no doubt staked enormous self-interest. In 1867, he disputed with another member of his local college that an observation of the planet Venus in 1839 should be understood as an augur of the war that broke out that year between China and the Western powers. In a pedagogical reaction that seems typical of his technical assurance and his faith in visual demonstration, he convinced his misguided opponent of the true state of planetary movements by drawing an intricate chart. When Zou Boqi taught a lesson, the art of knowing was inseparable from the act of seeing. Zou's ideas on seeing are what make him appear so modern.

Aside from a short tomb inscription, the most prominent local commemoration of Zou Boqi is the Zou Family Memorial Hall at the entrance to Michong. This also accommodates a display room of his mathematical instruments, photographs of the locality, and documents concerning his career. His descendants have collected a few recollections concerning his life, and someone has preserved ninety-seven letters addressed to him. His personal seals have also survived. The display includes a copy of his photographic portrait (see figure 3.1), but, curiously, nothing is said about his achievements in defining photography and perhaps taking his own portraits. A visit to Michong confirms the impression that Zou Boqi is above all celebrated for his achievements in mathematics, astronomy, and cartography. Indeed, of all memorials to his life and work, the most publicly visible is an extensive map that he and some of his students drew in the 1850s. This shows the river courses north of Michong, and, transferred onto a grand stone stele in 1874, it now stands among Guangdong province's most famous epigraphs outside the Guangzhou Museum. A monument to Zou's scientific ability and again witness to his interest in his locality, the retranscription of this precise design (and artwork) onto stone is also testament to the next generation's interest in his scientific interests at the forefront of new cultural concerns. By contrast, in 1853, during Zou's lifetime, intellectual orthodoxy had centered on quite different priorities of preservation. Then, members of the Guangzhou government college commissioned masons to make stone versions of carefully preserved Song (960–1127) rubbings of the famous stone drums, allegedly dating to the eighth century BCE. The earlier of these two subjects of stone carving represented learned society's self-assured convictions of Chinese antiquity's relevance to the future; of course, the later map projects a response firmly based in a new imagination of current—rather than past and mythical—conditions that had been furthermore empirically tested.

**Figure 3.1. Photograph of Zou Boqi by Zou Boqi, possibly ambrotype on glass, ca. 1850.**
*Source*: Guangzhou Museum, Guangzhou, China.

## The Rise of Photography

Before discussing Zou Boqi's interest in vision, it will be useful to contextualize it briefly within a few key moments of the rise of photography in the West. The earliest surviving photograph is a view credited to Nicéphore Niépce (1765–1833), a French physician and keen exponent of the burgeoning art of lithography. Niépce took his most well-known photograph, a view from a window, probably in 1824, after years of experimenting with the possibilities of fixing an image obtained in a camera obscura. Niépce's success reached the ears of Louis Jacques Mandé Daguerre (1787–1851), a theatrical illusionist and master of multimedia effects. The two men collaborated until Niépce's death, and in 1837 Daguerre had perfected a technique of obtaining an image on chemically sensitized copper plates. His process for what was announced as the daguerreotype was eventually acquired by the French state and published on August 19, 1839. The new process, which created single images, elicited intense international interest, so that the spread of the technology was rapid. In October of the same year, the first American daguerreotype was displayed on New York's Broadway. One of the earliest known photographers in China was Alphonse Eugène Jules Itier (1802–1877), who in 1844 took daguerreotypes of views of Macao and portraits of Chinese officials in Guangzhou (see figure 3.2), but Itier might well have been preceded by earlier practitioners whose names and actions went unrecorded.

During this early period of the new medium's development, in England, William Henry Fox Talbot (1800–1877), another physician and a passionate botanist, had long been experimenting with different methods. In 1839 he

**Figure 3.2. Photograph of officials in Guangzhou, by Alphonse Eugène Jules Itier, daguerreotype, 1844.**
*Source*: Musée français de la Photographie, Bièvres, France.

had completed his experiments for a sustainable negative-positive system that heralded the advent of the multiple photographic image. Advocates of Daguerre and Talbot's systems competed throughout the 1840s, and, besides Niépce, these two personalities are the most widely cited in accounts of photography's invention—indeed several inventions. However, recent revisions of photographic history now note that several other figures had perfected photographic processes even earlier than August 1839. It is no exaggeration to say that the verdict on who single-handedly invented photography is unlikely to be final.[4]

It would be some years before Talbot's principles of negative-positive transfer resulted in images precise enough to rival the daguerreotype. Consequently, Daguerre's method competed successfully as the preferred method of photographic image making for the first decade after its public announcement. By the 1850s, however, new chemical discoveries had improved the quality of negative images and lowered exposure times. A significant discovery was a solution of collodion (gun cotton) that could be applied to glass supports for the creation of extremely sharp negative images. One of the methods that this gave rise to in 1852 was the ambrotype, which provided not only a qualitative rival to the daguerreotype but also the true potential for multiple reproduction. The ambrotype was a collodion-coated negative on glass, first underexposed, then treated, and finally displayed against a dark background. Zou Boqi's portrait reproduced in figure 3.1, if not an ambrotype, was made by a similar method.

From Niépce's success onward, and throughout Zou Boqi's lifetime, the chief developments of photography were largely due to chemistry research aimed at fixing the photographic image. Zou Boqi did not document whether he carried out his own chemical experiments. Therefore, it might seem superfluous to ask whether Zou also invented photography. Some historians of photography in China propose that he did, and their claims are by no means to be discounted out of hand. But, without better evidence, it remains a moot point. Quite certainly, however, wherever photography was practiced, the technology that facilitated the reception of the image was the box camera—or plate camera—whose logical antecedent was the camera obscura. It is generally assumed that this was a purely European device that had entertained its users, guided scientific and artistic observation, and helped to conceptualize ways of seeing in Europe since the Renaissance. However, the camera obscura also possesses a Chinese history. And, it was the view through this device—an engagement with camera vision—upon which Zou Boqi had the most to say.

## Camera Vision in Nineteenth-Century China

Zou Boqi completed two important essays: *Science Updates* (*Geshu bu*) and *Notes on a Mechanism for Capturing Images* (*Sheying zhi qi ji*). Also, never one to squander an opportunity for empirical demonstration, he built a box camera and developed his own photographs. In an intriguing hint of his lasting relevance to Guangzhou cultural life during the early Republican period, Zou Boqi's photographic implements are recorded to have been on display there before disappearing in the chaos of the Sino-Japanese War. In 1962, investigators at his old property recovered some more equipment as well as a number of his images taken on glass plates in varying states of preservation. Although it features in several publications, the portrait reproduced again in this chapter is the only one so far published.

*Science Updates* deals with a number of subjects, but, particularly relevant to the history of vision, it summarizes ancient Chinese principles of optics. It reviews the considerable Chinese literature on lenses, and it explains methods for constructing telescopes and microscopes. Finally, it sets out the theoretical principles for constructing camera lenses. Zou's other work, *Notes on a Mechanism for Capturing Images*, provides a lucid account of the principles of the camera obscura and, equally, the earliest plate cameras. Since it does not touch on the chemical procedures for fixing the camera image on a supporting medium, *Notes on a Mechanism* is an account of only the optical principles of photography. Evidence that Zou Boqi did experiment with fixing images on glass—and might also have employed his own discoveries to produce his own portrait—is circumstantial and inadequately published but nonetheless plausible. Given what *Notes on a Mechanism* reveals of his activities in Guangzhou at the time of writing, it is quite likely that he completed it in or before 1844. If truly so, that was remarkably early.

His opening description of how to apply optical phenomena in pursuit of obtaining images in a camera obscura will be entirely familiar to the reader of almost any basic explanation of photography: "If you have a sealed room and you open a single aperture in its front wall to let in light then all objects outside the room will appear as reverse images on the back wall."[5] This was old knowledge. The fourteenth-century antiquarian and bibliophile Tao Zongyi (ca.1320–ca.1402) had already noted, "In the Tiger Hill pavilion in Pingjiang [Suzhou] they use a board with a hole in it. When the sunlight is bright and clear they hold a large white paper to receive an image [*ying*]."[6] Observations such as this no doubt continued uninterrupted. In seventeenth-century Beijing, for instance, the Tianning Monastery was known for providing visual entertainment similar to that long enjoyed in Suzhou, by then the center of nearly all Chinese enterprises in the visual arts.

In *Notes on a Mechanism*, Zou Boqi also explained the principles of focal length applied by inserting an adjustable lens on the front of a box. Here, too, he had ample Chinese sources on which to depend. During the Yuan dynasty, the astronomer Zhao Youqin had first performed experiments with lenses to prove the direct relationship between focal length and the angle of light. Western knowledge of lens making as well as usable specimens were imported to China by the seventeenth century. The manufacture of glass—which might be construed as *the* material base of modern science—was a technology in which China had once been deficient. Nevertheless, much progress took place during the Qing. In the Kangxi reign (1662–1722), Sun Yunqiu (b. ca. 1630) achieved renown as a lens maker in Suzhou. He also wrote a *History of Lenses* (*Jingshi*), which has not survived. One of his products was a kind of projecting lens, an invention that he ascribed to European origins. Even if such implements did owe their existence to Western discoveries, their use in new technical strategies of vision was equally indebted to Chinese inventiveness. The subject of lantern slide projection, for instance, has attracted the attention of several historians of cultural exchange. The first European teacher known to have made serious use of this form of visual presentation during his lectures at Louvain, in the Spanish Netherlands, now Belgium, was Martin Martini (1614–1661), but it is highly significant that this priest had previously resided for many years in the Jesuits' mission to Beijing.[7] This is an interesting revelation of no doubt both elite and popular Chinese interest in the lens-projected image, itself a technology and art of illusion that later in both European and Chinese contexts became a foremost heuristic tool for apprehending the science of photography.

To Zou Boqi, a more recent and equally remarkable source of knowledge was Zheng Fuguang (b. 1780), who, in 1835, completed a lengthy work on applied optics. Published in 1846, this treatise was an indispensable manual for creating camera lenses. Zheng Fuguang, whose given name means "Reflecting Light," was, like Zou Boqi, a government academy student. He turned to optics and camera studies after watching a lantern slideshow in Yangzhou. One of the chapters in his treatise was titled "The Dark Box for Painting Paintings." He also provided diagrams for building these boxes. Reflecting his life and career in a region more famous than any other for garden design, Zheng advocated the use of his box—quite plausibly a portable camera obscura—for drawing gardens; he also extolled its use for drawing human portraits.

Finally, Zou Boqi's description outlines the possibilities of receiving images on transparent paper or glass screens and observing these images from a view hole on the back of the camera. In introducing this modification, his description departs from the norms of building a camera obscura, which allowed light to be projected either onto the camera's inner wall or else onto a semitransparent screen to allow a viewer to see the image from outside. Figure 3.3 shows a French camera obscura of a type that still circulated quite widely in the 1850s. Its user looked down on the image, which appeared on the viewing screen shaded by the raised baffles. Zou Boqi proposed to put a viewing aperture at the back of a box similar to this to allow the observer to see into it and to observe images on an internal screen. Zou Boqi's proposal to modify a camera obscura in this way could have stood as reliable instructions for a cabinetmaker to construct a box camera ready to receive photographic plates.

Highly significant in *Notes on a Mechanism* is Zou's statement that the camera image records *all* objects within its optical range. He grasped what fascinated millions the world over: the camera's seemingly magical delivery of an exact and all-inclusive transcript of whatever the operator pointed it at. At the same time, however, his reactions were typically those of the camera obscura viewer who observed that the mechanism delivered visions of the external world in color: "On paper the shapes, colors and positions do not err by a fraction."[8] These were indeed the common properties of the camera obscura image.

Zou Boqi strove, nevertheless, to find a method of making the image permanent. He is perhaps the first Chinese theorist to use the expression "capturing images" (*sheying*). This remains today the Chinese word for all kinds

**Figure 3.3. Camera obscura, ca. 1820.**
*Source*: Musée des Arts et Métiers, France.

of photography—plate, film, and digital. Thus, Zou Boqi's name for a process using the camera obscura has endured without any modification to describe the operation of the photographic camera. This apparent seamlessness in describing two distinct—albeit related—processes is intriguing. It suggests that in the nineteenth-century Chinese construction of sight, looking with—or in—the camera obscura did not differ substantially from the conception of vision as it emerged with the growing availability of photographic processes. One notion of camera vision served alone to describe two processes. By contrast, the invention of photography in Europe initiated a frantic quest not simply to understand what the new process involved but also to agree what to name it. Early terms for the process that ultimately became known exclusively as photography—constructed from the Greek morphemes *phōs* "light" and *graphē* "writing"—were by no means stable in the first few years of the new medium's appearance. Chinese *sheying* was not the only term in China, but it dates directly to the inception of photography in China. *Sheying* is formed of a verb and its object, meaning "to capture the/an image." If Zou Boqi was the first to coin *sheying*, this early denomination was extremely modern. Not simply did "capture" anticipate a central Sontagian notion,[9] but *sheying* became an ontological figure existing in marked isolation from other knowledge of visual representation, most notably painting. This clear separation was an imaginative and precocious coup, all the more obvious considering how consistently Zou Boqi's contemporaries and other observers during the rest of the century used expressions for photography that made it analogous with painting. Most commonly, they borrowed Chinese terms for portraiture, which is not surprising, since portrait making in China soon employed photography so vigorously that almost all the other useful functions of the medium escaped further comment. But, Zou was more sensitive to how photographic vision would change the viewer's recognition of what had been norms of visual representation.

## A New Construction of Vision

Although Zou was fully aware of photographic portrait practices, he staked a claim also for the camera's agency in a much broader scopic regime of scientific exploration and observation. He put no limit on the number of applications that the camera could serve, but he emphasized in particular its usefulness for mapping terrain and for drawing astral charts: "In methods for composing pictures/maps nothing is more precise than this."[10] Such a remark provides a fascinating sidelight to his stone-engraved map now standing outside the Guangzhou Museum.

More remarkably, however, the new mechanism of vision was for Zou "the most enlivening of all painting manuals."[11] This is a highly telling metaphor in which Zou compared the camera favorably with what had long been the major heuristic tool for visual knowledge. Painting manuals (huapu) had existed since the Song dynasty, if not earlier. As one of the central commodities of the lucrative commerce of art publishing, the painting manual circulated as a production ranging from deluxe editions—collectors' items—to highly ephemeral pamphlets on poor-quality paper. Cheap encyclopedias also contained lengthy sections on how to paint representations of a broad range of things.

If a painting manual instructs its user how to paint, what does a camera do? Cameras, of course, do not provide decisions concerning what the world looks like, but Zou's comparative metaphor is at least a revelation of his thinking that the camera—more accurately photographic vision—teaches. Also, the nature of the comparison itself is intriguing: the camera reveals reality to a degree that far exceeds previously available resources for acquiring the knowledge and skills needed for visual representation.

Zou's recognition that photography offered a sense of reality quite different from painting certainly does not mean that he believed one medium superior to the other in its potential to convey visual messages. In fact, his own self-portrait is an excellent example of how successfully painterly codes dominated the visual composition of photographic portraits. This portrait shows him as he wished to be seen: a literate gentleman and a scholar-official not only enjoying access to books but also dependent on them to define his status. The portrait also shows the sitter surrounded—and defined—by other luxuries, such as finely crafted furniture, porcelain vessels, and the choicest peony blooms quite probably raised and cut on his own estate. All of these furnishings—as well as clocks, tobacco pipes (note the pipe held by one of Itier's subjects in figure 3.2), and other items from the garden—were fast becoming the staple tropes of the Chinese photographic portrait.

In addition, early photographs were not isolated from the literary responses that painting enjoined in the form of poems, eulogies, and comments concerning their content and style. Such statements frequently appeared as inscriptions on the pictorial surface. Zou's portrait does not feature this manner of direct inscription, but he did compose poems to sum up his own reactions to looking at this portrait as well as the other three photographs attributed to him. The only poem to be published so far is one that he wrote in response to a photograph of himself dressed in white, holding a round white fan, and posed in front of his ancestors' tombs. Dated to 1868, the year before his death, these verses are a nostalgic reflection on the passage of time and his changing appearance. Such introspective musing was by no means an unusual reaction to portraits more generally. A melancholic tone was not only familiar in literary self-analysis but also characteristic of contemporary commentary on painted portraits. Given the greater historical depth of painting, it is obvious that its associated commentary must have strongly influenced the new genre of talking and writing about photographs. Nevertheless, in the same period, it is also clear that what might be called the affect of a photographic portrait influenced even the most adventurous painters' own discourse on portraiture. A famous example is the painted self-portrait by Ren Xiong (1823–1857),[12] whose lengthy biographical text beside this near life-size image uses familiar terms of the photographic image—the reversal of dark tones to light—to comment on the visualization of his own features. Such comments are intriguing evidence of the extent to which photographic constructions of vision had become enlisted in traditional techniques of representation during Zou Boqi's lifetime.

## A Chinese History of Photography

By no means does Zou Boqi represent solely the whole story of founding and developing photography in China. Indeed, a history of photography in China should be equally concerned with the town photographer, a figure who appeared with increasing frequency throughout the second half of the nineteenth century. However, only exceptionally did other early commercial and amateur practitioners ever document their existence and activities. Lu Xun (1881–1936), the celebrated writer and critic, recollected photographic studios in Shaoxing during his childhood but only in order to satirize them contemptuously. Such records are a fraction compared to what even Zou Boqi recorded, let alone better-known Western contemporaries who institutionalized themselves more thoroughly within the photographic societies of London, Paris, and Philadelphia.

Zou Boqi's true gift to the modern historian is his presence as an instrument with which to provincialize photography's European context. His theories and his photographic image are the arguments that China possesses an untold history of photography's early development. In particular, he presents his theories on the photographic image with an awareness of their intrinsic historical depth. In *Notes on a Mechanism for Capturing Images* several references to ancient Chinese knowledge of light and optics include mention of Shen Gua's (1033–1097) *Mengqi bitan*, the famous collection of scientific observations recorded in the Northern Song dynasty. The stylistic influence of this work on Zou's writing is readily apparent, and its content confirmed that a body of Chinese scientific theories was available with which to test and confirm the technological propositions now rapidly entering China in the wake of expanding Western trade, diplomacy, and war. Given the perilous conditions that reigned in vast areas of China from the 1840s onward, the emotional appeal of seeking explanations for new questions in a native source such as Shen Gua must have been irresistible. Politically it was also advisable, unless a writer during this period was willing to risk his career prospects by advancing Western theories without qualifying them as either deficient beside Chinese truths or else as simply derivative. In fact, Zou was willing to ascribe the Chinese scientific tradition to the even more elevated origins of the fifth-century BC philosopher Mozi, any of whose observations on engines, siege warfare, light refraction, and the notion of universal love (which Zou equated with Christianity) seemed eerily enough quite in step with nineteenth-century experience.[13] Zou Boqi's dependence on Chinese books also demonstrates the practical relevance with which nineteenth-century Chinese thinkers could still invigorate an ancient heritage of scientific knowledge. Crucially, too, Mozi's and Shen Gua's observations of light rays entering a pinhole and forming images of the external world on a facing wall was a precedent to the invention of photography just as valid as the European Renaissance's use of the camera obscura as both a gadget and a technique of vision.

That Zou Boqi could enunciate a theory of photography by drawing on Chinese knowledge concerning optics and light refraction demands some reconsideration of photography's history. The flaw in many narratives is the claim that photography was embedded within a technological determinism that the West experienced first and then revealed to others afterward. Zou Boqi's theories show that a story so favorable to Western scientific discovery is by no means sustainable. No less worthy of consideration is Zou Boqi's competence as a photographer and his own self-portrait, now located in the Guangzhou Museum, which counts as one of the earliest surviving Chinese photographs. The eventual gravitation of Zou's portrait to this public collection housed in the Zhenhai lou ("Tower guarding the ocean"), the grandiose Ming watchtower on Yuexiu Hill, in the northern sector of Guangzhou, is not without irony. This prodigious structure was one of the southern Chinese sites most frequently visited by Western photographers during the nineteenth century. Its image still features in numerous accounts supporting the notion of photography as an enterprise supported exclusively by nineteenth-century acts of Western and Japanese penetration into China.

Zou Boqi's achievements not only overthrow old historical assumptions that photography was imported into China as either a fully perfected technology or an absolute ontological novelty but also give rise to a richer social history of photography in China. Zou Boqi is a leading example of how Chinese photographers swiftly adapted the new medium to their immediate cultural conditions. In this unfamiliar pattern, it becomes impossible to assume that Western preferences still controlled what was a photographic subject, how exactly to compose its image, and how to make these operations culturally acceptable (and commercially successful). In 1859, Lai Afang (also known variously as Li Afang and Li Ahong), a Cantonese photographer, not only set up his portrait studio in Hong Kong but also hired a Portuguese assistant. Too little is known of this business's activities, but its presence—not least the constitution of its personnel—is a sure sign that the definitions and uses of photography were by no means alienated from Chinese priorities.

The failure to recognize the existence of a Chinese history of photography creates serious distortions. Most notably, it fails to account for the role that photography played in a major visual culture outside Europe; at the same time, it ignores how Chinese photographers repudiated or confirmed the norms of other established practices of visualization. This chapter has mentioned painting, but other visual arts would no doubt reveal more influences of photography in China. Such research would have to pay greater attention to the local contexts of photography's development outside the West. Recent anthropological work at least challenges the primacy of a European photographic vision, examining the medium of photography as globally disseminated *and* locally appropriated.[14] This dialectical approach is useful for modern critiques of photographs— including Zou Boqi's portrait. It also constructs a better framework for exploring the conditions under which Chinese photographers and Chinese subjects of photographs collaborated in a project to promote the visual at the forefront of rival concerns to define China's modernity.

## Zou Boqi and Modernity

Photography was a new technology, and "technology" is a key modernist notion that historians have long invoked to argue the rise of modern societies. It is not without some significance that, in the title given to his description of the camera obscura, Zou Boqi drew attention not to the outline of a theory but first and foremost to the properties of a mechanism. Like several leading contemporaries, he was aware that China faced the challenge of a machine age. More questionable, of course, was his willingness to engage with that challenge when invited to teach a generation of those preparing to control it. Nevertheless, as both compiler of the earliest treatise on camera principles and a photographer, Zou Boqi deserves recognition as an author in the rapid technological advances that Chinese intellectuals fostered from the mid-nineteenth century onward.

"Modern" is also synonymous with the new. Zou Boqi did not make the novelty of his findings explicit, but his stress on the accuracy that camera vision provided in certain practical applications was unprecedented. Even within the limits of describing the camera obscura, he grasped that viewing through a lens marked historically a pivotal point of rupture with the past. His understanding of science in this respect anticipated the next generation of thinkers who would stress even more forcefully how modern progress could be defined through the polarized contrasts of past and present. A similarly contrasting conception of modernity motivated one of the greatest modernist thinkers of the next generation, Liang Qichao, to feature Zou Boqi's name among the mathematicians that he listed in his history of Qing China's intellectual achievements, *History of Scholarship during the Last Three Hundred Years in China* (*Zhongguo jin sanbai nian xueshu shi*), completed in 1924. This brief inclusion in a key document of modern intellectual history, of course, convinces us that Zou Boqi was a force to be reckoned with in the late Qing advent of modernity, but it does not explain why this should have been so in any terms equal to Zou Boqi's own professed interests in vision.

The camera obscura and the photographic plate camera were simultaneously technological models and discursive objects that both in China and the West accelerated breaks with the past. The camera's accuracy and its registry of detail impelled Zou Boqi to forecast applications that would turn out to be crucial in China's modernization throughout the rest of the century. Precociously, too, he conceptualized the image anew when he identified photographic vision as a discontinuous element in the Chinese history of visual representation. By claiming that the potential of the photographic image exceeded that of the painted depiction, Zou Boqi had recognized that photography was the major component of a new visual economy of value and exchange, an economy in which painting would become progressively devalued in the greater number of its functions. If we consider that Walter Benjamin, one of the early twentieth century's leading theorists on the "photographic effect," said less about painting than all the other topics of visual experience that he examined, we will recall a historical reorganization of European visual perception in which painting hardly figures.[15] Of course, what was represented in European and Chinese painting in the nineteenth century was not premised on the same ideals, and reactions to photography in both cultures were correspondingly different.[16] Nevertheless, Benjamin's theories, although devoted exclusively to a consideration of European culture, then appear as a paradigm of visual modernity that Zou Boqi had also considered.

## Conclusion

Even after many hours' research, the persona of Zou Boqi remains somewhat shadowy. This is partly because engaging with the personal lives of all but the most important figures of the Chinese past is fraught by the scarcity of reliable sources. However, as this chapter has tried to show, it remains possible to reimagine quite a lot of his intellectual life, as well as to draw from its context in nineteenth-century modernity some useful social insights.

Zou's participation in Chinese modernity leads the enquirer to areas other than the usual panorama of academic, cultural, and political pursuits in China's great urban centers. Preferring a somewhat isolated existence for much of his career, Zou Boqi is an unfamiliar presence amid a larger group of scholars who contributed to a new culture of modernity in China. Many narratives of such figures' contributions to defining Chinese modernity depend upon a cosmopolitan urban background. But, unlike the next two generations of prominent thinkers, Zou lived too early to appear within the scholarly circles of Beijing and Shanghai, let alone the communities of Chinese students and distinguished exiles in Tokyo, Paris, New York, and so on. More specifically, histories of photography point to Shanghai as the most commercially vibrant center of late Qing intellectual, artistic, and commercial patronage. The importance of Shanghai as a new and rapidly modernizing urban culture can hardly be downplayed, and photographic studios and their personnel there were prominent as recorders and even agents of the city's history. Yet, despite the urban fixations of many cultural critics, paradigms of modernity need not be entirely city bound. If so, Zou Boqi is one of those figures who, in seeming paradox, leads historical strands of China's modernity into the relatively obscure circuits of old family estates and village life.

Another possible cause of Zou's relative obscurity was the extent to which subsequent debate on technical modernization was willing to ignore Chinese agency in favor of that controlled by Western authorities. Late Qing and early Republican histories of photography, photographic magazines—even those published in Guangzhou—and several science-oriented works of fiction say nothing about Zou Boqi. It is questionable that their authors had even heard of him. One particularly valuable Chinese treatment of photography appears in Wu Zhihui's (1865–1953) novel *Chats Comparing Old and New (Shangxia gujin tan)*, completed a few months before the end of the Qing dynasty in 1911. The setting is Beijing in or soon after 1900, following the Qing government and the foreign powers' suppression of the Boxer Rebellion. The novel's several chapters comprise an almost continuous exposé by a highly knowledgeable third-person narrator who recounts the histories of several technological marvels that have made life for him and his listeners in Beijing completely different from a generation earlier. In chapter 8, the talk turns to photography, so that this indefatigable talker can treat his listeners to an account of the achievements of Josiah Wedgwood, Niépce, Talbot, William Herschel, and Daguerre (in their chronological order) but no one from China. Wu Zhihui's characters refer to local conditions merely as the breeding ground of popular misconceptions and superstitions. The historical origins of photography are Western and therefore completely exotic. Highly significant also is the narrator's identity as a broadly traveled mariner, and no less interesting is his group of listeners composed of young women. One of these women provides a single glimpse into the rarely documented conditions under which Chinese individuals advanced photography in China. She recalls—silently—that her father was a high official and amateur photographer who, having long ago acquired his equipment on a trip to Guangdong, made photographs only surreptitiously and mentioned his hobby to neither work colleagues nor neighbors. Tolerance of photography as a social practice in North and South China differed considerably, and as late as 1900, a member of the capital's cultural elite who engaged in photography still caused mistrust. Zou Boqi, even had his name been mentioned at all, would no doubt have attracted the same opprobrium among the intelligentsia.

Claims, such as Edgar Allan Poe's, that photography was "the most extraordinary triumph of modern science"[17] today seem exaggerated, but there is no doubt that photography, like several other nineteenth-century technologies, emerged as a foremost index of modernity in many parts of the world. Zou Boqi's *Notes on a Mechanism* saw the light of day so late that their eventual impact on universalistic conceptions of technology was extremely limited. But, at this point, to consign Zou Boqi's findings to obscurity would wastefully neglect a history of modernity that foregrounds how individuals and groups in different cultures adopt, theorize, and use technology for new ends.[18] Zou Boqi is an excellent witness to Chinese priorities for technological modernization, to the shift from old methods of creating and recording knowledge to new, and to setting on record a new visual awareness among his contemporaries and later generations.

Zou Boqi was a master of technical issues, a competence that has never made him as celebrated a figure as his elder contemporaries Zeng Guofan and Guo Songtao or the following generation of reformers. Largely because historians of modern China tend to downplay the history of technology beside that of ideas, Zou Boqi remains a figure seldom examined beyond his place in a few scholarly footnotes. He lived in a period when China underwent foreign attack, internal rebellion, dynastic restoration, and—in comparison with what had gone before—a dramatic acceleration in the impact of Western thought systems on Chinese culture. His reactions were not atypical of many on the longer road of China's modernization during the close of the imperial era. But, less usually, just as his writings both illustrate traditional patterns of thinking and announce radically new ways of looking at the world, Zou Boqi combined an antiquarian esteem for the Chinese past with an urgent sense of modernity's demands. An original element in his lifelong commitment to science was his ability to connect ancient Chinese discoveries with modern applications.

Finally, Zou Boqi's status as a scientist within China's community of scholars also deserves comment. In China, the links between literary thought and politics have always been strong, and biographers make the links overt, not least when, in inverse proportion to even the most ignominious political career, the subject has proved to be an outstanding exemplar of literary achievement. Zou Boqi's life and work recall that science and politics combined another valid outlook on the part of that group long known in the West as the Chinese literati—nor was an emphasis on science in Zou's day a new phenomenon to be explained as a symptom of modernity, for the notion that a classically trained scholar might express a fascination for science was by no means unheard of. Zou Boqi was a late example of China's civil service–oriented elite who, while predominantly expert in the hermeneutics of a Confucian canon and the moral universe for which it argued, were time and again willing to comment on practical scientific know-how that lay far outside the epistemological framework of their education and careers. This was not new. Indeed, it was no less a paragon of the Chinese literati than Su Shi (1036–1101), who first observed how particular saline solutions used to write words and patterns on paper appeared only after exposure to light—an observation, that is, based on a different yet by no means irrelevant awareness of *phōs* "light" and *graphē* "writing."

## Further Reading

Bajac, Quentin. *The Invention of Photography: The First Fifty Years*. London: Thames and Hudson, 2002 (first published as *L'image révélée: L'invention de la photographie*. Paris: Gallimard, 2001).

Clunas, Craig. *Art in China*. Oxford: Oxford University Press, 1997.

Misa, Thomas, Philip Brey, and Andrew Feenberg, eds. *Modernity and Technology*. Cambridge, Mass.: MIT Press, 2003.

Pinney, Christopher, and Nicholas Peterson, eds. *Photography's Other Histories*. Durham, N.C.: Duke University Press.

# Notes

1. Jonathan Crary, *Techniques of the Observer: On Vision and Modernity in the Nineteenth Century* (Cambridge, Mass.: MIT Press, 1990).

2. Benjamin Elman, *From Philosophy to Philology: Intellectual and Social Aspects of Change in Late Imperial China* (Cambridge, Mass.: Council on East Asian Studies, Harvard University Press, 1984).

3. See the introduction to Xiaobing Tang, *Global Space and the Nationalist Discourse of Modernity: The Historical Thinking of Liang Qichao* (Stanford, Calif.: Stanford University Press, 1996).

4. This brief account of early photography is indebted chiefly to Quentin Bajac, *The Invention of Photography: The First Fifty Years* (London: Thames and Hudson, 2002) (first published as *L'image révélée: L'invention de la photographie* [Paris: Gallimard, 2001]).

5. Zou Boqi, *Zou Zhengjun cungao* (Shanghai: Zou Daquan, 1873), 18a.

6. Tang Zongyi, *Chuogeng lu*, juan 15.

7. Joseph Needham, *Science and Civilisation in China*, vol. 4: *Physics and Physical Technology*, part 1: *Physics* (Cambridge, UK: Cambridge University Press, 1962), 123.

8. Zou Boqi, *Zou Zhengjun cungao*, 19a.

9. Susan Sontag, *On Photography* (New York : Farrar, Straus, and Giroux, 1977).

10. Zou Boqi, *Zou Zhengjun cungao*, 18b.

11. Zou Boqi, *Zou Zhengjun cungao*, 18a.

12. See reproductions in Craig Clunas, *Art in China* (Oxford: Oxford University Press, 1997), 170; also at Richard Barnhart et al., *Three Thousand Years of Chinese Painting* (New Haven, Conn.: Yale University Press, 1997), 295.

13. On Mozi and Shen Gua's observations, see Needham, *Science and Civilisation in China*, sec. 26, 81–86, 97–98.

14. Christopher Pinney and Nicholas Peterson, eds., *Photography's Other Histories* (Durham, N.C.: Duke University Press, 2003).

15. Crary, *Techniques of the Observer*, 20.

16. Clunas, *Art in China*, 199.

17. Edgar Allen Poe, "The Daguerreotype," *Alexander's Weekly Messenger*, January 15, 1840, 2.

18. On this idea, see Thomas J. Misa, Philip Brey, and Andrew Feenberg, eds., *Modernity and Technology* (Cambridge, Mass.: MIT Press, 2003), 9.

# CHAPTER FOUR

~

# Ho Kai: A Chinese Reformer in Colonial Hong Kong

*John Carroll*

A barrister, financier, physician, and leader of the Hong Kong Chinese community, Ho Kai (He Qi) was part of a group of reformers who lived in Hong Kong and the Chinese treaty ports (especially Shanghai) during the late 1800s. He is credited with influencing the political ideas of Sun Yatsen, who is revered by Chinese people everywhere as the father of modern China. Like Kang Youwei and Liang Qichao, who were eager to reform China but opposed Sun's more radical republican ideas, Ho believed that China should be a constitutional monarchy rather than a republic. Unlike Kang and Liang, however, Ho called for using Western ideals of democracy and people's rights, rather than the Confucian classics, to reform China.

What distinguished Ho Kai most from other Chinese reformers of his age, however, was his conviction that the Western presence was beneficial, rather than detrimental, to China. More so than Sun Yatsen, whose rather vaguely conceived and poorly articulated "Three Principles of the People" could be appropriated and abused by Yuan Shikai, Chiang Kai-shek, and the scores of warlords who ravaged China after the 1911 republican revolution, Ho had a clear model for reforming China: Great Britain. Because he believed that China should be a constitutional monarchy rather than a republic, and because he served the Hong Kong colonial government, Ho has been often branded a "collaborationist patriot" or even a "running dog of British imperialism." Marxist historians in China have argued that Ho's own class background led him to overestimate the ability of capitalism to free China from feudalism, and that his call for a larger Western presence in China would have only increased China's humiliating "semicolonial" status. Other historians have argued that, despite his Chinese patriotism and interest in constitutional government, Ho was torn between his dual allegiances to Hong Kong and China.

Such arguments privilege Ho's "Chineseness," rarely asking what it meant to be Chinese in colonial Hong Kong. On the one hand, Ho is touted as a great Chinese reformer; on the other, he is condemned for not being sufficiently Chinese. These arguments assume that Chinese in Hong Kong necessarily suffered from a sense of insecurity, when in reality they could move very comfortably between East and West, and between Hong Kong and China. Ho Kai was greatly admired and respected in his own time, both in China and in Hong Kong, by Chinese and Europeans. Such arguments also overlook how Ho's Chinese identity was only one of several identities. For Ho was not only Chinese: he was a settler whose family had moved to Hong Kong after it became a British colony, a leader of Hong Kong's Chinese bourgeoisie, and a capitalist who was as concerned about his own class interests as he was about his home, Hong Kong, and his ancestral homeland, China. For many Hong Kong Chinese such as Ho Kai, their colonial experience was what helped them conceive of reforming China. Indeed, Ho's Chinese nationalism was formed as part of his experience in colonial Hong Kong.

## Ho Kai's Colonial Context

Born in 1859, Ho Kai was the son of Ho Fuk Tong (He Futang), a Protestant minister, land speculator, and merchant who had come to Hong Kong in the early 1840s, shortly after it became a British colony. The father was ordained in 1846 as the first Chinese pastor in Hong Kong and worked with the London Missionary Society until his death in 1871. He began investing in land soon after arriving in Hong Kong, and by the time he died his estate was one of the largest in the colony.

Ho Kai was educated entirely in British schools, both in Hong Kong and in Britain. He received his early education at the government-run Central School (which later became Queen's College), founded in 1861 to help train young Chinese from Hong Kong and the mainland as teachers, clerks, interpreters, and merchants—both for strengthening Britain's commercial position in China and for reforming China. Ho went to Britain in 1873 for further schooling, followed by training in medicine at the University of Aberdeen and in law at Lincoln's Inn (one of four Inns of Court in London where barristers of England and Wales are called to the Bar). In 1881 he married an Englishwoman, Alice Walkden. Ho returned to Hong Kong with his wife in 1882 as the first Chinese in Hong Kong to qualify in Western medicine. Ho soon quit his own medical practice when he realized that many Chinese residents would accept Western medicine only if it were provided free of charge. Instead, he began a distinguished career as barrister-at-law and, like his father, invested in real estate and local businesses, quickly becoming one of Hong Kong's most prominent Chinese residents. After his wife's early death in 1884, Ho married a local Chinese woman, Lai Yuk-hing (Li Yuqing). A rather tall, plump man with a Western-style moustache, Ho was one of the first Chinese in Hong Kong to wear Western dress.

Ho also had an illustrious career in public service. Instrumental in the development of a Chinese medical profession in Hong Kong, he was the main founder of the Alice Memorial Hospital (named after his first wife) and of the Hong Kong College of Medicine for Chinese, where he taught physiology and medical jurisprudence. Ho was on every major board in Hong Kong during the last twenty-five years of his life. He was a justice of the peace for twenty-six years and served three terms on the colonial Legislative Council, more than ten years on the Sanitary Board, and five years on the Public Works Committee. He was also a committee member of several elite Chinese organizations, including the District Watch Force (founded in 1866 to control crime in the Chinese sections of town), the Tung Wah (Donghua) Hospital (established in 1869 to provide traditional Chinese medicine), and the Po Leung Kuk (Baoliangju, founded in 1878 to end the kidnapping and trafficking of young women). For his services to the colony, Ho was awarded the Companion of the Order of St. Michael and St. George in 1892 and was knighted in 1912.

Ho Kai was part of a new Chinese business and professional class that arose in Hong Kong toward the end of the nineteenth century, by which time Hong Kong had become the center of a Chinese capitalist expansion that ranged from China to Southeast Asia. Apart from controlling trade with China and Southeast Asia, Chinese began to dominate the industrial sector of the Hong Kong economy. In September 1899 Governor Henry Blake wrote that "the growth in number and variety of the manufactures" over the past five years "shows that Chinamen are not too conservative to turn their capital and abilities into new directions."[1] By the early 1900s, Chinese also owned the most real estate in Hong Kong. Large numbers of Chinese businessmen and their families bought property and moved to the Mid-Levels on Hong Kong island, an area previously reserved for European merchants. The Chinese bourgeoisie had also developed new organizations to represent the interests of the local business community, organizations such as the Chinese Chamber of Commerce, founded in 1896 by prominent merchants and compradors—both to represent local Chinese commercial interests against the European-dominated Hong Kong General Chamber of Commerce and to promote a "modern" Chinese business class in Hong Kong.

The leaders of this Hong Kong bourgeoisie—mainly entrepreneurs, compradors, lawyers, and physicians who were usually born and educated in Hong Kong—saw themselves as members of a special, privileged class, not just in Hong Kong but also in the greater Chinese world and in the British Empire. With the British, they had not only transformed Hong Kong from a "barren rock" or "barren island" into a thriving commercial center and stable metropolis but also helped introduce new business techniques into China.

Three examples show how Ho and other leaders of the Chinese bourgeoisie distinguished themselves from the rest of Hong Kong's Chinese population. In March 1901 a group of wealthy Chinese businessmen petitioned the Hong Kong government to establish a special government school exclusively for their own children. The first signature on the petition was that of Ho Kai. Referring to themselves as representatives of "an important and influential section of the Chinese Community," the petitioners explained the need for "a suitable English School for the education of the children . . . of the upper classes of the Chinese resident in this Colony." They lamented how in Hong Kong education for Chinese had been "directed almost exclusively" toward the "lower and lower middle classes" at the expense of the "higher and more thorough training of the children of the more well-to-do classes." Schools such as Queen's College, which many of the petitioners had attended, were "excellent Government institutions in their way." But "the indiscriminate and intimate mingling of children from families of the most various social and moral standing, render them absolutely undesirable as well as unsuitable for the sons and daughters of respectable Chinese families." Given the "large increase to the Chinese population of a higher social status and permanently residing in this Colony," argued the petitioners, "it is time that some provision be made for a secondary education for their children."[2]

The 1901 school petition shows how these men saw themselves as privileged members of a special, respectable, and modern upper class. They were trying to affirm, protect, and perpetuate this status by grooming their children in their footsteps. By stressing how the new school would build closer ties between China and Britain, the petitioners reaffirmed the importance of their role in civilizing and modernizing China. At the same time, they declared that, as Chinese "permanently residing" in colonial Hong Kong, they were different from their counterparts on the Chinese mainland. Like the petitioners, colonial officials considered the new school essential, not only for the preservation of the "respectable" Chinese upper classes of Hong Kong, but also for the future of China, since it would train young men who would help reform China. Although some members of the Chinese community objected, the new school was built the next year.

In December 1911, only two months after the republican revolution in China, Ho Kai and seventeen other wealthy Chinese residents petitioned Governor Frederick Lugard for a special cemetery for "Chinese permanently residing" in Hong Kong. The petitioners, who referred to themselves as "eighteen of the leading Members of the Chinese Community of Hong Kong," explained that they were petitioning "on behalf of themselves and their fellow countrymen" who had made the colony "their home." They had "no intention of returning to China, save for temporary purposes—social, commercial or otherwise."[3] Because the colonial government was eager to cultivate a "colonial feeling" and a "class who desire to identify themselves with the Colony," it approved the petitioners' request. The land was to be used solely as a cemetery for "persons of Chinese nationality permanently resident in the Colony."[4] When in 1927 another group of Chinese requested an extension to the permanent cemetery, the colonial official in charge of Hong Kong's Chinese population explained to the British government that the cemetery had created a "closer bond with the colony" for upper-class Chinese residents.[5] The following year, the acting governor approved the extension, noting that the cemetery had been "entirely successful in attaining its primary object—the strengthening of the ties which bind true Hong Kong Chinese to the Colony."[6]

## Colonial Hong Kong and Chinese Nationalism

Even as many wealthy Chinese in Hong Kong came to see themselves as a special group of Chinese, like many Chinese around the world they grew increasingly concerned about the fate of China, especially after its humiliating defeat by Japan in the Sino-Japanese War of 1894–1895. Hong Kong played an important role in China's nation building in the late 1800s and early 1900s. Graduates of local schools such as the Central School served widely in the Chinese Civil Service and the Imperial Chinese Maritime Customs. Other Hong Kong–educated Chinese ended up working in China as teachers, doctors, scientists, and engineers. Local entrepreneurs invested heavily in commercial and industrial activities in South China, and donated to philanthropic and charitable, educational, public works, and medical projects in their native districts. Hong Kong was also the main remittance center for South China, handling over 50 percent of the money remitted to China by overseas Chinese. Many Chinese in Hong Kong also participated in nationalist boycotts such as the Anti-American Boycott of 1905–1906, after the American government prohibited Chinese workers from entering the United States, and in the Anti-Japanese Boycott of 1908, after the Japanese government forced the Chinese government to apologize for seizing a Japanese freighter that had been smuggling arms and munitions into Guangdong.

Although the cession of Hong Kong to Britain in 1842 is known in modern Chinese history as the beginning of the "unequal treaties" and China's "century of humiliation," Hong Kong played an important role in the 1911 Revolution, which ended the Qing dynasty and established the Republic of China. Sun Yatsen, the leader of this revolution, was educated partly in Hong Kong—first at the Central School and later at the Hong Kong College of Medicine for Chinese. Hong Kong served as a base for recruiting and training Chinese revolutionaries. Here Sun established a local branch of the Revive China Society, which he had founded earlier as a student in Honolulu. A local branch of another revolutionary society, the Literary Society for the Promotion of Virtue, was founded in 1892, while the United League, a revolutionary group founded by Sun in Tokyo in 1905, was also active in Hong Kong. The first revolutionary uprising in Guangzhou in 1895 was planned from Hong Kong, as was the second uprising, which occurred in 1900 in Huizhou—only ten miles from Hong Kong's New Territories. An aborted uprising planned for January 1903 outside Guangzhou was also partly orchestrated in Hong Kong. The colony was home to a host of local organizations that supported the revolutionaries, and local Chinese businessmen offered financial support for the movement.

Hong Kong's colonial situation itself played a critical role in the growth of Chinese nationalism. Given Hong Kong's relatively wide freedom of the press, revolutionary newspapers such as the *China Daily*—published in Hong Kong and distributed to overseas Chinese communities—could not only debate more conservative newspapers advocating less radical reforms for China but also openly call for revolution. Hong Kong also served as a sanctuary for Chinese reformers and revolutionaries. Sun Yatsen took refuge there after the failed 1895 uprising, and in March 1896 Governor William Robinson rejected a request by Guangdong authorities to extradite one of Sun's followers. When the moderate reformer Kang Youwei fled to Hong Kong with help from British authorities after the aborted Hundred Days' Reform in the summer of 1898, he was protected by the colonial government until he stayed with friends. Hong Kong's education system also helped encourage the growth of Chinese nationalism by including topics such as parliamentary government. In a speech at Hong Kong University in 1923, Sun Yatsen declared that he had developed his revolutionary ideas "entirely in Hong Kong." The extreme contrast between the peace and order in Hong Kong and the disorder and corruption in China, Sun explained, had made him a revolutionary. While in Hong Kong, Sun began to wonder "how it was that foreigners, that Englishmen could do such things as they had done, for example, with the barren rock of Hong Kong, within 70 or 80 years, while China, in 4,000 years, had no places like Hong Kong."[7]

## Ho Kai and the Chinese Reform Movement

Given Sun Yatsen's glowing impressions of the colony, it should hardly be surprising that Ho Kai was very proud of Hong Kong. More prosperous and more politically stable than any Chinese city, and its government less corrupt and repressive than that of the Qing, Hong Kong seemed to represent the best of two worlds: British free trade and liberal government and the enterprise of Chinese merchants, free of the restrictions and prohibitions they faced on the mainland. This explains why in 1898 Ho so adamantly refuted Kang Youwei's criticism of Hong Kong Chinese as little more than British lackeys and defended the local colonial administration. Unlike the Chinese government, Ho argued, the Hong Kong government appointed and promoted officials on the basis of their talent, merit, and worth, rather than on their knowledge of the Confucian classics. It provided schools that trained students in science and technology, schools at which more than 90 percent of the students were Chinese. Most important, argued Ho, colonial Hong Kong offered many ways for Chinese to rise, in both government and business.

Ho's pride in Hong Kong and his commitment to the colony's welfare did not, however, conflict with his concern for his ancestral homeland—nor did he make any attempt to hide this concern. In a letter to a local English newspaper in February 1887, Ho declared, "I deeply sympathize with China in every wrong which she has suffered, and I long with every true-hearted Chinaman for the time to come when China shall take her place among the foremost nations and her people be welcomed and esteemed everywhere."[8] In fact, Ho's occupational, financial, and political position in colonial Hong Kong enabled him to take an active interest in Chinese affairs. As the only Chinese faculty member at the Hong Kong College of Medicine for Chinese, of which he was also the main founder, in 1887, Ho was ideally positioned to share his liberal ideas with young Chinese students from Hong Kong and the mainland.

One of these students was Sun Yatsen, who in 1892 became one of the school's first two graduates. Having become a Christian while attending school in Hawaii, Sun had moved to Hong Kong in 1883 after being expelled from his native village in Xiangshan, Guangdong, for vandalizing a statue in the village temple. Although historians disagree on when Ho and Sun became associated with each other, the two probably knew each other well at the College of Medicine: the small school often graduated only four students per year, and teachers knew their students individually. Sun also received much of his clinical training at the Alice Memorial Hospital, which Ho had founded. Some scholars have argued that many of Sun's political ideas derived partly from Ho's theory of popular sovereignty. Another student at the College of Medicine, Kwan Sun Yin, Sun's roommate during their five years at the school and a member of Hong Kong's new medical elite, later formed a club called the "Cut Queues but Unchanged Clothing Association." As a symbol of their opposition to the Qing dynasty, the members cut their queues but continued to wear traditional Chinese robes.

Ho Kai was involved with the Chinese reform movement and played an important role in the history of the Revive China Society. Along with several other local Chinese merchants, he helped finance the society's revolutionary newspaper, the *China Daily*. Ho also helped organize the aborted 1895 uprising in Guangzhou; during the planning of the Huizhou uprising in 1900 he tried to use his Hong Kong connections to obtain British support for Sun Yatsen's revolutionaries. Although Ho's involvement with the revolutionary movement appears to have diminished greatly after the 1900 uprising, as do his attempts to act as a middleman between the Chinese revolutionaries and the Hong Kong government, this does not mean that he was no longer concerned with Chinese affairs or, as some historians have assumed, that his allegiance to Hong Kong was greater than his allegiance to China. Convinced that China should be a constitutional monarchy like Britain rather than a republic, Ho had come to believe that the republican ideas of Sun and his revolutionaries were too radical. As a longtime friend and fellow legislative councillor, Wei Yuk (Wei Yu), once explained, "in all his life," Ho was "in favour of Reformation and not Revolution."[9] Ho would in fact remain deeply committed to the welfare of China for the rest of his life. Indeed, as we shall later see, it was Ho's interest in Chinese affairs that eventually caused the Hong Kong colonial government to lose confidence in him.

## The Role of the West: Hong Kong as a Model for China

Like many Hong Kong Chinese, Ho believed that Hong Kong could be a commercial and political model for China and that, like Britain, China should be a constitutional monarchy. Ho therefore never saw any difference between what was good for Hong Kong and what was good for China. Because it had made Hong Kong more prosperous and stable than China, Ho argued, the cure for China was commerce, supported by British-style liberalism and parliamentary government. With his friend Hu Liyuan, Ho expressed this belief in a series of political treatises in the late 1880s and 1890s. In 1900 these essays were published in a six-volume work called the *True Meaning of New Government*.

For example, Ho and Hu were convinced that Hong Kong's role as a commercial center, rather than a British military base, was the reason for its success. Thus, they were very critical of the military and technological reforms advocated by the Self-Strengthening Movement officials. In one of their earliest essays, written in 1887, Ho and Hu refuted the writings of Zeng Jize who, as the eldest son of general and reformer Zeng Guofan, argued that military reforms must be China's first priority. Although Ho and Hu agreed that China must develop a strong army and navy, they argued that China's first priority must be political, social, and economic reforms. China's real problem was not its military weakness but its loose morality and its ingrained, debased social and political practices. Before attempting military reforms, the government must first revamp the process for appointing civil and military officials.

Ho was especially critical of Zhang Zhidong's famous formula of "Chinese learning for the essence, Western learning for the application." A key figure in the Self-Strengthening Movement, Zhang had founded military academies and technical schools, established foundries and arsenals, promoted China's technological and industrial development, and sent students to Japan—all the time hoping to preserve China's Confucian essence. Insisting that it was futile simply to borrow Western military technology to learn the secret of Western power, Ho and Hu argued that China's essence itself needed to be changed. Whereas Zhang had argued that China needed more schools, Ho and Hu argued that China needed universal education to prepare the populace for official appointments and as parliamentary representatives.

In "Discourse on New Government," written in 1894, Ho and Hu called for broad, sweeping reforms for China. The antiquated civil service examination must be overhauled completely, examination quotas should be abolished, and the new examination should include practical subjects such as law. The government must establish schools for training lawyers, teachers, physicians, and scientists. The government itself should be reorganized, with ministries of finance, commerce, industry, justice, education, foreign affairs, and defense, all under the leadership of a competent prime minister elected by a national assembly. Arguing that enterprises such as the China Merchants Steam Navigation Company—supervised by officials but financed and managed by merchants—had been a failure, Ho and Hu stressed the role of private enterprise. Unfettered by oppressive government restrictions and interference, private foreign and Chinese capital would build a nationwide railway and shipping network, and fully exploit the potential of China's natural and agricultural resources. Finally, Ho and Hu argued that no serious reforms could be achieved without changes at the local level. The government must develop a reliable system for collecting revenue to finance public services and form police forces to ensure peace and stability. These changes must not be directed only from above: the government must encourage the growth of a popular press to spread information and solicit public opinion.

Because he did not see any difference between what was good for Hong Kong and what was good for China, Ho was not critical of the Western presence in China. Rather, he blamed China's weakness on leaders who ignored Western ideas and failed to develop China's economy. Ho argued that the Western presence had brought foreign capital and new business techniques to China and that Western missionaries had provided important medical, social, and educational services. In an "Open Letter on the Situation," addressed to "John Bull" and published in a local English newspaper as the foreign powers occupied and pillaged Beijing during the Boxer War in August 1900, Ho called for Britain to force the Qing into reforming China's government and economy along Western lines. Ho did not dispute that many Chinese were oppressed and humiliated, both in China and around the world. But, unlike reformers such as Kang Youwei and Sun Yatsen, Ho did not blame the West for this situation. Instead, he blamed this oppression and humiliation on China's own weakness. In "Review of Kang's Speech," Ho and Hu criticized Kang Youwei for blaming the West for China's plight. The real blame, they argued, lay not with the West but with Chinese leaders who ignored Western ideas. By clinging to the idea of China as the center of the world, officials such as Lin Zexu (the Qing official who confiscated the Europeans' opium in 1839) and Ye Mingchen (the governor-general of Guangdong and Guangxi during the Second Opium War) had been responsible for the opium wars and China's subsequent humiliation by the West. By focusing on military and technological reforms but refusing to forsake the superiority of Chinese culture, reformers such as Zeng Guofan, his protégé Li Hongzhang (the famous general and statesman known to foreigners as "the Bismarck of China"), Zuo Zongtang (a military leader and Qing official who most recently had fought in the Sino-French War), and Zhang Zhidong had all deluded themselves into thinking that China might eventually stand up to the West.

In "Foundations of New Government" and "Administration of New Government," both published in 1897, Ho and Hu blamed China for the Western domination of China's mines and railways. Given that China had failed to develop its own economy and exploit its own natural resources efficiently, how could foreigners not be expected to dominate? Also, they argued, the Western enterprise in China was not necessarily damaging to China. The Western presence provided much-needed foreign capital and new efficient business techniques to China. By introducing Western business techniques, foreign merchants had brought a new sense of fair play to the Chinese economy. Christian missionaries in China had opened free schools, orphanages, and hospitals, led campaigns against opium and foot binding, and organized efforts for flood and famine relief, while Western educators had translated Western scientific, medical, and political texts.

Ho's support for the Western presence in China was not, however, a wholesale acceptance of this presence. It was Britain and not the other nations that impressed Ho. Impressed especially by Britain's government, jurisprudence, and education, he saw Britain as the power on which nations like China should be modeled. But Ho did not always accept the British presence in China uncritically. In "Discourse on New Government," for example, he and Hu condemned Britain for expelling Chinese from its Asian colonies in Southeast Asia. In his prefaces to "Practice of New Government" and "Foundations of New Government," Ho chastised Britain for its aggressive behavior in China and for taking Zhoushan, a small island off the coast of Zhejiang province, during the Opium War. Ho also criticized the British for coveting Weihaiwei, a seaport in Shandong province (after Russia leased Port Arthur and Dalian, on the Liaodong Peninsula, for twenty-five years in 1898, Britain leased Weihaiwei for as long as the Russians retained Port Arthur and Dalian; it relinquished control of Weihaiwei in 1930).

## Conflicting Interests: Ho Kai the Capitalist

Whereas Ho Kai has often been criticized for having a dual allegiance to China and Hong Kong, it is perhaps his dual allegiance to the Chinese community of Hong Kong and to his own financial interests that were harder to reconcile. On the one hand, Ho often tried to protect the local Chinese working classes from colonial injustices. For example, during a popular strike in 1884 by Chinese workers and boatmen in response to the Sino-French War, Ho and several European lawyers agreed to defend the strikers. (France had invaded Vietnam, historically a Chinese dependency, in the late 1850s and early 1860s —supposedly to protect Catholic missionaries and their converts—and in

1874 had forced Vietnam to sign a treaty making it a French dependency. China and France went to war in 1884, and tensions in Hong Kong escalated in mid-September 1884 when the colonial government, ignoring a petition from local Chinese merchants, permitted French naval vessels to use Hong Kong's harbor for supplies and repairs.) Ho also frequently used his position in the colonial political machinery for the good of the working classes. In 1901, as a member of the Legislative Council, Ho made sure that a new bill allowing the Tramway Company to operate on Hong Kong Island included lower prices for workers. And when in 1908 some three thousand rickshaw pullers went on strike after the rickshaw owners raised the daily rental rate, Ho Kai helped the government negotiate with the rickshaw owners, convincing them not to raise the rents.

On the other hand, Ho could be remarkably callous toward Hong Kong's poorer classes. In 1893, he and sixteen other wealthy Chinese and Eurasians opposed the colonial governor's prison reforms. They were especially opposed to the proposed extension of the colony's main jail to provide separate cells, arguing that this would only encourage poorer Chinese to commit crimes so that they might be sent to prison, "where they can have a lot of amusement and pay nothing." Whereas jails in China were designed so that "bad characters are afraid of committing crimes in case they may be lodged in them," the petitioners argued that the colonial jail "does not inspire much fear, and it would inspire still less if made more comfortable which would most certainly lead to an increase of crime, as criminals will have no dread of entering it." Instead of expanding the jail to reduce crime, Ho and the other petitioners urged the government to "use more freely the power of banishment and the rattan, and to make the prisoners' life not so much a life of ease as it is at present." Existing jail space was already sufficient, and prisoners enjoyed even more space than they had when they were not in jail. The petitioners argued that expanding the jail, which was already "looked upon as a paradise by many a rascal" in China, would only "bring harm to the community, and would lead to a large influx of criminals into the Colony, and a great increase in crime."[10]

Although Ho Kai was committed to improving the colony's health standards (he helped establish a hospital and a medical college), he sometimes opposed health measures that he knew would benefit the colony and its inhabitants. In 1887, for example, Ho opposed as "wholly unnecessary" a proposed bill to improve sanitation in houses—a bill that he had helped draft several years earlier as a member of the Sanitary Board—and argued that the bill violated Chinese customs and that the Chinese of Hong Kong should be left to live as they pleased, regardless of overcrowding and unsanitary conditions. Ho complained how his European colleagues on the Sanitary Board

> are constantly making the mistake of treating Chinese as if they were Europeans. They appear to forget that there are wide constitutional differences between a native of China and one who hails from Europe. They do not allow for the differences of habits, usage, mode of living and a host of other things between the two. They insist upon the theory of treating all nationalities alike however much they may differ from one another physically, mentally, and constitutionally. . . . One might as well insist that all Chinese should eat bread and beefsteak instead of rice and pork, just because the two former articles agree better than the latter with an English stomach.[11]

Were the proposed bill to be passed, Ho maintained, poor Chinese tenants "would be forced to pay enormous rent for space less than before, plus all sorts of Sanitary improvements which, however good in themselves from a European stand point, they do not care for, and which they think at least their constitutions do not require." Legislating changes in sanitation would be tantamount to claiming that local Chinese "are so ignorant of what is good for themselves that they must be taught, and forcibly too, by means of severe legislative measures."[12]

Like many local Chinese elites, Ho often referred to the British government's proclamation in 1841 that all Chinese in the colony shall be governed according to the laws and customs of China in his warnings against government interference in the daily lives of the Chinese population. When criticizing the 1886 sanitation bill, for example, he insisted that "as long as we govern the Chinese according to our promise . . . to govern them as much as possible in accordance with their manners and customs, and to respect their religion and prejudices, we must of a necessity modify our laws in order to meet their peculiar requirements."[13] If the colonial government were to interfere in its Chinese subjects' living conditions, asked Ho, where would this interference end? Would the government, for example, force Chinese to convert to Christianity or forbid Chinese doctors to practice traditional Chinese medicine? In 1901 Ho opposed another sanitary bylaw on similar grounds. Ho was not unaware of the absurd hypocrisy of a colonial government trying to enforce legislation for the health of its Chinese subjects while these subjects enjoyed no political representation. But in both cases he placed his interests as a capitalist over his concerns as a physician. Similarly, during the antiopium debate of 1908 Ho and other Chinese capitalists argued that, although banning the sale of opium in Hong Kong would be good for the Chinese public, it would hurt both government and merchant revenues.

## The Tram Boycott of 1912–1913 and Ho Kai's Forced Retirement

Despite his many years of loyal service to the Hong Kong government, Ho Kai's political career ended in March 1914 after he angered Governor Francis Henry May by waiting too long to help end the tram boycott of 1912–1913. In April 1912 the Hong Kong government banned the circulation of Chinese coins. Chinese currency had long been used in Hong Kong even after it became a British colony, but as conditions in Guangdong deteriorated after the 1911 Revolution, the colonial government became worried about the effects of an influx of depreciated Chinese coins. In November 1912, Governor May ordered the Star Ferry Company and the colony's two tramway companies to refuse to accept Chinese coins. Although the government insisted that the move was purely economic, many Chinese in Hong Kong naturally took it as an insult to the new Chinese Republic. A colonywide boycott of the tramway companies broke out. Eager to end the boycott but worried about encouraging anti-British sentiments in the wake of the republican revolution, in late 1912 Governor May encouraged local Chinese leaders to help end the boycott by traveling in the trams themselves. May insisted that the boycott would only hurt both Hong Kong and China since so much Chinese capital was invested in the tram companies.

Although the tram boycott was over by early February 1913, May was upset that Ho Kai and his friend Wei Yuk, both unofficial members of the Legislative Council, had waited so long to help end the boycott. May reported to Colonial Secretary Lewis Harcourt in August 1913 that he had "lost confidence in Sir K'ai Ho K'ai," accusing him of corruption and meddling in Chinese affairs. Although May admitted that he lacked concrete evidence of these charges, he insisted that the rumors were "not without foundation." Rumors also circulated in Hong Kong that Ho was looking for a position in the new Chinese government. Ho had been "intimately connected" with the Guangdong uprising against the Qing and with the Guangdong government "ever since" the republican revolution. Furthermore, the governor reported, Ho was related by marriage to Chen Shaobai, a newspaper editor, friend of Sun Yatsen, and first legal advisor to the Guangdong government. Most important, Ho Kai, who had been knighted only two years earlier for his loyalty and service to the British Crown, was no longer of any use to the colonial government. "Formerly," May wrote to Harcourt, "Sir K'ai could be relied on for information and advice when the Government wanted it. Now this is not so." During the tram boycott, Ho had given "practically no assistance to the Government." Ho was no longer keeping the government abreast of local Chinese affairs. In short, "Sir K'ai Ho K'ai no longer represents the Chinese community, whose confidence he has lost, as he has lost that of the Government."[14]

May tried to avoid confronting Ho by suggesting to the Colonial Office that Ho not be given another term on the Legislative Council after his four six-year terms expired in 1914. He suggested that the senior British official in China, Sir John Jordan, might persuade the new Chinese president, Yuan Shikai, to give Ho a position in the Chinese government where he could "utilise his knowledge of English and his undoubted ability" in the Chinese diplomatic service.[15] If this plan failed, May would have to tell Ho himself that four terms on the Legislative Council was enough. In the end, the Colonial Office helped May by passing a new rule regulating terms for colonial legislature members. In January 1914 the local colonial secretary informed Ho that, "save in very exceptional circumstances," unofficial members of legislative councils in the colonies were not to be reappointed for more than one term. Aware of the situation and eager to avoid embarrassment, Ho replied that his weak health would prevent him from accepting a further term on the council even if he were reappointed. Ho expressed his satisfaction at having been able to serve the "Colony in which I was born and bred."[16]

Ho Kai thus ended his distinguished political career in early 1914. In a letter that March to the Colonial Office, May wrote that "Sir Kai's loss will be felt in the Legislative Council where his acumen and knowledge were very useful factors in debate."[17] In his address to the council on Ho's last day in office, March 25, 1914, May thanked Ho for his twenty-four years of service, noting how Ho had "devoted his intellect and his energies to the advancement of the best interests of the Chinese community and for the good of the Colony as a whole."[18] In his farewell speech to the council, Ho insisted that he had always "tried to do my best in the discharge of my public duties." Never had he "permitted my personal inclination or self-interest to interfere in the discharge of my public duties both inside and outside this Council."[19] Ho died at the age of fifty-five in July 1914, only four months after his forced retirement from the Legislative Council. He is buried in the Colonial Cemetery in Happy Valley.

# Conclusion

As Hong Kong reverted to Chinese sovereignty in 1997 after more than 150 years of colonial rule, Ho Kai's experience has both historical and contemporary implications. Ho's experience is emblematic of how Hong Kong challenges standard assumptions about Chinese nationalism and "Chineseness," both of which were inextricably linked with the colonial nature of this Chinese city outside of China proper. Too often we assume that there is such a thing as an undifferentiated, transcendent Chineseness, ignoring that human beings, like nations, defy rigid categorization. By the end of the nineteenth century, some Chinese in Hong Kong had come to consider themselves members of a special group of Chinese. Although these Chinese distinguished themselves from their counterparts on the mainland, they could nevertheless care deeply about China's welfare. Because Ho Kai believed that British domination had made Hong Kong into a vibrant commercial center, he genuinely felt that Hong Kong, because of its Britishness, had an important role to play in the development of a new, strong China. And because Ho saw commerce and liberalism as the reasons for Hong Kong's great success, he believed they could do the same for China, given the proper political environment.

His sense of being a special kind of Chinese in a special kind of place intensified in the twentieth century, especially during the chaotic years after the 1911 Revolution, when Sun Yatsen's dream of a Chinese Republic quickly gave way to a nightmare of political chaos and territorial disintegration. As they contrasted the stability of Hong Kong with the turbulence in China, many local Chinese increasingly came to identify with Hong Kong even while they remained committed to China's welfare. After Japan launched its full-scale invasion of China in 1937, local organizations such as the Chinese Merchants' Relief Association and the Chinese Women's Relief Association helped raise money for the Chinese war effort. A Western political scientist who visited Hong Kong on the eve of World War II observed that "one factor which has played a part in creating a class of Chinese who regard Hong Kong as their home is the insecurity which prevailed for many years in China."[20]

This identification with colonial Hong Kong became even stronger after the Chinese revolution of 1949 and the founding of the People's Republic of China (PRC). When riots broke out in Hong Kong in 1967 during the Cultural Revolution, many Hong Kong people identified with the colonial regime rather than with that of the PRC. This sense of belonging intensified in the 1970s, mainly because of Hong Kong's rising economic prosperity but also because of renewed ties with China. Visits to China in the late 1970s and early

1980s showed Hong Kong people how different Hong Kong was from the mainland. In 1985, shortly after the Sino-British Joint Declaration that Hong Kong would revert to Chinese sovereignty on July 1, 1997, a survey showed that three-fifths of Hong Kong's Chinese population preferred to see themselves as "Hong Kongese" rather than "Chinese." When hundreds of thousands of Chinese in Hong Kong took to the streets in June 1989 to protest the Tiananmen Square Massacre, they did so both as Chinese nationalists and as Hong Kong Chinese. Tiananmen intensified their Chinese nationalism and patriotism, but it also alienated them from the Chinese government.

Since 1997, Hong Kong and the rest of China have become more closely integrated than any time since the 1949 revolution. Yet even while more Hong Kong people than ever before travel across the border between Hong Kong and Guangdong, they frequently differentiate themselves from Chinese on the mainland. A 1992 survey found that Chinese in Hong Kong and on the mainland had negative impressions of each other that increased the more often the two groups came into contact with each other. Although more recent polls show that people in Hong Kong increasingly identity themselves as Chinese, there is little evidence that these mutual suspicions have changed dramatically since the 1997 transition. Even as they help to build the mainland's booming economy today, many people in Hong Kong continue to see themselves as a special group of Chinese.

## Notes

1. Henry Blake to Neville Chamberlain, in *Hong Kong Annual Report, 1898* (Hong Kong: Government Printer, 1898), 13.

2. Great Britain, Colonial Office, *Original Correspondence: Hong Kong, 1841–1951*, Series 129 (CO129), Public Record Office, London, CO 129/306, September 24, 1901, Henry Blake to Neville Chamberlain, 672–73; also in *Hong Kong Legislative Council Sessional Papers, 1902*, 14.

3. Colonial Office, *Original Correspondence*, CO 129/391, July 20, 1912, Francis Henry May to Lewis Harcourt, 110.

4. Colonial Office, *Original Correspondence*, CO 129/391, July 20, 1912, May to Harcourt, 107–9.

5. Public Records Office of Hong Kong, Hong Kong Record Series (HKRS), HKRS 58.1.60 71.

6. Public Records Office of Hong Kong, Hong Kong Record Series (HKRS), HKRS 58.1.60 71.

7. Quoted in Brian Harrison, "The Years of Growth," in *University of Hong Kong: The First 50 Years, 1911–1961*, ed. Brian Harrison (Hong Kong: Hong Kong University Press, 1962), 52.

8. Ho Kai, letter to editor, *China Mail*, February 16, 1887.

9. Letter from Wei Yuk to Henry May, August 20, 1914, enclosed in Colonial Office, *Original Correspondence*, CO 129/413, September 11, 1914, May to Harcourt, 272–77.

10. "Memorial to the Registrar General (Lockhart) Respecting Gaol Extension, from Wei A Yuk, Lau Wai Chün, Seung Sz Kai, Ip Juck Kai, Ho Fook, Chan Pan Poo, Law Yam Chuen, C. Chee Bee, Poon Pong, Ho Kai, Chan A Fook, Wong Shing, Chow Peng, Chen Quan Ee, Kaw Hong Take, Woo Lin Yuen, Ho Tung," in *Hong Kong Legislative Council Sessional Papers*, January 6, 1893, 72.

11. "Dr Ho Kai's Protest against the Public Health Bill, Submitted to the Government by the Sanitary Board, and the Board's Rejoinder Thereto," *Hong Kong Legislative Council Sessional Papers, 1887*, 404.

12. "Dr Ho Kai's Protest," 405.

13. "Dr Ho Kai's Protest," 404.

14. Colonial Office, *Original Correspondence*, CO 129/403, August 18, 1913, May to Harcourt, 124–27.

15. Colonial Office, *Original Correspondence*, CO 129/403, August 18, 1913, May to Harcourt, 128–29.

16. Colonial Office, *Original Correspondence*, CO 129/409, March 5, 1914, May to Harcourt, 410–12.

17. Colonial Office, *Original Correspondence*, CO 129/409, March 5, 1914, May to Harcourt, 410.

18. Francis Henry May, address to the Legislative Council, *Hong Kong Hansard, 1914*, March 25, 1914, 28–29; also enclosed in Colonial Office, *Original Correspondence*, CO 129/409, March 5, 1914, May to Harcourt, 414–15.

19. May, address to the Legislative Council, 29; also enclosed in Colonial Office, *Original Correspondence*, CO 129/409, March 5, 1914, May to Harcourt, 414–15.

20. Lennox A. Mills, *British Rule in Eastern Asia: A Study of Contemporary Government and Economic Development in British Malaya and Hong Kong* (London: Oxford University Press, 1942), 390.

# CHAPTER FIVE

# Der Ling: Manchu Princess, Cultural Advisor, and Author

*Shuo Wang*

The setting is Beijing, early spring of 1905. Rivers were still frozen, and trees had not grown new leaves. A carriage came out of the magnificent palace, the Forbidden City. Inside sat a young lady, Der Ling (1884–1944), a Manchu princess who later became a well-known author in the Western world.[1] Many years later in California, Der Ling commented on her physical surroundings: "The houses [where] I lived in the Forbidden City or Summer Palace were much bigger and more splendid than my house here. But I love my home in America because this is my own world where I can enjoy freedom."[2]

Princess Der Ling was daughter of Yu Keng, a high-ranking official and diplomat who served as a minister of the Qing government to Japan, England, and France in the last decade of the nineteenth century. Der Ling's mother was of mixed blood, Chinese and American. This unique family background gave Der Ling the opportunity to study English and other foreign languages in her early age when she lived abroad with her parents. Der Ling received her education in missionary schools and later became a Christian in France. All of these experiences helped her grow up as an open-minded woman who accepted and appreciated other cultures and traditions. On returning to China in 1903, she became the first "lady-in-waiting" to the Empress Dowager Cixi (1835–1908) who dominated court politics for some four decades during the late nineteenth and early twentieth centuries. In 1907

Der Ling married Thaddeus C. White, the American consul in Shanghai, and moved to the United States. She died in a car accident on November 22, 1944.

During her lifetime, Der Ling wrote several books about her overseas life and her experiences in the palace. From her writing, it is interesting to see her dual identity as both Manchu and Chinese, depending on the context. Indeed, one's ethnic identity or the understanding of "my people" is not something objective and immutable but involves the creation of "others." When Der Ling was in China she was well aware that she belonged to the ruling ethnic group, the Manchus, and thus distinguished herself from the majority of the population, the Han. However, when she lived in Europe, she considered herself as Chinese, because "other people" in this context were no doubt Westerners, not the Han people working for her father.[3]

Der Ling's books were all based on her personal observations of the Qing court life, and thus provide us with firsthand information about China during the last decades of the Qing dynasty (1644–1911) when Manchu rulers faced two major challenges: saving themselves from assimilation by the Chinese and protecting China from being carved up by imperialist powers. It is in this context, and with Der Ling and her works as a lens, that this chapter will examine China in a tumultuous time.

## Childhood (1884–1894)

Der Ling was born in 1884, the year that China was defeated in the Sino-French War. Indochina (territory that includes today's Laos, Cambodia, and Vietnam), once China's protectorate, now fell under the control of the French. Ten years later in the war with Japan, China lost again. Taiwan, the Pescadores, and the Liaodong region of southern Manchuria were ceded to the Japanese; Korea, a tributary of China, became an "independent" state, actually, a Japanese protectorate; China had to pay Japan two hundred million ounces of silver as indemnity and open four more treaty ports. As a little child, Der Ling thus witnessed the downfall of the Qing and a changing world order.

The Qing dynasty was established by the Manchus, an ethnic group originally inhabiting northeast China. The majority of the Manchus were ethnically related to the Jurchen, a tribal people who conquered a vast area in northeastern Asia in the twelfth century and founded the Jin dynasty (1115–1234). In the early seventeenth century, a powerful leader, Nurhaci (1559–1626), unified all the Jurchen tribes, incorporating the Mongols, Chinese, Koreans, Sibo, and other peoples who lived in Manchuria under one ruler. In

1635, Nurhaci's successor Hong Taiji (r. 1626–1643) changed the name of Jurchen to "Manchu." From an ethnic perspective, the new name is significant because it became a universal label for all the peoples under Hong Taiji's rule regardless of their ethnic origins. It suggests that from the very beginning the Manchus as an ethnic group were actually not one single people but rather an ethnic community.

The formation of the Manchus determined the nature of "Manchuness." The Manchus distinguished themselves from Han Chinese primarily by cultural traits and social organizations, rather than ancestral inheritance or other biological-related qualifications. As result, the ethnic boundaries between the Manchus and Chinese were flexible and, sometimes, ambiguous. This flexibility was reflected in the banner system, founded in 1601 by Nurhaci. Originally, there were only four banners. Each had its assigned color—yellow, white, red, and blue. In 1615, as the banner population increased, Nurhaci added four more banners to the original ones with a red border added to the flags (the red flag was bordered in white). Between 1634 and 1642, the system was expanded to twenty-four banners by adding eight Mongol banners and eight Chinese banners (also called *Hanjun* or Chinese martial).[4] Literally, "banner people" only referred to people's military and social affiliation, having nothing to do with their ethnic identification. However, in the conversation of people's daily life and in most of the Qing documents, the term "banner people" was frequently conflated with the Manchus themselves. By the twentieth century, it formally became an equivalent for Manchus. In addition to the ambiguity of names, all banner people, regardless of their original ethnic background, shared the same cultural traditions and enjoyed political and economic privileges as a ruling ethnic group.[5] A comparison between the lives of Chinese banner people and Chinese commoners revealed broad distinctions, while there was only slight difference between the people in different divisions of the banners. In other words, ethnicity in the context of Manchu rule in China was primarily determined by people's social identity, not by their ethnic origins.[6] Der Ling's family is a good example. Although registered as Chinese banner people, they all followed the Manchu traditions, respected the rules for the Manchus, and considered themselves Manchu.

After consolidating power in the northeast through implementation of the banner system, the Manchus settled down in the capital of Beijing and in nineteen garrisons around the country. The very first challenge they met was how to rule the Chinese, who always considered any outsiders as barbarians. The Manchus learned lessons from the failure of earlier conquest dynasties that resisted adopting Chinese culture and eventually became short lived. They seemed to agree with a Chinese maxim: one might conquer but not rule a country on horseback. During their 267-year rule in China, the Manchus made a great effort to compromise with Chinese culture and adopt Confucian traditions to legitimize their rule. However, by doing that, they risked acculturation by the Chinese, who outnumbered them approximately forty-nine to one.[7]

To rule the country successfully and, at the same time, maintain their ethnic identity, the Manchus advocated a strategy of diarchy in their political, social, and cultural practices. They allowed Chinese officials to share power with them in government. Chinese troops—the Green Standard Army—existed as a supplement to the banner forces. Manchu rulers also prohibited Manchu-Han intermarriage, especially in the case of Manchu women, and assigned separated living quarters for banner people. Culturally, Manchus and Chinese could be distinguished by language, religion, costume, size of women's feet, jewelry, style of hair, and so forth. Although by the end of the dynasty the Manchus were to a great extent acculturated, they still had maintained their ethnic identity.

In one of her books, Der Ling recalled an incident that occurred when she was about six years old. One day, two Chinese officials came to visit Yu Keng at his home in Shashi.[8] They met Der Ling in the courtyard. After conversing with the little girl, one official said, "She is very smart and pretty." "Yes, she is. But what a pity that she has big feet!" said the other.[9] Der Ling looked down at her feet—they seemed quite small and dainty. So, she felt confused. She did not understand that what the official meant by big feet actually referred to normal unbound feet. The practice of foot binding was a Chinese tradition that probably started in the eleventh and twelfth century when the Song rulers had to share power with some non-Chinese states, such as Liao, Xi Xia, and Jin. It was one way to distinguish Chinese women, the "civilized," from "barbarian" women under that historical circumstance. In the Qing period, although the Manchus accepted many Chinese traditions, they refused to compromise on foot binding. To the Manchus, it was one of the hallmarks of their ethnic identity. But most Chinese looked down on this Manchu tradition and saw women's flat unbound feet as a sign of savagery.[10]

Another issue that concerned Manchus was intermarriage with Chinese. During most of the Qing dynasty Manchu rulers implemented a policy of prohibiting intermarriage to help maintain the ethnic boundary. However, unlike European experiences in colonial Asia and Latin America that discouraged all the Europeans from marrying indigenous people, the Manchus strictly forbade intermarriage between Manchu women and

Han men but allowed, though without encouraging, bannermen to marry outside of banners. This gendered duality reflected the main concerns of Manchu rulers regarding their ethnic security—since a child's ethnicity would be determined by his or her father, only female exogamy had the power to harm their interests by reducing the Manchu population. Der Ling's mother, half Chinese and half American, was not registered in a banner before she met Der Ling's father. It was the marriage that made her a bannerwoman, and her children (including a son from her previous marriage) were unquestionably Manchus.

From Der Ling's autobiographical novel *Kowtow*, we learn that, in addition to the policy of controlling intermarriage, cultural conflicts between the two peoples—especially the general Chinese feelings of disdain for the Manchus—also made the Chinese reluctant to marry Manchus. Der Ling recalled that, when she lived in Shashi where her father took a post as city tax inspector, the magistrate of Shashi (a Chinese) was a frequent guest of her family. The magistrate's seven-year-old son became a playmate of Der Ling who was about the same age. One day the boy's nanny brought him to Yu Keng's place to play with Der Ling. She and Der Ling's nanny started to gossip. The conversation turned unpleasant when they talked about whether it was possible to arrange a marriage between the two little children. "I do not think so," Der Ling's nanny said, "because my master's rank is higher than the rank of your master." The Chinese servant countered back, "Come to think of it, our master probably would not hear to the match at all because your master is ONLY a Manchu!" "And what has that to do with arranging a marriage between this boy and Der Ling?" Der Ling's nanny asked. "Because she is a Manchu, too, and she has big feet."[11]

According to Der Ling's memories of her childhood, she often felt hurt when Chinese criticized her for having big feet and being a Manchu. She even cried and came to her father with questions such as why she was a Manchu and why Chinese hated Manchus. Yu Keng comforted his daughter, introducing her to the glory of the Manchu conquest and the pride of Manchu cultural traditions. He told Der Ling, "Our Manchus have no reason to be ashamed of being Manchus! We were a great people and we still are. The Chinese hate us, yet we are their masters!"[12] Yu Keng's words planted a seed in the heart of little Der Ling. Many years later when Der Ling gave a speech to an American audience at Kansas City in the United States in 1931, she insisted on wearing a full Manchu court dress (a gift of Empress Dowager Cixi). It indicated that, although the Qing dynasty was gone and she was to some extent Westernized after living in America for decades, she still considered herself a Manchu and was proud of it.

## Living Overseas (1895–1902)

China opened the door to the outside world after the Opium War. Many Westerners settled down in Beijing and other big cities. To respond to the new treaty obligations, in 1861 the Qing court established the Zongli Yamen (Foreign Affairs Office), a new bureaucratic unit under the Grand Council. Located at Dongtangzi Street, one mile east of the Forbidden City, it was responsible for all diplomatic affairs, including executing and signing treaties with other countries, managing international trade and tariffs, and the troublesome problems of extraterritoriality as it applied to Christian missionaries and other foreigners.[13] In order to meet the ever-increasing demands of dealing with foreigners, the first foreign language school in China was founded in June 1862, offering English, French, Russian, German, and Japanese language courses, as well as courses that were called Xixue (Western learning), such as mathematics, physics, chemistry, biology, geography, and laws. At the same time, the Qing court sent many diplomatic envoys abroad as its representatives overseas. These diplomatic initiatives indicate that the Qing government wanted to (though reluctantly) adjust their attitude toward foreigners and foreign affairs to help China fit into the changing world.

In 1895, Yu Keng was sent to Japan as the Qing's foreign minister. The whole family moved to Tokyo. Foreign cultures and customs were not completely unfamiliar to Der Ling because, from a very early age, she and her sister Rong Ling had studied Western literature, arts, dance, and music under the guidance of their mother. However, living in another country was a different experience.

Yu Keng was a wise man. He knew that the world was becoming more interconnected and China had to deal with other powerful countries. He believed that people who knew foreign languages and understood other cultures would play a significant role in international affairs in the coming years. Therefore, he encouraged all his children to study foreign languages—English, French, and Japanese—as well as foreign cultures and customs. During the four years she stayed in Japan (1895–1899), Der Ling had learned Japanese and could speak that language fluently. She also highly appreciated Japanese culture and received formal training in the art of flower arrangement and traditional dancing. In 1899, Yu Keng was dispatched to France, and the family moved to Paris. There Der Ling and her sister studied with Isadora Duncan, the founding mother of modern dance. They also danced classical ballet—they were probably the first Chinese ballerinas in the world!

From 1899 to 1902 Der Ling spent the happiest years of her life. She was deeply immersed in Western culture and to a great extent was Westernized.

However, some conservative Chinese staff at the legation found Der Ling's open-minded attitude unacceptable because in many aspects Western values were incompatible with Chinese traditional culture. For example, when Der Ling was in Paris, a friend invited her to act in a play called *Sweet Lavender*. One scene in the play was designed to have the boy actor comfort the heart-broken girl (acted by Der Ling) by touching her hair, perhaps even kissing her. On the day of rehearsal, the whole staff of the Chinese legation was invited to watch. In the middle of this scene, the wife of the secretary got up and took her ten-year-old son out of the theater because she felt that the scene was too indecent for him to witness. The secretary later said to Yu Keng, "As a Manchu gentleman of your rank, you even allow your daughter to associate with a man! It is not according to the custom and your daughter's reputation will be ruined!" He even threatened to report this to the throne in China.[14] This incident left an indelible mark in Der Ling's heart and helped her realize the cultural differences between the West and China. In her later career as lady-in-waiting to the Empress Dowager Cixi, and as a professional author after she moved to the United States, Der Ling made every effort to bridge the gap between East and West. Such enthusiasm might be attributed to these early experiences.

Living overseas also helped Der Ling see China's position in the world. She realized that, although China had a long history and brilliant culture, it was now left behind and had become a victim of the imperialist powers. These countries looked down on China and showed contempt for Chinese culture. When they lived in Japan and France, Der Ling and her sister had the opportunity to attend dinner parties and other social engagements where they met the family members of other ministers. Der Ling recalled that at one reception held by a Japanese friend she heard the German minister criticizing Chinese use of chopsticks. The minister thought that eating with two sticks was ridiculous and Chinese should learn from "civilized people" by using knives and forks. He also criticized the way Chinese and Japanese greeted guests (with deep bows) and said to Yu Keng, "What a silly custom! A grown man crawls around on his knees before his guests. You Orientals are a servile lot."[15] The German minister's comment really hurt Der Ling's feelings. As a person with a dual identity of both Manchu and Chinese, Der Ling saw China as her country and the Chinese people as her people. Today, in a multicultural environment, people learn to appreciate different traditions. One hundred years ago people tended to evaluate cultures from an ethnocentric perspective. Der Ling realized that Westerners thought China was weak and without status in the world and therefore discriminated against

Chinese culture. She hoped that someday China would become powerful and her culture respected.

The Boxer Movement in 1900 brought fundamental changes to Chinese society and to Der Ling's personal life as well. After the Opium War (1839–1842) the Qing court signed a series of unequal treaties with the major Western powers, including Great Britain, France, Russia, and the United States, opening treaty ports and then all of China to foreign merchants, who could conduct commercial activities freely. The treaties also granted these countries extraterritoriality, exempting their citizens in China from the jurisdiction of Chinese law. Moreover, the treaties allowed Christian missionaries to build churches in the treaty ports and spread the Gospel. By the late nineteenth century, foreign merchandise poured into the Chinese market and Christian churches stood in many areas of the country. The growing numbers of Western missionaries and Chinese converts exacerbated social problems that had accumulated since China opened to the West. In addition to the conflict between the faith of monotheist Christianity and Chinese traditions of ancestor worship, rumors about Christianity spread widely in Chinese society with some saying that missionaries drugged Chinese to trick them into becoming Christians, or that missionaries kidnapped Chinese children, then gouged out their eyes to make medicine.[16] To the Qing court, the growth of Western powers in China threatened their political rule. Therefore, when the Boxers initiated an antiforeign movement aimed at Christian churches and missionaries, the Qing court backed them up in the hope that the Boxers could use their magic powers, such as practicing breath techniques and speaking spells, to expel all Westerners from China. On June 21, 1900, the Empress Dowager Cixi issued a declaration of war, supporting the Boxers against the imperialist powers. In the decree, she stated, "The foreigners have been aggressive towards us, infringed upon our territorial integrity, trampled our people under their feet. . . . They oppress our people and blaspheme our gods. . . . Thus it is that the brave followers of the Boxers have been burning churches and killing Christians."[17]

The violence of the Boxers jeopardized the interests of imperial powers in China. In August 1900, the imperial powers sent allied troops to China to suppress the uprising. When the troops marched into Beijing, the Qing court fled to Xi'an and left Li Hongzhang (1823–1901), governor-general of Zhili (the capital area) and the leading Chinese statesman of the nineteenth century, to negotiate with the foreigners. In September 1901, the Qing signed the Boxer Protocol with eight countries—Japan, Russia, Britain, the United States, France, Italy, Germany, and Austria. This treaty forced China to give up more interests and sovereignty. Among other terms, China had to pay an indemnity of 450 million taels of silver and allow permanent foreign guards and emplacement of defensive weapons to protect foreigners' property in China. China was in danger of being colonized.

The incident brought disaster to Yu Keng and his family in France. Rumors that French minister Stéphen Pichon had been assassinated by the Boxers in Beijing led to a demonstration in Paris. Although Yu Keng disagreed with the Qing court's support of the Boxer Movement, he was threatened by resentful people who surrounded the Chinese Legation, shouting, "Kill the Chinese minister! Kill his secretary! Burn the legation!!" Meanwhile, Yu Keng received a telegraph from Beijing asking him and his people to leave for China immediately. Yu Keng refused to go back and insisted on staying in France to solve the crisis through formal diplomatic channels. However, when some radicals in the Qing court, led by Prince Duan (Zaiyi, 1856–1922), learned that Yu Keng refused to come back to China, they assumed that he sympathized with Westerners and might be trying to sell out China to the foreign powers. Prince Duan sent his underlings to Yu Keng's residence in Beijing, and they burned the house to the ground. When the Boxer uprising ended with a humiliating treaty, Yu Keng sighed in great sorrow, "This, I think, will be a much needed lesson to the Manchus. I am a Manchu, and I am proud of my line, but we are so conservative we are not fit to rule!"[18]

Der Ling saw it all. As the daughter of a diplomat, she knew that social crises involving other countries should be solved through peaceful negotiations. She felt deeply ashamed for the Qing rulers, who simply thought that violence could scare away the imperial powers. She believed that China's failure in international affairs reflected ignorance of the Qing court about the modern world. She felt that it was necessary to introduce Western cultures and customs to the Qing court and to Chinese people in general. But how could she get close contact with Qing policy makers in the court? How could she bridge the gap between East and West? What could she do for her country? Der Ling waited for an opportunity.

At the end of 1902, Yu Keng had completed his service as Qing minister in France and prepared to return to China. By then Der Ling was already an eighteen-year-old young lady, had finished her formal education, and had been baptized as a Christian. Many years later Der Ling recalled how she felt about leaving France: "We were returning home to China though I must admit that I never truly regarded China as home, because I had lived most of my life in other countries, had been educated outside China, and was a thorough cosmopolite."[19]

## Two Years in the Forbidden City (1903–1905)

In the early spring of 1902, the Empress Dowager Cixi and the Guangxu emperor (r. 1875–1908) came back to Beijing from Xi'an. Cixi began dominating court politics in the 1860s and was still the matriarch of the Qing ruling house. She never forgot the terrible experience of disguising herself as a common rural woman as she fled Beijing when the allied foreign troops approached. She finally realized that the Qing government was not powerful enough to use military means to expel the foreigners from China. She had to deal with them through diplomatic contact. However, her knowledge about the outside world was very limited. Before the Boxer incident, Cixi had believed that there were only two countries in the world—China and England. Other countries, such as France or Spain, were simply England by other names—a strategy to claim more indemnity from China by appearing to be several countries. Until then Cixi had never received foreign guests in the Forbidden City. Now she began to meet diplomats and their ladies from various countries. Sometimes she even invited them and their family members to banquets in the palace. These activities made the Empress Dowager feel it necessary to find someone to help her with translation as well as introduce her to Western customs. For example, what posture should she adopt when she received foreign envoys? What questions should she answer? What was she supposed to say when greeting those guests? If the wives of diplomats bent their knees to salute her, should she raise them up with her arms or return a salute by doing the same? Clearly, the Empress Dowager Cixi needed someone who knew foreign customs to help her. Der Ling's opportunity had arrived.

On January 2, 1903, Yu Keng and his family arrived at Shanghai on their return from France, where he had been Qing minister for four years and had met several influential court figures. In 1902, when Prince Zaizhen traveled to Europe to attend the coronation of King Edward in England, he passed through Paris and visited Yu Keng's residency. He met Der Ling and her sister Rong Ling. Zaizhen noticed that the two sisters had lived overseas for many years and could speak English, French, and Japanese, as well as a little Russian. They were also very familiar with foreign cultures and customs. Therefore, he recommended the sisters to the Empress Dowager.

On the first day of March 1903, Der Ling entered the palace with her mother and sister. The Forbidden City was a completely new world to Der Ling. Ever since she was little, she had heard that Cixi was a conservative woman with a very fierce temper. She also knew that there were many regulations and rules for people who served in the palace. Der Ling felt a little nervous.

The first meeting was arranged in the Audience Hall in the Summer Palace. With special permission, Der Ling did not wear Manchu costume when she appeared at the palace. Instead, she wore French-style clothes—a red velvet gown, a lovely red hat trimmed with plumes, and the same color shoes with stockings to match. The Empress Dowager acted kindly to Der Ling. She was especially interested in Der Ling's Paris gown and Louis XV high-heel shoes, and even asked Der Ling to wear clothes like this all the time. When she learned that Der Ling could speak many languages, she said, "I am proud of you and will show you to the foreigners that they may see our Manchu ladies can speak other languages than their own."[20] Before long Der Ling found that the Empress Dowager was not as old-fashioned as outsiders had assumed. She was actually very interested in new things and eager to show the foreigners that she was knowledgeable. For example, she insisted on Der Ling wearing the Parisian gown to receive the Russian minister's wife, Madame Plancon. Her reason was simple: "I want them to see you in foreign clothes in order to let them understand I know something about the way they dress."[21]

The arrival of the sisters opened a small window for Cixi to view the Western world. At the same time, some aspects of Western lifestyle were introduced into the palace. Before 1900, imperial feasts never included wine. Now the Empress Dowager started to drink wine to accompany those diplomats and their ladies. She also noticed that Westerners placed a piece of cloth on their chest when they ate. So she found a square-shaped silk scarf and attached it below her chin, too. In order to make her guests comfortable, banquets were to provide not only Chinese cuisine but also Western-style food and drinks. Forks and knives were provided for the guests. At each banquet Cixi told her servants not to forget to prepare some "black water" (her words for coffee) since Westerners liked to drink that. Although she did not like coffee, she drank it anyway when she had dinner with foreign guests to show her politeness and to make her guests feel comfortable, though she had to add a lot of sugar in her cup. Cixi also learned from the guests to smoke cigars. What is interesting is that she smoked cigars by attaching them to her long-stemmed pipe (a typical Manchu style of smoking).

The Empress Dowager also followed Der Ling's recommendation on adding some Western-style decorations and furniture in the palace—for example, a statue of Venus, full-length mirrors, and chime clocks—so that Westerners would think that the Qing rulers appreciated their culture. Der Ling told Cixi that, according to Western customs, people celebrated birthdays with cakes, flowers, and gifts. Cixi took Der Ling's advice and sent a peach-shaped cake (a Chinese-style cake meaning long life) to Mrs. Conger, the American minister's wife, on her sixtieth birthday, which made Mrs. Conger very happy. Cixi also invited the wives of diplomats to the palace every year for her own birthday party and on holidays. With Der Ling's help, she felt more comfortable and confident dealing with Westerners.

Der Ling's efforts helped the matriarch gradually accept Western culture. In 1904, the Empress Dowager commanded the Board of Works to construct a new Audience Hall in the Forbidden City at the same site as the original one that had been destroyed by fire during the Boxer Movement. Up to that time all the structures in the palace were in Chinese style, but this new building was a cultural mixture. It was furnished throughout in Western style, with the exception of the throne, which retained its Manchu appearance. The Empress Dowager compared the different styles of furniture with the catalog Der Ling had brought with her from France and finally decided on the Louis XV style, but everything was to be covered with imperial yellow, with curtains and carpets to match.[22] This is a good example of what the Qing court generally did in cultural borrowings—they tried to modify foreign cultures and make them somewhat acceptable.

All the changes mentioned above reflected the bigger picture of China's situation in the late Qing and the position of China in the world. The last decades of the dynasty witnessed peasant rebellions, secret societies, and revolutionary associations all over the country. The defeat of China in the Sino-Japanese War followed by the Treaty of Shimonoseki in 1895 exposed China's weakness to the world, encouraging the imperialist powers to take more advantages from China, which resulted in an increasing number of foreign factories, partitioned into spheres of influence, and foreign control of the economy. It was under this situation of crisis that the Qing court attempted to implement some new military and educational policies similar to those suggested by Kang Youwei (1858–1927) and Liang Qichao (1873–1929) in the late nineteenth century.[23]

Political system reforms came later.

During her stay in the Forbidden City, Der Ling observed that, although the Empress Dowager implemented a series of new policies, she was reluctant to start constitutional reform, making changes on the government structure along the lines of the Meiji model of Japan as well as on the diarchy system by reducing Manchu-Han differences. However, under the pressure of officials, both Manchu and Chinese, such as Tieliang (1863–1938), Duanfang (1861–1911), Zhang Zhidong (1837–1909), and Yuan Shikai (1859–1916), Cixi agreed to allow limited political reform after 1905.[24]

Der Ling knew that the Empress Dowager was eager to learn what was going on in the outside world, so she suggested that she read her all the latest news from newspapers. Cixi loved this idea. Then Der Ling asked her father to subscribe to some foreign newspapers and bring them to the palace. Every morning during her audience, Der Ling translated the main contents of the newspaper to the Empress Dowager. During those days, one of the most sensitive issues was news about the 1898 reformers who were in exile. Der Ling remembered that one day she learned from the newspaper that Kang Youwei had arrived at Singapore from Batavia. She translated it to the Empress Dowager. The news seemed to irritate the matriarch, which frightened Der Ling. The Empress Dowager told Der Ling that Kang Youwei had caused all the trouble by introducing the ideas of reform to the Guangxu emperor, which was definitely not good for China at that time. When she stopped the reform, she ordered the capture of Kang Youwei, but he had fled overseas. Now, when Cixi learned that Kang had arrived at Singapore, she said to Der Ling, "I do not understand why the foreign government offered protection to Chinese political agitators and criminals? Why could not they leave China to deal with [their] own subjects?"[25] She asked Der Ling to keep a lookout for any further news of Kang Youwei and report to her immediately.

Actually, Der Ling was very sympathetic to the reformers of 1898. The experience of living overseas made Der Ling knowledgeable about the development of the outside world and China's position in the world. She knew that the Guangxu emperor had supported the 1898 reforms, but he was only a figurehead in the Qing court. The real political power was in the hands of Empress Dowager Cixi and her supporters, who saw no need for China to reform. From the first day she entered the palace, Der Ling had made up her mind and even promised her father Yu Keng that she would try her best to influence the Empress Dowager to change her attitude regarding reform.[26] However, after two years in the palace, Der Ling realized that Cixi and the conservative powers around her were only willing to take some steps of moderate reform, for example, building up a new army with Western-style training and equipment (1903); adding a new ministry of commerce (1903); and abolishing the old civil examination system and establishing new schools along the line of Western education (1905), and so on. Yet, they did not want to push the reform in a political direction because they feared that reform of the governmental system would shake the foundation of the empire and threaten their own power. Der Ling felt that she was too weak to fight against the conservative forces and to change China's situation. So when the Guangxu emperor ventured that she did not seem to have made much progress with the Empress Dowager in the matter of reform, Der Ling explained to the emperor that many things had been accomplished since her arrival at the court (she mentioned the new Audience Hall as an instance), but the time for a bigger change in China had not come yet.

## Leaving the Palace and After

Life as a lady-in-waiting to the Empress Dowager was full of pressure and intensity. According to Manchu tradition, when girls came of age at twelve, they should go through the *xiunü* (beautiful women) inspection by the court. Only when they were not chosen as candidates for imperial marriage in this inspection could their parents and banner leaders arrange a marriage for them. Imperial daughters or daughters of high officials with a title like Der Ling would marry someone assigned by the Empress or Empress Dowager under the system of *zhihun* (directed marriage). In the summer of 1904, the Empress Dowager found someone for Der Ling. The man was the son of Ronglu, a confidant of the Empress Dowager. Because Ronglu was very powerful in the court and his son was a millionaire, most people would see this arrangement as a great honor for the prospective bride and her family. But to Der Ling, a woman who grew up overseas with a Western education, marriage without romantic love was unacceptable. She politely declined the Empress Dowager's arrangement. Many years later, Der Ling recalled this incident:

> I resolved to defy Her Majesty, something that no one had ever succeeded in doing. [The American-educated revolutionary] Sun Yat-sen had done it, and was an exile from China with a price on his head. Kang Yu Wei [Youwei] had tried it, and China knew him no more. Others had tried it, and their heads had been cut off. But I resolved not to marry this man Her Majesty had chosen. And when I returned to court I gave my answer, and from that day on expected to be decapitated for disobedience.[27]

During the summer of 1904, Der Ling had plenty of leisure time and devoted about an hour each day to helping the emperor with his English. These lessons gave Der Ling a good opportunity to get to know the emperor. According to Der Ling, the emperor was a very smart but lonely individual. He told her all the troubles he experienced during the reform of 1898 and his sorrows about China. He wanted to know how the outside world criticized him and the Qing court. On one occasion the emperor complained, "I have plenty of ideas regarding the development of this country but am unable to carry them out as I am not my own master. I don't think the Empress Dowager herself has sufficient power to alter the state of things existing in China at present, and even if she has, she is not willing to. I am afraid it will be a long time before anything can be done toward reform."[28] The emperor also expressed his wish to travel abroad and move from place to place like the European monarchs did. He wanted to visit Europe and see for himself how things were carried on there. But it was only a daydream.

The Guangxu emperor had a pessimistic point of view about China's future and advised Der Ling to give up the idea of influencing the Empress Dowager to reform. The emperor even implied that Der Ling should leave the palace because he knew that Der Ling would never be able to settle down permanently to court life after spending so many years abroad. He promised that he would put no obstacles in the way of her leaving the court if she desired to do so.[29] The development of their friendship of course could not escape the vigilance of the Empress Dowager. The bond of sympathy between the emperor and Der Ling made her worried and uncomfortable. Therefore, when Der Ling asked the Empress Dowager to let her go to Shanghai to visit her father, whose health had seriously declined, she received permission.

In March 1905 Der Ling left the Forbidden City. On the way to Shanghai, Der Ling seemed to hear what her father had said before they left Paris for China: "I am worried about you because you are different from other girls. You are a Manchu, and have been reared as an Occidental. The Chinese will never understand you, and if you marry among your own kind you will be unhappy."[30]

Shortly after Der Ling left the court, relations between the Manchus and Han took a bad turn. Starting with Kang Youwei and Liang Qichao some Han officials serving the Qing court and the local gentry class developed some anti-Manchu sentiments, blaming the Manchus for all the humiliations the foreign powers brought to China in the past fifty years. At the beginning of the twentieth century Manchu-Han relations became very intense. The widely circulated anti-Manchu publications, such as Zou Rong's *Gemingjun* (The Revolutionary Army), Chen Tianhua's *Meng huitou* (A Sudden Look Back), *Jingshi zhong* (An Alarm to Awaken the Age), and *Shizi hou* (Lion's Roar), called for all Chinese to join the revolution and drive the alien Manchus out of China. At the same time, more revolutionary organizations, including Sun Yatsen's Revolutionary Alliance (1905), appeared in China and overseas. Using nationalism as their flag, these groups played a significant role in organizing Han people into a nationwide anti-Manchu movement that eventually ended the Qing rule in 1911. The Manchu-Han tensions within the court also contributed to the Qing's fall. Observing the problems of the banner system during the military conflicts with imperialist powers, many Han-Chinese officials such as governor-general Zhang

Zhidong saw an urgent need for reformation. They pushed the Qing court, headed by Cixi and other conservative Manchu nobles, to eradicate all the boundaries between Manchus and Han, and to abolish the Manchus' monopoly on administrative positions in the banner system.[31] They also suggested other reforms to the court to eliminate the differences between Manchus and Han, including giving bannermen freedom to leave banners and become civilians; encouraging bannermen to make their own living by farming and trading; and making Manchu and Han subject to the same criminal law. However, Manchu rulers worried that these changes would take away the privileges of Manchus as a ruling ethnic group and eventually destroy the Manchus as an ethnic group. As a result, the Qing court only made some minor changes, which did not satisfy the Chinese but only created resentment, unrest, and disappointment among the Manchus. The Revolution of 1911 solved all these problems: with the Qing downfall Manchus lost all their special privileges.

Knowing what happened in Beijing during the last years of the Qing, Der Ling never returned to the palace after her father died in December 1905. While in Shanghai, Der Ling made many new friends, among them Thaddeus C. White, the American consul. After they married in May 1907, they moved to the United States and settled in California, where Der Ling became an American citizen.

Yielding to the urgent solicitation of friends, Der Ling began to write books about her experiences. Her first book, *Two Years in the Forbidden City*, was originally published in English in 1914 and later was translated into Chinese. This book tells us how the Empress Dowager Cixi lived her life within the walls of the Forbidden City. Due to the male-centered tradition of Chinese historiography, information about the lives of women is hard to find, even such significant historical figures as the Empress Dowager, who influenced court politics for nearly half a century. Obviously, Der Ling's book is significant because of her firsthand observations and evaluations of the Empress Dowager and court life in general. She also wrote *Old Buddha* (1928), *Kowtow* (1929), *Imperial Incense* (1933), and *Son of Heaven* (1935), all published in the United States.

In her books, Der Ling expressed her love for China. In one, she expressed her wish for "the day when China shall wake up and take her proper place among the nations of the world."[32] In her time, most of her American audience felt China and its people were mysterious. Der Ling's personal experiences within the Forbidden City made her books popular among the American readers. Thus, she played a significant role in introducing and interpreting China to Americans. However, Der

Ling's books confirmed some older Western prejudices about China and Chinese culture because of some bias and misunderstanding about China held by the author herself. In one of her books, Der Ling admitted that she at heart was a foreigner and unable to fully understand China's situation in the changing world and harbored biases against aspects of Chinese culture. These limitations, however, should not compromise her reputation as a cultural advisor who opened a window for Americans to see inside China.

## Further Reading

The main sources for this essay are Der Ling's books, published in the United States between the 1910s and 1930s, as well as Chinese translations published in Taiwan and mainland China after her death. *Kowtow* (New York: Dodd, Mead, 1929) is a memoir of Der Ling's childhood. It also provides information about how the Manchus attempted to maintain their ethnic identity in the last decades of the Qing dynasty. *Two Years in the Forbidden City* (New York: Moffat, Yard, 1914) and *Old Buddha* (New York: Dodd, Mead, 1928) mainly describe Empress Dowager Cixi's life within the Forbidden City. Since Der Ling had served two years in the palace as Cixi's attendant, these two books provide some insights not available in official histories, books, and archives. To know the Guangxu emperor, his attitude toward the 1898 reform, and the last years of his life, *Son of Heaven* (New York: D. Appleton-Century, 1935) is good informational reading.

For background regarding Manchu identity and ethnic consciousness, Pamela Kyle Crossley's books, *A Translucent Mirror: History and Identity in Qing Imperial Ideology* (Berkeley: University of California Press, 1999) and *Orphan Warriors: Three Manchu Generations and the End of the Qing World* (Princeton, N.J.: Princeton University Press, 1990), are the best readings. Mark Elliott's *The Manchu Way: The Eight Banners and Ethnic Identity in Late Imperial China* (Stanford, Calif.: Stanford University Press, 2001) is the most comprehensive research on the banner system. On relations between Manchu and Han, the New Policies of the late Qing court, and the status of bannermen, see Edward Rhoads, *Manchus and Han: Ethnic Relations and Political Power in Late Qing and Early Republican China, 1861–1928* (Seattle: University of Washington Press, 2000). Joseph Esherick's *The Origins of the Boxer Uprising* (Berkeley: University of California Press, 1987) and Diana Preston's *Boxer Rebellion: The Dramatic Story of China's War on Foreigners that Shook the World in the Summer of 1900* (New York: Walker, 2000) are for those who want to know more about the movement.

# Notes

1. Der Ling had no blood relation to the Qing imperial clan. Empress Dowager Cixi bestowed the title of "princess" as a special honor.

2. Der Ling, *Puyi waizhuan* (unofficial biography of Puyi) (Taipei, Taiwan: Zhonghua yi lin wenwu chuban youxian gongsi, 1976), 42.

3. To some extent, Der Ling's dual identity as both Manchu and Chinese is comparable with that of Ho Kai, an ethnic Chinese and British colonial subject living in Hong Kong in the late nineteenth century. See chapter 4 of this book.

4. Der Ling's family was a member of the Chinese banners and registered in the Plain White Banner.

5. For the discussion on the overlap of the Manchu identity and banner identity, see Mark Elliott, *The Manchu Way: The Eight Banners and Ethnic Identity in Late Imperial China* (Stanford, Calif.: Stanford University Press, 2001), 43–44. In this chapter, I use the term "Manchus" and "bannermen/women" interchangeably.

6. Pamela Kyle Crossley discusses the ethnic identity of Chinese in *A Translucent Mirror: History and Identity in Qing Imperial Ideology* (Berkeley: University of California Press, 1999), chap. 2, 89–128.

7. Evelyn Rawski, "Ch'ing Imperial Marriage and Problems of Rulership," in *Marriage and Inequality in Chinese Society*, ed. R. S. Watson and P. B. Ebrey (Berkeley: University of California Press, 1991), 171.

8. Shashi is a city in today's Hubei province in South China.

9. Der Ling, *Kowtow* (New York: Dodd, Mead, 1929), 20.

10. In addition to becoming a symbol of non-Chineseness, unbound feet also came to indicate low class. For example, women from poor peasant families usually did not have bound feet, which prevented them from working in the fields. Chinese also saw Hakkas, a group of the Han people that migrated to the south, as crude partly because they did not bind their women's feet. For more details about foot binding and its significance, see Dorothy Ko, *Every Step a Lotus: Shoes for Bound Feet* (Berkeley: University of California Press, 2001), and *Cinderella's Sisters: A Revisionist History of Footbinding* (Berkeley: University of California Press, 2005).

11. Der Ling, *Kowtow*, 43.

12. Der Ling, *Kowtow*, 49.

13. At the request of the foreign powers, the Zongli Yamen was renamed and upgraded into the Waiwubu (Ministry of Foreign Affairs) in 1901 as one of the four newly created ministries in addition to the existing six.

14. Der Ling, *Kowtow*, 298.

15. Der Ling, *Kowtow*, 243.

16. Der Ling, *Two Years in the Forbidden City* (New York: Moffat, Yard, 1914), 176–77.

17. Victor Purcell, *The Boxer Uprising: A Background Study* (New York: Cambridge University Press, 1963), 299–300.

18. Der Ling, *Kowtow*, 296.

19. Der Ling, *Kowtow*, 315.

20. Der Ling, *Two Years in the Forbidden City*, 36.

21. Der Ling, *Two Years in the Forbidden City*, 49.

22. Der Ling, *Two Years in the Forbidden City*, 371–72.

23. For more information about Manchu-Han tensions and New Policies (*Xinzheng*) of the Qing court in the early twentieth century, see Edward Rhoads, *Manchus and Han: Ethnic Relations and Political Power in Late Qing and Early Republican China, 1861–1928* (Seattle: University of Washington Press, 2000), 73–95.

24. See Rhoads, *Manchus and Han*, 95–104, for the constitutional reforms in the late Qing.

25. Der Ling, *Two Years in the Forbidden City*, 370.

26. Der Ling, *Two Years in the Forbidden City*, 149–50.

27. Der Ling, *Kowtow*, 319.

28. Der Ling, *Two Years in the Forbidden City*, 291.

29. Der Ling, *Two Years in the Forbidden City*, 374.

30. Der Ling, *Kowtow*, 316.

31. Rhoads, *Manchus and Han*, 76.

32. Der Ling, *Two Years in the Forbidden City*, 382–83.

~

# CHAPTER SIX

# Li Chenggan: Patriot, Populist, and Factory Patriarch

## *Joshua H. Howard*

I love sports. I can swim and like to do so in the countryside. I don't smoke, drink, gamble, or womanize. I am socially inept and don't like to attend meetings. I dislike giving speeches. In my spare time I try to improve my moral character, exercise, and expand my knowledge, nothing less nothing more.

I am an optimist in all matters whether in my studies or my work. I believe that there is a solution to every problem. I am not willing to become anxious and vexed without reason, thus it could be said I'm an optimist. I often tell my colleagues, "Doing is always better than not doing," meaning that as long as one works hard in all matters, there will be some result. Moreover, one shouldn't be too cautious or hesitant. After considering if one can complete an action, one should boldly proceed. This is the so-called doing or active outlook. I also dislike civilities and empty talk. I don't like shallow propaganda. As far as my character is concerned, it is best described as an "emphasis on practice."

I have already reached an advanced age. I have no great hopes for my life but I wish to use my experience and what I have learned to promote industrial reconstruction. In the defense industry, I can join the ordnance group or the national defense economic group. . . . If I can exert all my efforts for our country's people, work for the welfare of the broad masses of the people and create happiness for humanity—my desires will have been fulfilled.[1]

Reflecting on his life in 1944 at the age of fifty-six, Li Chenggan's autobiography captures the essence of this industrial reformer and engineer. Born in the twilight of imperial China's last dynasty, Li inherited the literati's stress on learning and moral cultivation. As director of the Jinling Arsenal, one of the first arsenals built in China during the nineteenth-century self-strengthening movement, and its successor, Arsenal No. 21, Nationalist China's largest arms plant during the Anti-Japanese War, Li's managerial ethos and paternalism manifested his commitment to retaining a sense of traditional cultural values. At the same time, and in seeming contradiction to his eventual post, Li held populist sympathies, scorning hierarchy and the division of mental and manual labor so prominent in industry. Li's nationalist sentiments offered a partial resolution to this contradiction. A lifetime advocate of "industrialization for national salvation" (shiye jiuguo), Li became involved in China's struggle to modernize, resist imperialist invasion, and become self-reliant. Starting in the early 1930s, he stood at the forefront of China's state-guided military industrial modernization. Li's prominence attests to the emergence of a professional stratum of technical managerial elites throughout industry, an emergence fostered by the state. Moreover, Li's reforms in technology and social welfare demonstrate the Nationalist government's increasing prominence in managing the economy and mobilizing society. At the same time, Li's life was affected by the profound social transformations ushered in by the Anti-Japanese War. The challenges and contradictions posed by the rapid and forced wartime industrialization and class formation to Li's Nationalist project might have ultimately led him to cast his lot with the ascendant Communist movement. Like other members of the urban elite during the Chinese civil war of 1946–1949, Li became increasingly alienated from the Nationalist regime, facilitating the Communist revolution.

My account of Li's life and his ideas draws heavily from his autobiography and memoirs. By his own admission, Li was a man of few words; nevertheless, he wrote extensively in 1944 and in 1947 as he took leave of his arsenal post. In part, he wrote these documents in compliance with orders from the Ministry of Defense. Seeking to commemorate the victory against Japan and strengthen dwindling popular support, the Nationalist government asked each arsenal to compile a factory history and catalog its achievements during the War of Resistance. The writing of his memoirs took on both a personal and political significance for Li. He could honor the sacrifices of his employees and criticize, albeit in a very indirect fashion, the increasing corruption of the Nationalist regime. By emphasizing his own patriotism and upright moral leadership, Li in the best Confucian tradition sought to serve as a role model for his employees and also to suggest that these qualities were exactly what was most lacking among official circles.

Born July 7, 1888, on the outskirts of Changsha, Hunan province, a center of late Qing reform and revolution, Li's education was a mixture of traditional and modern elements. Li conducted his first studies at home with his father, the local schoolteacher, who duly impressed upon Li the neo-Confucian principles of self-cultivation and regulating the family as necessary to bring order to state affairs. After attending various rural academies, Li had mastered the eight-legged essay, a standard written format required of the civil service examination, and could write couplet poetry by the age of fourteen. Li's traditional education heavily shaped his future managerial style and ethical outlook. Chinese historians suggest that the Ming scholar Wang Yangming might have influenced Li's stress on reform and practice. Wang's activism, epitomized by the concepts of *wushi* (dealing with concrete matters in work) and "uniting thought and action," was prevalent among Li's generation, especially in Hunan, where local gentry had developed a "muscular Confucian" statecraft in response to the devastation wrought by the mid-nineteenth-century Taiping rebellion. In the past, such learning would have also served as the springboard for competing in China's "examination hell" and potentially landing a lucrative bureaucratic post. But the Qing government's abolition of the civil service examination system in 1905 alongside the promotion of Western learning as part of its New Policy reforms foreclosed such a career path and pushed Li toward a lifelong study of manufacturing. Li entered the field of science and technology just as Chinese intellectual currents shifted to stressing industrialization as a precondition for wealth and power. By the late 1890s, prominent reformers such as Kang Youwei downplayed the promise of commerce as the key to China's prosperity, while advocating "vigorously developing industry to strengthen the country." Growing up too when China was in danger of being "carved up like a melon" by imperialist powers, the young Li Chenggan became an avid proponent of "industrialization for the nation's salvation" (*shiye jiuguo*). Only through industrialization, Li believed, would China become a strong and prosperous country able to resist foreign aggression.

To this end, Li left his home at the age of seventeen and went to study at the Hunan Provincial Manufacturing Academy in Changsha. "I was nurtured by instructors . . . who were all the older generation of revolutionaries," Li noted of his teachers. Li's pursuit of scientific knowledge and participation in revolutionary activities took a decisive turn the following year (1906) when the provincial leader and pioneering industrialist Zhang Zhidong, founder of the renowned Hanyang Ironworks, sponsored Li to study abroad in Japan. Li attended middle school in Osaka for two years and then spent four years in Tokyo at the Number One high school of Tokyo and the Gangshan Number Six high school. That China's 1911 Revolution was "made in Japan" was by no means a truism for Li Chenggan. While in Japan, he became influenced by the democratic revolutionary thought of Sun Yatsen and the National Revolutionary Alliance. Li recounts in his autobiography how he "frequently associated with revolutionary comrades," such as Alliance member Wu Yuzhang and the leftist writer Guo Moruo.

Li viewed both economic development and political revolution as necessary for China to progress. Recalling his bourgeoning political awareness on the eve of the 1911 Revolution, he said,

> I strongly felt my country could not achieve political order unless we overthrew the autocracy; we could not become strong unless we vigorously developed industry. I liked math, mechanics, and engineering, so at an early age vowed to pursue manufacturing. Although I yearned to do revolutionary work, I rarely was an active participant in political and military revolutionary activities and only returned to China in 1911 when I went to Wuchang [Hubei province] to fling myself into the revolution. At this point, I felt my personal studies were secondary [to the revolution].

Upon hearing of the mutiny in Wuhan that would spark the overthrow of the Qing dynasty, Li embarked for China. He joined Sun Yatsen's associate, Huang Xing, and fought for twenty days at the front in Hanyang, where battles raged between revolutionary forces and the Qing army. After the establishment of the Republic in 1912, Li resumed his studies in Tokyo. Li later justified his return to Japan as a product of his social awkwardness and disdain for official circles. "I didn't like to interact and was socially inept. I wasn't suited for political life, in particular I wasn't suited to be an official, so I vowed to devote myself to industrial reconstruction and not disperse my energies in other matters."

Li attended the prestigious Tokyo Imperial University and graduated with an honors degree in electrical mechanical engineering, "the rage in Japan." He recalls how his teachers encouraged him to become an entrepreneur, yet Li's interest in technology convinced him that he was better suited to an engineering career. Moreover, the "chaotic political situation" of the warlord era in his view left him no alternative but to "concentrate on industrial reconstruction" when he returned to China in 1917. Li's first job was at the Hunan industrial bureau. Despite opposition from father and friends, Li resigned as section chief, a post "full of bureaucratic airs," within a matter of days and took a lower-paying technical position. For much of the next decade, Li worked as an engineer in his native Hunan and Fujian as well as at the Hanyang Arsenal. These experiences shaped Li's populist sympathies and ascetic lifestyle. "When I started working at the Changsha electric lamp company in 1918," Li recalled, "I shared with workers the hardships and difficult experiences. I had firsthand experience with poverty, so I became accustomed to leading a simple and diligent lifestyle." The decade also marked Li's first entry into the arms industry. After the Northern Expedition, Chiang Kai-shek's military campaign to bring the warlord powers to heel and thereby unify China, and the establishment of the Nationalist government in Nanjing, Li Chenggan transferred jobs in 1928 to become the production board section chief of the Nanjing-based Jinling Arsenal. Within a year he was promoted to bureau chief and in 1931 became factory director, a post he would hold for the next sixteen years.

Employment at the Jinling Arsenal would seem to have been the perfect place for Li Chenggan to fulfill his *shiye jiuguo* aspirations. Founded by the viceroy Li Hongzhang in 1865, the arsenal was the first of its kind in China and a prominent symbol of the late Qing's self-strengthening movement. Between 1861 and 1895, seeking to resist the dual threat of Western encroachment and internal rebellion, the imperial state embarked on a program of rapid military industrialization. Arms were crucial to the empire's salvation and future glory. As the leading advocate of the self-strengthening movement argued, "Eventually we must consider manufacturing, repairing, and using weapons by ourselves. . . . Only thus will we be able to pacify the empire; only thus can we play a leading role on the globe; and only thus shall we restore our original strength, and redeem ourselves from former humiliations."[2] One of the largest arsenals, the Jinling Manufacturing Bureau (renamed the Jinling Arsenal in 1928), initially consisted of a gun and cartridge works. During the next three decades, the arsenal added two machinery workshops, a steel-rolling factory, and a copper smelter. Most prominently, a large machinery plant was established in 1887, which would eventually be converted to produce guns and still be in use by the early 1930s.

When Li arrived in Nanjing, he found Jinling in dire need of reform. Because so much of China's military buildup had taken place in the late nineteenth century, the plant's machinery was dilapidated and in need of constant repair. Outmoded machinery exacerbated reliance on labor-intensive technology. Long hours and poor working conditions characterized arsenal employment. Workers toiled in dark workshops guided only by a single light-bulb hung over their machines. Fourteen-hour workdays lasting until 10 p.m.

worsened conditions, because operatives could inadvertently mangle their arms in machine shafting. Despotic labor regimes compounded these arduous working conditions. Managers used coercion and the threat of conscription to discipline workers. "The director stated that it was well known among the laborers that if any disaffection was noted the guilty ones would be sent for assignment to the front."[3]

Production was still largely craft based; machines were belt driven by overhead shafting, and many operations depended on hand labor. Although key components such as gun barrels were imported for assembly, artisans continued relying on their experience to replicate parts and by necessity resorted to crude production techniques. Machinists assembled machine guns, rifles, and revolvers with parts and bolts, which had been hand filed to achieve a fit. "Mechanism roughly machined and parts are therefore often not interchangeable," a U.S. Consul noted of Chinese-made rifles in 1930.[4] Imprecision and subpar standards had fatal consequences for soldiers on the battlefield. "There is a deplorable lack of appreciation of exactness and precision (common to all arsenals in China) which results in faulty weapons and munitions turned out to the troops in the field; this is particularly true in the case of small arms ammunition, to the extent that gun jams are the rule rather than the exception," a foreign military observer noted.[5]

Although Li would focus his attention on resolving these production problems, his immediate criticisms were directed at the factory administrators. During his first year at Jinling, Li began to "rectify the long-standing abuses of China's arm industry that had accumulated over dozens of years." Jinling had become a hotbed of corruption and graft. "Administrators embezzled funds and some were even opium addicts," recalled Yu Zhuozhi, a fellow engineer and eventually Li's successor as arsenal director.[6] Another of Li's colleagues, who joined him in 1928, asserts that the factory director and managerial staff were military men by training who knew nothing about technology. Most prominently, Huang Gongzhu, Jinling's factory director between 1927 and 1931, was a Whampoa cadet who had served as artillery brigade chief under the "Christian warlord" Feng Yuxiang. Li had the audacity to scold him in public for his laziness and corrupt ways. "We come to work on time, while you only arrive by nine or ten o'clock. We wear work clothes, while you administrators wear well-pressed Western suits. . . . Can you even match the work performance of a lowly clerk in the production board?"[7]

Li Chenggan's disdain for Huang climaxed in 1930 and catapulted him into the top administrative post. An increase in the government's budget for state-run enterprises prompted debate within the arsenal on how to use the surplus funds. Li prevailed over dissenting views in advocating using the entire surplus to increase production capacity. Huang Gongzhu felt Li's idea ran counter to his clique's interests. Huang, too, was infuriated with Li's incorruptibility. Li had blocked Huang's scheme to smelt excess copper plates, ordinarily used for bullet production, and to resell them for profit as primary materials. Hoping to bring about Li's dismissal, Huang thus mobilized workers to strike on the pretext that Li opposed giving workers an end-of-the-year bonus. With some workers calling for "the overthrow of Li Chenggan," Li was forced to go to Shanghai to seek approval for his job from the Ordnance Department, the Nationalist administration overseeing the defense industry. After meeting with the Ordnance director Chen Yi, an investigation was conducted of the factory. Huang was ordered to restore order. Li returned triumphantly to Jinling, greeted to the tune of firecrackers. In a face-saving maneuver and sop to the influential Whampoa faction within Nationalist military circles, Huang was transferred out to become director of the Hanyang Arsenal. Within months, Chen Yi appointed Li as the new arsenal director.[8]

At the helm of Jinling, Li Chenggan implemented sweeping reforms that echoed military industrial modernization efforts spearheaded by his boss, Yu Dawei, director of the Ordnance Department between January 1933 and December 1945. Both men were impelled by a sense of national crisis and likely shared the sense of urgency voiced by their industry's bulletin. "In this twentieth century of ours, eagles glare and tigers stalk; the weak fall prey to the strong. In an era where the mighty are duplicitous, if we lack weaponry, we cannot speak of war; if we are not self-sufficient in arms production, how can we talk of nation building?"[9] The Manchurian Incident and the impending threat of war with Japan forced the Nationalist government to initiate several key reforms to increase production and achieve a more self-sufficient defense industry. Launching a Five-Year Plan, the Ordnance Department began to incorporate arsenals controlled by provincial militarists, establish new war plants, and modernize older ones. German military and technical aid was crucial to Yu Dawei's modernization program. By 1931, ten of the sixty German advisors helping to reorganize the Nationalist army and establish a blueprint for industrial reform were assisting the Ordnance Department. Yu used complete sets of German machinery, introduced mass-production methods, and adopted German managerial methods. Realizing the limitations of importing advanced technology without an adequate base for its use, Yu Dawei promoted research and education, greatly expanding technical and administrative personnel. Technological reforms also transformed production processes. The Ordnance Department used arms transactions, especially with Germany, to acquire technology that facilitated interchangeable manufacture as well as weapon standardization. These two advances ushered in mass production before the Anti-Japanese War erupted in 1937.

Li started modernizing Jinling by implementing a cost accounting system overseeing cost estimates, wage calculations, auditing, and accounting. This reform reduced production costs and improved product quality. Another cost-saving measure was to exercise self-reliance. Rather than import mortars from Germany, for instance, Jinling began its own production. While each imported mortar had cost twelve yuan each, by 1936 mortars produced at Jinling cost five yuan each and were superior in quality to the import. By 1936, the average cost of other major products, such as 7.9 mm cartridges, 82 mm mortar shells, and the Maxim heavy machine gun had decreased by a third.[10]

Li invested US$800,000—money saved from increased productivity—to update equipment, buy new machinery, and install new workshops.[11] Between 1932 and 1937, the arsenal added new plants totaling fifty thousand square meters and constructed fifteen dormitories. To assist in the factory modernization, Li hired an entire corps of engineers who had studied abroad in Japan, France, England, Germany, and the United States, and then assigned them various tasks, such as improving foundry techniques, testing materials, and modernizing equipment. By the mid-1930s, Jinling was producing sixteen different types of weaponry and had become a primary manufacturer of mortars, gas masks, TNT, cartridges, and heavy machine guns. By the eve of war, Jinling employed almost three thousand workers, a sixfold increase since 1928.

Among Li's various reforms, the production of gauges was most noteworthy. Reflecting Li's support for the manufacture of precision tools and interchangeable manufacture, a full third of the construction budget went to build a gauge tool workshop, the first of its kind in China. Defense plants used two types of gauges, the master block and working gauge. Master blocks tested the tolerance of working gauges, while the working gauge, as its name implies, measured the precision of parts. Gauge departments assiduously protected the master block from being touched, in order to prevent wear, and only used the tools to test tolerance, the variance in dimension between the original and copied parts. Extremely skilled workmen made working gauges, which they placed alongside the master block to see if they sealed hermetically, a mark of success. The level of precision obtained by these gauges reached up to 1/100,000 of an inch, making them the most precise in China. Their use helped produce bores for weapons, such as the widely used 7.9 mm caliber rifle, which maintained a tolerance level less than .04 millimeters, thinner than a strand of hair. Workers and technicians in assembly and repair shops used fairly high-level working gauges to inspect gun barrels, stocks, and shell parts for quality control.

The importance of gauges is difficult to exaggerate. By achieving far greater precision, they facilitated interchangeable manufacturing for standardized-caliber guns, a cornerstone of Western gun manufacturing since the mid-nineteenth century and an important precursor to mass production. Mass production in turn rendered the industry more self-sufficient and reduced the constant and severe shortages afflicting the poorly equipped Nationalist army during the early 1940s. Mass production changed the social landscape of the shop floor. Gauges accelerated production and altered power relations by diminishing management's reliance on experienced artisans to check precision. Although the production of gauges required extremely skilled workers, once the gauges had been produced, machine operatives could use them to make individual parts more easily. Widespread use of gauges reduced dependence on the ranks of the highly skilled artisan during the War of Resistance and opened the factory gates to less skilled workers and Sichuan's rural proletariat.

The development of precision production and interchangeable manufacture led to greater uniformity of weapons. Standardization of weapons was urgent, given that critics had mocked the army as "an exhibition gallery for weapons from 10,000 countries."[12] After World War I and throughout the 1920s, Chinese warlords' voracious appetite for arms and a surfeit of cheap weapons in Europe benefited arms merchants in search of new markets. Although China might have increased its supply of weaponry at a cheaper cost, most arms were discards from the Great War. The production and maintenance of so many different weapons delayed the standardization of small arms and impeded mass production. Repairs caused tremendous backlogs, as machinery had to be coordinated with the various caliber makes.

Whereas political rivalries during the warlord era had impeded uniform advances in military technology, Nationalist unification improved conditions for standardization. The Nationalist government's close ties with German military advisors further accelerated the standardization of arms that were primarily based on German prototypes. The Ordnance Department achieved considerable success in standardizing weapons through technology transfers that accompanied large-scale armament transactions with Germany between 1933 and 1935. Specifically, the transfer of gauges allowed arsenals to manufacture their weapons based on German models, hence eliminating the plethora of foreign makes. China's military leaders purchased weapons not only for their immediate use but also to study their manufacture so that they could eventually produce the same weaponry.

Reverse engineering allowed China's military industry to standardize and establish prototypes for much of its weaponry prior to the outbreak of war in 1937. Under Li Chenggan's tutelage, Jinling played a key role in standardizing the mortar. After purchasing the French 1930-make Boulanger 81 mm trench mortar, the arsenal's subsequent replica and modification to an 82 mm caliber became a national standard weapon and was produced on a mass scale. Reflecting the armament industry's technological advances and its ability to adapt and innovate, by 1934 Jinling had manufactured a complete set of gauges. The Ordnance Department's success in standardizing armaments and introducing interchangeable manufacture radically improved the quality of weaponry and facilitated mass production of various light weapons.

While Li's factory reforms coincided with the military modernization plans of the Nationalist government during the Nanjing decade (1927–1937), his moral outlook led him to develop a distinctive managerial ethos. Li stressed the need for factory managers to set a moral example for the rank and file, akin to Confucius's advocacy of rule by personal virtue: "The virtue of the gentleman may be compared to the wind and that of the commoner to the weeds. The weeds under the force of the wind cannot but bend." To foster personal integrity, Li pursued a frugal ascetic lifestyle.

> One should make every effort to leave a simple life . . . and only thus will one succeed in one's affairs. All employees should be determined to distance themselves from corruption, and immerse themselves in their profession, not wallow in the mire with unworthy people. They should especially have a spirit of sacrifice, be willing to suffer hardships and setbacks. If they work hard and set an example for others, comrades will eventually fall in line and prevailing customs will change.[13]

At the same time, Li promoted a respect for public property so that his staff would economize and avoid engrossment. "Machinery, resources, manpower, funds and all equipment should all be recognized as our country's capital. The fruits of people's labor must be cherished. It is appropriate to economize."[14]

To be sure, Li could also resort to harsh "legalist" methods in waging his moral crusade against corruption. When Li discovered during the war that a section chief by the name of Yuan had pocketed money after giving an inflated figure for a procurement report, he handed the official over to the military tribunal of the Ordnance Department, which sentenced him to execution. Li might have felt a sense of remorse at the verdict, but he publicly used the case to reaffirm his commitment to a Confucian-style leadership based on moral suasion.

I was distraught when I heard he was sentenced to death. I regretted that I had not been sufficiently vigilant before the case and could not rescue him after the verdict and let him make a fresh start. But I told everyone in the factory that Yuan's case was a lesson for us. I strengthened my faith in our factory maxim ['Treat others with care and sincerity; be faithful in discharging your post; be fair and honest; be industrious and pursue knowledge'], thus Mr. Yuan's death helped our factory.[15]

Besides exhorting his colleagues, Li practiced what he preached. After his promotion to factory director, Li rejected a 30 percent salary increase and maintained his Spartan lifestyle by living in a single room that contained only a wooden desk, chair, and a plank bed covered with several cotton quilts and mosquito netting.

The outbreak of the Anti-Japanese War in 1937 and the forced relocation of the arsenal to Chongqing, the Nationalist wartime capital, reinforced Li's commitment to frugality and sacrifice for the national cause. Obeying Ordnance Department orders to remain in Nanjing until the last possible moment, Li urged his employees to continue producing weaponry to defend Shanghai against the Japanese offensive. Once the arsenal finally moved in mid-November, however, the tremendous speed of relocation and subsequent assembly minimized disruption of production. In a breathtaking sixteen days Li oversaw the transport of over four thousand tons of equipment from Nanjing to Chongqing. Using patriotic appeals, like "go to work as if you are going to battle," the fiery Nationalist exhorted his workers and even slept alongside them on the floor of an old depot while supervising the rebuilding of the arsenal. In record time, production resumed in the spring of 1938, within one hundred days of having left Nanjing.[16]

Defying the strict military hierarchy of the defense industry, where all managers and staff members were military officers who tended to lord over the workers, Li often rubbed shoulders with arsenal laborers, rare for a man of his rank (major general) and times. Enduring perceptions of a natural social division based on mental and manual labor continued to inform management practices and underscored staff members' sense of superiority relative to workers. Li faced an uphill battle in trying to combat these prejudices, which he noted in a 1947 parting speech to the skilled workers' school: "Our country's people have in ignorance retained the long-standing habit of scorning workers."[17]

Li's populism was largely a product of the Anti-Japanese War, which convinced him that all factory employees played a crucial role in the resistance effort. "Factory affairs must depend on pooling the wisdom and efforts of everyone" to shoulder "the heavy responsibility of national defense," Li stated. Li made no distinctions of hierarchy. "Because their skills and learning vary, the positions of staff officers, workers and soldiers are inherently different; nevertheless, they are all the masters and partners of this factory." Thus, "colleagues should not make distinctions amongst themselves, there should be one room for fraternity and courtesy."[18] As an example of how Li tried to foster fraternity, Li encouraged his staff to wear simple blue cotton clothes to work rather than Western suits or Sun Yatsen suits.

As a man of action and committed patriot, Li also exerted all his energies in protecting the arsenal to fight the Japanese. With material and manpower shortages during the war, Li frequently went to the river ports to haul up material with his employees and thus save public funds. One former employee recalled how Li led a team of laborers hauling up two thousand hectoliters of rice from the river port to prevent their destruction from air raids or flooding. It was quite rare for a factory director to engage in manual labor side by side with his employees.

He was called the "big boss" (da laoban) by workers, and a strong paternalist flavor marked Li's managerial style, which Li put into practice with elaborate social welfare programs at Arsenal No. 21. One can attribute these practices to both Confucian benevolence and Machiavellian strategy. In large part, the rapid increase in the number of arsenal employees necessitated such measures. Starting in July 1938, Li incorporated three other factories and established a branch factory in neighboring Yunnan province, leading the "mother" arsenal to oversee more than thirty thousand employees and their immediate family members. Given that the arsenal was located in a new industrial district on the outskirts of Chongqing proper, to better shield it from Japanese air raids and to have ready access to river transport, the factory became the focal point of workers' communities as well as the distribution center for daily goods. Thus, within months of moving to Chongqing, Li established several grain purchasing offices in rice-rich counties throughout Sichuan so the arsenal could provide grain rations for employees and dependents. Moreover, the arsenal distributed monthly provisions of cheap vegetable oil, cloth, matches, and coal. Below-market prices offset the deep wage cuts workers endured throughout the 1940s. Real wages declined so dramatically that by December 1942 industrial workers' actual income was only worth 20 percent of its 1937 value. In keeping with his ethos of self-reliance, Li also allotted small plots of land to employee families living inside the factory compound so they could raise pigs, cultivate vegetables, and produce bean curd and soy sauce.

The arduous conditions of arsenal work and low wages pushed thousands of workers to leave the defense industry each year, prompting management to use housing policy as an instrument of social stability. By the early 1940s, factory housing had become the most basic welfare policy of munitions plants. In order to alleviate housing shortages and high rents caused by the massive influx of war refugees and migrant workers, each arsenal provided free housing—dormitories for single employees and dwellings for employees with family members. The factory also set up mess halls, showers, barber shops, and consumer cooperatives, and provided free medical care to employees and their dependents at the factory clinic and employee hospital. Li went so far as to establish a dating service for the many single men living in the factory compound and oversaw several collective marriages at the arsenal. Nevertheless, as a reflection of his Nationalist sentiments, Li advocated late marriage and birth control.

> It is unhealthy to marry prematurely before one has fully grown. Early marriage before finishing one's education will lead to a loss of ambition. Thus, it is truly not late for men to wed at the age of 30. Moreover, if one marries at an early age, unavoidably one will have too many children. It will be difficult to attend to their education leading our people to become physically weak and ignorant. Not only will this prevent individual prosperity but it will harm the nation.[19]

Perhaps because he placed his utmost loyalty to the nation rather than the family, Li remained single and rejected offers of marriage, joking, "The Xiongnu [Huns] have not yet died out. Why should I marry?"

Li became a forceful advocate of education to achieve a public-spirited citizenry. At the Chongqing Arsenal he established a remedial school for staff members and workers, a skilled workers' training school, several elementary schools, and a middle school for employees' children. Li viewed education as a means of strengthening China, which in his view was locked in a Darwinian struggle for survival.

> I have often told my employees, the strength or weakness of a country depends on citizens' spirits, not on the number of people. If citizens bestir themselves and are public minded and selfless towards their country, then their country will undoubtedly prosper. By contrast, if citizens indulge in corruption and have listless spirits, simple and crude knowledge and become degenerate, even if there are multitudes of people, inevitably they will progressively become extinct.[20]

Li's concern to strengthen the Chinese citizenry through factory welfare programs was most evident in his promotion of sports. By the early 1940s, Li oversaw the construction of a four-hundred-meter track, a soccer field, numerous basketball courts, and a twenty-five-by-fifty-meter swimming pool with high and low platform diving boards. Every autumn Li presided over a factorywide athletic meet lasting three days. Moreover, the factory held an annual marathon and a long distance swimming race across the Jialing River. Li's emphasis on sport was fueled by his fierce nationalism and desire to advance China's industry. In a speech to colleagues and factory workers on the day of the meet, Li emphasized that sport could strengthen the Chinese people so they would not be bullied by other nations.

> A strong and healthy physique is the basis for all undertakings. No matter the extent of your wisdom or your morality, if you do not have a strong body, then you will not be able to achieve in your endeavors. What a disgrace that foreigners call us the "sick man of Asia." Not only are we unable to catch up with Britain, the United States and all advanced countries in science, industry and all material conditions, but our physique and manpower also lag far behind.

After noting that China's average life expectancy was one-third less than that of Japan and Germany and that the average career spanned half the time of those employed in more advanced countries, Li remarked, "If our common citizens do not work hard for China's prosperity and do not first exercise, after the victory in the War of Resistance, we will still be unable to compete with other people, we will still be bullied and oppressed, and we will still be unable to avoid worrying about national subjugation and genocide."[21]

Li's concern over the fate of China was viscerally felt at the sight of his employees and the health crisis affecting his industry. "I feel distressed every time I see some of our factory colleagues with their lean and haggard looks and weak constitutions." Among twelve thousand employees and dependents, there had been over 230,000 clinical visits during 1943, an average of nineteen visits per person. Reports and surveys conducted by the arsenals indicate the carnage that went on during the war. From available records for seven arsenals, a total of 1,348 workers lost their lives between 1937 and 1946, roughly 2 percent of the workforce. Sheer exhaustion caused many workers to succumb to disease and injury. "You ate on the job so that the machines kept running," Li Chenggan recalled. "You did not sleep until late at night, or volunteered to extend [your] working hours for over fourteen hours with no rest at all. Workers who made concerted efforts and vied to rush through production became sick from not sleeping. Exhaustion spread among those relying on this death-defying, sweat-drenched spirit of dedication to our country."[22]

No doubt Li's own paternalistic altruism and *shiye jiuguo* sentiments inspired these welfare benefits, but they were also a response to workers' demands for greater security. A striking example of how workers played on Li's paternalist reputation to demand benefits occurred soon after the factory had moved to Chongqing, when over a hundred workers collectively wrote Li Chenggan. Appealing to his sense of Confucian propriety and nationalism, the workers urged Li to provide economic aid for their dependents in the Japanese-occupied areas so they could reunite in the Nationalist war capital. "Our children in the occupied territory will receive an education of enslavement. As descendents of the Yellow Emperor, we are the future generations of warriors to reconstruct our country, but how can we be used if the talent of youth is buried?" After noting the low wages received amid inflation, the petitioners asked, "How can workers have enough to save their elders, brothers and sisters from the abyss of misery and deliver them inland? We are dedicating our lives to the cause of the country, but we do not have the economic means to save them. . . . We believe your Excellency treats workers like his family and will prevent workers from worrying."[23] Responding to his workers' pleas, Li secretly arranged for the migration of their relatives to Chongqing in the spring of 1940. Several hundred family members were first brought to the British Concession in Shanghai and then placed on a British steamship for Hong Kong and then Vietnam. From Hanoi the migrants went by train to Kunming, where they were picked up by truck and sent to Chongqing.

But Li was not always so accommodating to his workers' demands and could take a hard-line stance. Arsenal No. 21 was subject to two labor disputes involving a convergence of workers' economic and moral grievances.[24] In the first instance, workers challenged management's use of a compulsory savings plan when Chiang Kai-shek began consolidating control over Sichuan. Prior to the local Chongqing machine gun plant's merger with the Jinling Arsenal, management had kept 3 percent of workers' monthly wages and placed them in individual savings accounts. The plan proved unpopular with workers, who demanded their full wages and proceeded to strike for three days. Management's ability to divide workers along economic and regional lines and fire workers' representatives temporarily defused potential conflict. Workers were further appeased when the director of the machine gun plant agreed to return employee savings if his successor consented. But when Li Chenggan took control over the arms plant and subsumed it under Arsenal No. 21, he refused to terminate the plan. Li argued that the savings plan worked as an incentive for workers to stay put because they would lose their savings if they left their posts. His stance prompted Communist activists to capitalize on widespread dissatisfaction among the workforce by threatening a slowdown if the savings were not redistributed. Police reported that activists threatened a factorywide strike if management did not respond to workers' demands within a week of the slowdown. Apparently the issue was resolved in favor of the arsenal workers without recourse to violence.

Perhaps buoyed by their success, workers challenged social welfare policy regarding subsidies for family members. In 1940, workers from six departments coordinated a four-day slowdown to protest the selective distribution of ten yuan as a provisional subsidy to workers with dependent family members. Workers perceived the measure as a form of economic discrimination designed to divide the workforce. The coordination among departments needed to mount the slowdown suggests the rancor caused by economic discrimination stemming from managerial policies intended to favor one segment of the workforce over another. Ultimately, Li acquiesced and distributed the ten yuan to the entire workforce.

Just as labor disputes forced managerial compromise, the development of social welfare benefits at Arsenal No. 21 and throughout the defense industry was in large part a response to workers' flight, the most frequent form of industrial action among workers in search of better working conditions. To be sure, workers saw arsenal employment as a patriotic act. "We work for the War of Resistance against Japan," a young worker explained. "As long as everyone undergoes equal hardship, as long as we are in high spirits, we prefer to withstand lowly treatment."[25] That sense of self-sacrifice might explain how they could tolerate poor working conditions, low wages, and risk the fatal dangers that permeated arsenal work. Patriotism notwithstanding, the combination of grueling work conditions, a repressive political environment, and low pay relative to other industries led workers to exit en masse. By the early 1940s, over ten thousand workers were leaving the defense industry each year in search of other jobs. Extensive labor mobility prompted Ordnance leadership to devise new means of discipline, offset worker hardships, and create a force of loyal retainers. By 1941, all Nationalist arsenals had established welfare boards to oversee arsenal farms, hospitals, entertainment, schools, consumer cooperatives, and resident areas. By the mid-1940s, fringe benefits became increasingly elaborate to compensate for abysmally low wages and to prevent flight. As Colonel Walter Sylvester, liaison with the Chinese Ordnance Department, noted, "The wage scale for these ordinary or unskilled laborers is very low. However to keep them from being attracted to more lucrative jobs, the arsenals have provided gratis, quarters, certain food stuffs, medical care, and educational facilities."[26]

As the leading industrial sector in an increasingly state-driven economy, the defense industry was a pioneer in promoting fringe benefits. Welfare services in the arsenals had assumed increased significance for several reasons. The geographic isolation of most arsenals and large workforces necessitated social welfare services such as hospitals and company housing. Management sought to use welfare to discipline an emerging proletariat and overcome its resistance to factory life but above all to maintain and reproduce a stable workforce as economically as possible. The demands of wartime production pressured state managers to offer incentives other than wages to enhance productivity. Payment in kind was replacing cash wages owing to the currency devaluation caused by the hyperinflation crisis that worsened throughout the 1940s. Finally, conflict between workers and management—as manifested in mobility and other forms of resistance—forced arsenal directors to offer benefits. The making of social welfare packages, as elsewhere, thus derived from a process of "negotiated loyalty."[27]

Despite an absence of violent clashes between labor and managers under Li Chenggan's tenure—perhaps a measure of his success in implementing social welfare—the arsenal was not immune to workers' resistance. The increasing use of piece rates led workers to contest the issue of time and, indirectly, raise questions of control over the labor process. In a 1939 speech to employees regarding the trial implementation of shorter shifts and piecework, Li admonished workers for slacking off. Li charged that for every twelve hours of the workday, workers' output equaled only four to five hours of actual labor, because workers zealously prevented competition to boost rates. Workers exerted greater control over their labor by slowing the pace of work, fearing rate cutting if they earned more than the standard wage scale. "After we set work deadlines and gave incentives through bonuses and piecework, workers not only continued to lack enthusiasm, but even obstructed other workers from doing more."[28] Workers continued to flout the rules during the late 1940s even when payment by result became more widespread. Workplace infractions such as damaging objects, breaking tools, pilfering, leaving one's post or even the factory, arriving late or leaving early, neglecting work, and ignoring directions had become habitual.[29]

Concerned that the various social welfare measures adopted by Li and other industrial managers were insufficient to win over the hearts and minds of the arsenal labor force, Nationalist Party leaders resorted to mass recruitment and indoctrination into the Nationalist Party (Guomindang or GMD). The wartime defense industry became a key site for partification. At its peak, in 1941, the district party branch affiliated with the defense industry supervised eighty-four subdistrict branches and included forty thousand party members.[30] Mass recruitment in the defense industry was in part a legacy of the Nationalist Revolution of the 1920s, when the GMD developed a social base in the military. More immediate causes, such as high labor turnover and the unraveling of the United Front, the political alliance between Communists and Nationalists, also forced the GMD to foster ideological cohesion in an industry so vital to the state's survival.

After the New Fourth Army incident of January 1941, when Nationalist forces ambushed Communist troops, Chiang Kai-shek authorized a new wave of repression against his Communist rivals while fortifying Nationalist Party ranks. Thus, he ordered all staff officers in the defense industry to join the Guomindang or face dismissal. Having sworn never to join the party because of his distaste for official circles, Li preferred to leave his post as factory director and tendered his resignation three times. But Guomindang officials were reluctant to let Li leave his post and so sent the Supervisory Commissioner Zhang Xun to discuss the matter with Li. Despite his status as a veteran revolutionary, party elder, and former mentor of Li's, Zhang Xun had minimal effect. Only after Chiang Kai-shek agreed to modify his rules on condition that technical staff members swear allegiance to the Three People's Principles did Li agree to remain director.

Li remained at his post until 1947, but the incident reflected his growing disenchantment with the Nationalist regime. Party corruption alienated Li; GMD mass recruitment methods smacked of hypocrisy if party leaders were morally corrupt.

> In a conversation with a certain party official [Zhang Xun], I noted that I have seen party officials disrespect the instructions handed down by the Father of the Republic [Sun Yatsen] and violate the Three People's Principles. Although I am not a party member, I can swear that my words and actions have not violated the Three People's Principles or the Father's testimony. This person knows me well as someone who doesn't boast. I often feel that in order to save China and become prosperous and strong and healthy, superiors and subordinates must sincerely follow the Three People's Principles. Party members and corps members should emphasize the quality not quantity of members, so that they can set an example for others. Not being corrupt and not doing things in a perfunctory way or putting one's interests above others will increase people's faith [in the party], provide a model for the citizens, and enable them to work in common for the country.

Li and his superiors also disagreed over the postwar reconstruction of China and the question of how the growing Communist-Nationalist impasse would be resolved. Immediately after V-J Day, Li was appointed deputy Ordnance Department director while retaining his post as director of Arsenal No. 21. Defying the short-term interests of the arms industry and in opposition to Yu Dawei, Li advocated reducing arms output while increasing machinery and machine tool production to "benefit the people's livelihood and strengthen the nation's foundation." Li's hopes for civilian conversion, however, were dashed when full-scale civil war broke out during the summer of 1946. Frustrated over his inability to affect political reconciliation, Li used reasons of health (high blood pressure) to tender his resignation. In February 1947 he was allowed to resign his post as Arsenal No. 21 director. As deputy ordnance director he went to the United States that summer to inspect military industries and receive medical assistance. While in America he had contact with Feng Yuxiang, who was inspecting irrigation works. Feng had publicly condemned Chiang Kai-shek as a dictator, for which he was expelled from the GMD. Pronounced guilty from association with Feng, Li was also dismissed as deputy director of the Ordnance Department.

By the eve of the Communist ascension to power in 1949, Li seems to have placed himself firmly in the Communist camp. One source goes so far as to claim that Li had already joined the Communist underground during World War II. Li's distaste for political parties, however, was not restricted to the Nationalists. "What GMD, what CCP [Chinese Communist Party], they're both a gang of scoundrels," he allegedly remarked in a speech to students at an athletic meet. Throughout the war, however, Li did maintain loose ties to the Communists, especially when his younger sister, Li Liuping, joined the CCP at the Yan'an base area in 1938. To retain contact, Li Chenggan would send her parcels and mail via the distributor of the Communist daily in Chongqing. Li also developed an interest in Marxism, placing the classic works of Marx on his bookshelf as well as Stalin's book *Liening zhuyi wenti* [Problems in Leninism]. Li never commented on Stalin, but he did express interest in understanding how the Soviet Union had industrialized so quickly.

Li gravitated toward the Communists not so much for their political appeals but because of their commitment to industrialization, a stark contrast to the Nationalists' last-ditch attempts to sabotage their own industries before fleeing to Taiwan. Upon returning to China, Li was invited in July 1948 to assume the post of assistant manager of the Nanjing Yongli chemical company and director of its sulfuric acid factory. In November 1948, under pressure from the GMD to relocate the factory to Taiwan, Li stood his ground. "As long as I'm here, this factory will not disband." Li actively began raising money and stored grain for his employees while establishing an alliance among workers, staff members, and administrators known as the "collegial mutual aid association" to mount a factory protection movement. By the summer of 1949 Li accepted Communist proposals that he inspect factories in the northeast, which they had recently occupied. Despite having left the Nationalist defense industry, Li continued to enjoy considerable prestige among acting arsenal directors. When Li attended the first meeting of the Chinese People's Political Consultative Congress at Beijing in October 1949, he wrote back to Yu Zhuozhi, his former secretary and successor at Arsenal No. 21. Li urged Yu to save his political skin and ally with the Communists. "The situation is already settled. . . . Conduct yourself carefully."

In the last few years of his life, Li assumed various honorific posts. After a stint as the manager of the Yongli chemical company, he became director of China's newly established Measurement Department. On January 15, 1959, Li passed away in a Beijing hospital from heart problems. True to his ascetic and frugal lifestyle, Li's only possessions were found to be two wooden soap-boxes holding a change of clothes and some books.

But Li left behind a much larger legacy that has bridged China's struggle to both create a socialist society and modernize. Li's disregard for hierarchy and officialdom combined with his criticisms of society's disdain for manual labor would find resonance in the industrial policies of the 1950s. Given his own values, one imagines that Li would have applauded Mao Zedong's efforts to promote a revolutionary ethos of self-sacrifice and self-reliance with prac-tices that tried to bridge the gulf between leaders and followers by encourag-ing cadre participation in physical labor. Moreover, Li's factory welfare pro-grams, which he had established in response to workers' resistance, the economic crises affecting wartime China, and his own melding of Confucian and Nationalist ideals, became the norm for industrial welfare programs of the People's Republic of China (PRC). To be sure, there were distinct differ-ences between Li's implementation of social services and the PRC's work unit system, urban residential and work communities administered by state enterprises. The absence of labor markets, the "iron rice bowl," and perma-nent unemployment that distinguished the work unit system were not char-acteristic of the 1940s. In other respects, however, Li's promotion of sport, medical care, housing, subsidized daily goods, and schooling for his employ-ees anticipated the social services offered to Chinese workers during the Maoist era. Ironically, while workers are now stripped of these benefits and Chongqing's arsenals enter into joint-venture agreements with Japanese mo-torcycle companies, contemporary Chinese historians conveniently sidestep Li's progressive views—his criticisms of political dictatorship, his belief that revolution and modernization were inextricably linked, and his belief in the sacredness of labor. Befitting the current mainland Chinese scholarship that looks at the past for lessons on how to achieve economic development and social harmony, Li's patriotism and factory paternalism are placed in a broader revisionist narrative of the Anti-Japanese War that celebrates the Nationalist regime's contributions to the war effort against Japan and the patriotism of the Chinese people.

## Further Reading

Li Chenggan's publications have been compiled in Zheng Hongquan, ed., *Huainian yu zhufu: jinian Li Chenggan xiansheng tingchen 110 zhounian ji gonghe Yu Zhuozhi xiansheng 90 huating zhuanji* [Remembering and Celebrating: Biographies in Commemoration of Li Chenggan's 110th Birthday Anniversary and Yu Zhuozhi's 90th Birthday] (1998), and this publication is based on Li Chenggan, *Zhigong jia yan lu* [Collected Speeches of Li Chenggan], found in the Chongqing Municipal Archives.

English-language publications dealing with the history of China's armaments industry include Joshua H. Howard, *Workers at War: Labor in China's Arsenals, 1937–1953* (2004), and Thomas Kennedy, *The Arms of Kiangnan: Modernization in the Chinese Ordnance Industry, 1860–1895* (1978). Those interested in engineers and the role of Germany in China's military modernization should consult William C. Kirby, "Engineering China: Birth of a Developmental State, 1928–1937," in *Becoming Chinese: Passages to Modernity and Beyond*, edited by Wen-hsin Yeh (2000); and William C. Kirby, *Germany and Republican China* (1984). For a recent study of the origins and development of China's industrial welfare practices, see Mark W. Frazier, *The Making of the Chinese Industrial Workplace: State, Revolution, and Labor Management* (2002).

## Notes

1. Unless otherwise noted, this and other quotations are from Li Chenggan's autobiography reprinted in Zheng Hongquan, ed., *Huainian yu zhufu: jinian Li Chenggan xiansheng tingchen 110 zhounian ji gonghe Yu Zhuozhi xiansheng 90 huating zhuanji* [Remembering and Celebrating: Biographies in Commemoration of Li Chenggan's 110th Birthday Anniversary and Yu Zhuozhi's 90th Birthday] (Chongqing, China: Chongqing Chang'an qiche youxian zeren gongsi, 1998), 7.

2. Feng Guifen, "On the Manufacture of Foreign Weapons," in Ssu-Yu Teng and John K. Fairbank, *China's Response To the West: A Documentary Survey, 1839–1923* (Cambridge, Mass: Harvard University Press, 1954), 54.

3. U.S. Military Intelligence Reports: China, 1911–1941 [henceforth abbreviated as MIR], Reel 6, Report no. 398: "Additional Reports on Various Arsenals," July 28, 1930.

4. U.S. Department of State, Records of the Department of State relating to the Internal Affairs of China, 1930–1939, 893.2421/28, May 13, 1930.

5. MIR Reel 6, Report no. 392: "The Taiyuanfu Arsenal," Lieut. Col. Field Artillery Nelson E. Margetts, December 10, 1930.

6. Yu Zhuozhi, "Kang Ri Zhanzheng zhong Jinling binggongchang de bianqian," *Jiangsu wenshi ziliao* 28 (1989): 91.

7. Li Jingwei, "Li Chenggan xiansheng huiyi pianduan," in *Huainian yu zhufu: jinian Li Chenggan xiansheng tingchen 110 zhounian ji gonghe Yu Zhuozhi xiansheng 90 huating zhuanji* [Remembering and Celebrating: Biographies in Commemoration of Li Chenggan's 110th Birthday Anniversary and Yu Zhuozhi's 90th Birthday], ed. Zheng Hongquan (Chongqing, China: Chongqing Chang'an qiche youxian zeren gongsi, 1998), 157.

8. Zheng Hongquan, "Aiguo binggong zhuanjia Li Chenggan" [The Ordnance Industrial Patriot, Li Chenggan], *Chongqing wenshi ziliao* 35 (1991): 119.

9. *Binggong yuekan*, July 15, 1929.

10. Zhao Zhizhong, "Jinling binggong Chang—di liushi binggongchang" [From the Jinling Arsenal to Arsenal No. 60], *Jiangsu wenshi ziliao* 28 (1989): 62.

11. "Yu Dawei wei Jinling binggong Chang yi jieyu jingfei gaijin changwu gei Chiang Kai-shek qiancheng gao," ZJBGS 3 (October 3, 1934): 769.

12. Wang Zhenghua, *Kangzhan shiqi waiguo dui Hua junshi yuanzhu* [Foreign Military Aid to China during the War of Resistance] (Taipei, Taiwan: Huanqiu shuju, 1987), 17.

13. Li Chenggan, "Kangzhanzhong fuwu binggong huiyilu" (1947), in *Huainian yu zhufu: jinian Li Chenggan xiansheng tingchen 110 zhounian ji gonghe Yu Zhuozhi xiansheng 90 huating zhuanji* [Remembering and Celebrating: Biographies in Commemoration of Li Chenggan's 110th Birthday Anniversary and Yu Zhuozhi's 90th Birthday], ed. Zheng Hongquan (Chongqing, China: Chongqing Chang'an qiche youxian zeren gongsi, 1998), 25.

14. Zheng Hongquan, "Aiguo binggong zhuanjia Li Chenggan," 125.

15. Li Chenggan, "Kangzhanzhong fuwu binggong huiyilu," 24.

16. Zheng Hongquan, "Binggong zhuanjia Li Chenggan" [The Ordnance Expert Li Chenggan], in *Peidu renwu jishi* [Accounts of Wartime Capital Biographies] (Chongqing, China: Chongqing chubanshe, 1995), 353–54.

17. Li Chenggan, "Zai gaobei jixiao shisheng shu" (May 16, 1947), in *Huainian yu zhufu: jinian Li Chenggan xiansheng tingchen 110 zhounian ji gonghe Yu Zhuozhi xiansheng 90 huating zhuanji* [Remembering and Celebrating: Biographies in Commemoration of Li Chenggan's 110th Birthday Anniversary and Yu Zhuozhi's 90th Birthday], ed. Zheng Hongquan (Chongqing, China: Chongqing Chang'an qiche youxian zeren gongsi, 1998), 61.

18. Zheng Hongquan, "Aiguo binggong zhuanjia Li Chenggan," 129.

19. Zhao Zhizhong, "Li Chenggan zhuanlue," *Jiangsu wenshi ziliao* 28 (1989): 126.

20. Li Chenggan, "Kangzhan zhong fuwu binggong huiyilu" (February 1947), in *Huainian yu zhufu: jinian Li Chenggan xiansheng tingchen 110 zhounian ji gonghe Yu Zhuozhi xiansheng 90 huating zhuanji* [Remembering and Celebrating: Biographies in Commemoration of Li Chenggan's 110th Birthday Anniversary and Yu Zhuozhi's 90th Birthday], ed. Zheng Hongquan (Chongqing, China: Chongqing Chang'an qiche youxian zeren gongsi, 1998), 25.

21. Li Chenggan, "Tiyuji gao tongren" (September 9, 1944), in *Huainian yu zhufu: jinian Li Chenggan xiansheng tingchen 110 zhounian ji gonghe Yu Zhuozhi xiansheng 90 huating zhuanji* [Remembering and Celebrating: Biographies in Commemoration of Li Chenggan's 110th Birthday Anniversary and Yu Zhuozhi's 90th Birthday], ed. Zheng Hongquan (Chongqing, China: Chongqing Chang'an qiche youxian zeren gongsi, 1998), 48–49.

22. Joshua H. Howard, *Workers at War: Labor in China's Arsenals, 1937–1953* (Stanford, Calif.: Stanford University Press, 2004), 130, 134.

23. Chongqing Municipal Archives [henceforth abbreviated as CQA], 20 Chang, 1352 juan.

24. Howard, *Workers at War*, 261–62.

25. Anonymous factory machinist, "Shoubuliao feili yapo, hanlei likaile gongchang," *Xinhua ribao*, June 15, 1940, 4.

26. Franklin D. Roosevelt Library, American War Production Mission, Munitions Production Box 16, Major Walter G. Sylvester, Ordnance Department, "Notes on Chinese Arsenals," 1945.

27. Gerald Zahavi, *Workers, Managers, and Welfare Capitalism: The Shoeworkers and Tanners of Endicott Johnson, 1890–1950* (Urbana: University of Illinois Press, 1988), 105.

28. Li Chenggan, "Shixing suoduan gongzuo shijian tigao gongzuo xiaolu zhi xunhua," *Zhigong jia yanlu*, July 7, 1939, 39.

29. Howard, *Workers at War*, 144.

30. CQA, 50 Chang, kuaiji, 3981 juan, p. 11, ZJBGS 3:1059; Cao Haosen, *Zhongguo Guomindang junzhengbu tebie dangbu di er zhounian gongzuo gaikuang* (1941), in Nationalist Party Historical Archives (Dangshihui), Taipei, Taiwan, 495 lei, 95 hao.

~

# CHAPTER SEVEN

# The Beijing University Students in the May Fourth Era: A Collective Biography

## Fabio Lanza

### An Event and a Tradition

Sunday, May 4, 1919: the cloudy and windy morning was rapidly giving way to one of those beautiful, blue-skied Beijing afternoons. Seeing how the weather had turned for the better, many among the more affluent urban residents were heading toward the central area of the old capital: close to what is now Tiananmen Square was Beijing's first public park, Central Park. That day, however, the very modern pleasure of strolling in the fenced green area was interrupted by some kind of commotion taking place just south of the park. The park visitors, as well as many others who were in the neighborhood for work or simply passing by, found themselves curious spectators of an unprecedented event.

The focus of the excitement seemed to be the area just in front of Tianan Gate, the southern entrance of the old imperial palace, where dozens, then hundreds of students were quickly gathering, carrying signs and distributing leaflets to bystanders. They were demonstrating against the Versailles Treaty that, rather than returning German colonial possession in China to the Chinese, instead passed them on to Japan. At Tiananmen, students argued briefly with the local police and then, for the first time in Chinese history, they marched through the old capital, staging the first of the demonstrations that spread across China and quickly came to be known as the May Fourth Movement.

The Beijing demonstration ended with minor violence and the arrest of several students by the police and the army. Weeks of protests followed, during which Beijing residents were treated to the very unusual spectacle of students giving speeches on street corners, more arrests, and even the complete sealing off of the university area—literally a siege—by a full-blown army deployment. In the end, students both won and lost. They won their battle with the Chinese government, which under their pressure refused to sign the Versailles Treaty, but they lost the larger fight as Japan was granted control over the former German territories. China's missing signature at Versailles remained a symbolic gesture.

And it is in symbols that we have to look for the significance of the May Fourth Movement, its historical consequence being more that of a foundational and iconic event than of a tale of success or failure. In the Chinese narrative of nation and state building, May Fourth has come to represent the awakening of the national consciousness of the intellectuals, the turning point that led to the foundation of the Communist Party in 1921 and to the rise of the Nationalist Party in the 1920s. In each and every textbook in the People's Republic of China (PRC), Taiwan, and even Hong Kong, modern Chinese history starts precisely on May 4, 1919. Modernity, from this perspective, became intimately connected with students and student activism. The "modern student" was the figure that heralded modernity itself, and student activism continued to play a crucial role in China's twentieth century; most of the cardinal moments in recent Chinese history have been accompanied by an upsurge in student activism, up until 1989, when in the crushed bodies of protesters around Tiananmen Square we might see the exhaustion of a political tradition centered on the figure of the student.

One institution and its students stand out in this tradition of activism, as they stood in the front line of political action both in 1919 and in 1989: Beijing University (Beijing Daxue, usually referred to as Beida). The first and most famous university in China, Beida owes its fame as much to being a hotbed of student activism as to its long-standing excellence in scholarship. That legacy of activism has been embraced consciously or subconsciously by subsequent generations of Beida students as a mark of identity. Many of the student leaders in 1989 were from Beijing University, and their acts and gestures made continuous references to a mythology of heroism and exceptionality springing from May 4, 1919. It was student at Beida who, on May 4, 1989, issued a "New May Fourth manifesto," calling on the students to fulfill the historical role of heralds of modernization. And when the 1989 students occupied Tiananmen Square, they spoke and addressed the crowd from the

Monument to the People's Heroes, where a bas-relief celebrates in vivid (albeit inaccurate) details the student activists of seventy years earlier.

What gets lost in the legacy of May Fourth, in the mythology of activism that sprung from 1919, are, in many ways, the students themselves. When the gestures, the iconic symbols of 1919, are inscribed into a tradition, we lose track of the fact that those university students who marched for the first time on the streets of Beijing were, first of all, youths. They had come to Beijing and to Beida from different places and different backgrounds; afterward they followed different, often divergent paths. But for a few years at the end of the first decade of the twentieth century, they lived together, sharing halls, classrooms, and dorms. They were "new" at this, and not just individually, as any freshman is new to college life, but as a group, as "students." The very idea of a university was new to China, and Beida's at that time had existed for fewer than twenty years; there was therefore no tradition to rely upon. In late 1910s, the young students at Beida had to figure out not only a new life, a new place, and a new city but also what it meant to be a modern student.

What follows is an attempt to write a collective biography of the Beijing University students in the May Fourth years (roughly 1917–1923). Who were these students; what did their lives look like? What, if anything, was different about everyday life at Beijing University? How did the students' communal experience shape their political activism? A collective biography is per se an exercise of imagination and invention but not one disconnected from historical sources. This story represents a myriad of daily experiences, hundreds of lives, but no single "real" individual. We will try to highlight the path students followed from admission exams to dorms, classes, and extracurricular activities. While this is in no way meant to be a stereotypical description (as we will see, there were no "stereotypical" Beida students), the goal is to show hints of an atmosphere, a set of shared experiences, a place: China's first modern university and first modern students at the moment of their emergence into—and creation of—national history.

## The Place

In 1919, Beijing University was the first and the only public university in China. Founded in 1898, the only surviving remnant of a failed attempt to radically reform imperial institutions, it had never functioned properly. Its mandate remained split between the ideal of a Western modern university (devoted to research) and the legacy of the imperial examination system (producing officers for the state). Even after the founding of the Republic in 1912 (when its name was changed from Imperial Academy to National

Beijing University), Beida remained plagued by careerism and bureaucratic influence, and its students were notorious more for brothel hopping and gambling than for academic achievement. Located in an old imperial residence within walking distance of the Forbidden City, even its physical surroundings were reminiscent of the lingering entanglement of the school with the state and its bureaucracy. But by the early 1910s, the promises of the new Republic had collapsed into warlordism, leaving the university with no legitimate state-based educational routine to fall back into.

Already in the mid-1910s, echoes of the so-called New Culture Movement—a critical rethinking of every single aspect of Chinese cultural and social practice[1]—started to reverberate in the halls of the schools, when new (usually young) professors introduced new subjects and new (Western) methods. This process of change drastically accelerated in 1917, when Cai Yuanpei became the president of the university. Both a successful imperial scholar and a graduate of Leipzig University in Germany, Cai had an eclectic mind, well versed in classical Chinese texts as well as in Western philosophical trends. More importantly, Cai firmly believed he had found a position from which he could—and so could any Chinese intellectual —negotiate the troublesome relationship in the modern world between an essentially Western concept of knowledge and the preservation of a Chinese legacy. Science, by which Cai meant the scientific method of investigation, implied a neutral judgment of "value" that could be applied regardless of the national origins of the object studied. Scientific truths (writ large) were neither Chinese nor Western; they were universal. The scientific method had reorganized Western learning, shaping modern disciplines such as history, philology, and archeology, while discarding "traditional" myth and religious accounts; the same method could be applied to Chinese learning as well. The Chinese past, Chinese history, and Chinese beliefs had to be scientifically reevaluated and rescued to be part of a universal field of "true" knowledge.

This was clearly an idealistic project, one that masked the precariousness of the Chinese intellectuals in a world in which the very existence of their country and culture was at stake. But Cai's attitude had practical implications as it structured the radical reform of the university. Following the idea that the university is a place devoted exclusively to pure research in the sciences and the humanities, which abdicated any state-related function, Beida expunged entire colleges (engineering, economics). In the end, of all the "applied" disciplines, only the school of law survived at Beida, along with sciences and humanities. The borders between disciplines and departments were progressively broken down, and students were not simply allowed but were strongly pushed to find their personal paths outside the rigidity of disciplinary inquiries. This freedom was also extended to the faculty, which acquired several new members from the leading intellectuals of the so-called New Culture. Looking at the faculty roster under Cai's presidency, one sees a veritable collection of major figures, the "who's who" of cultural radicalism in early twentieth-century China, as well as some of the Chinese pioneers of modern disciplines such as archeology, history, and philology.

Cai Yuanpei's presidency brought also less noticeable but no less important changes. It was not only boundaries between disciplines that were torn down, for under his presidency the university campus itself was open. Because of its location in the center of Beijing, Beida had always been urban, but it was only after its gates were finally unlocked and symbols of separation were removed that it became integrated with the surrounding city. As Cai himself reminded his students in 1918, the idea behind this change was to overcome the "ivory tower" syndrome of the school and to stress instead the need for an osmotic relationship with society and the world.

> In the past, outsiders were forbidden to enter this place, now everybody can. Once upon a time, just outside the Beijing University building at Mashenmiao, there was a sign, shaped as the head of a tiger. Everyone who saw it knew that this was a school and that he did not have the right to enter. People considered it the highest educational institution in China and only students and professors could get in. This idea was common especially among the people who lived near the university. Now, we got rid of that sign.[2]

Cai also tried to rid the schools of bureaucratic vestiges that survived in students' everyday practices. He encouraged students to adopt a respectful and supportive attitude toward the many laborers of the university; he sponsored an ethical association for the promotion of virtue, whose members promised to renounce gambling, whoring, and bureaucratic employment. In general, Cai promoted a more informal atmosphere in and around the university by, for example, creating a public forum for discussion on administration, school policies, and events in the form of the *Beijing University Daily*, which started its run in late 1917.

By early 1918, Beijing University presented itself to the new students as a place in turmoil, its physical boundaries as unsettled as its intellectual position, and its relationship with the state—which paid for its functioning but did not have authority over its content—increasingly precarious. Beida was asking by its very existence what the scope of action and the goals of a modern university and of modern intellectuals were. For a young man in early twentieth-century China, it was a place with few certainties but much promise.

## Testing In

But how did a promising young man, possibly living hundred of miles from Beijing, gain admission to Beida? Each summer, major newspapers and magazines carried advertisements of the admission exams, which were held in two sessions, August and September. Those applying in 1918 were particularly lucky: the university administration had just decided to increase admissions, and exams for the first time were held not only in Beijing but also in Shanghai.

Statistically speaking, the largest number of perspective students came from the rich Jiangnan area, the Lower Yangzi region. In 1918, about 25 percent of Beida students (as well as many of the professors) were from Jiangsu and Zhejiang provinces. The opening of an exam session in nearby Shanghai was probably welcomed by most applicants, who could save the onerous economic burden of a trip to Beijing. Still, even in Shanghai, taking part in the exam was not without costs: a small administrative fee, lodging, and transportation. Plus, to think that he could actually pass the exams and be admitted to Beida, any applicant must have had a certain confidence in the education he had received up to that point. He probably had gone to a modern middle or high school, which in turn implies his family was not of scarce financial means and could spare the work of one of the sons as well as the disposable income to pay for his schooling up to that point.

Passing the admission exams was not an easy task. All the exams had a section on Chinese, which tested not only linguistic abilities but also familiarity with Chinese literary and cultural references, as well as sections on English language—or another foreign language of choice—mathematics, geography, and history, usually, but not always, divided between Chinese and Western (or foreign) history. There were also questions on physics, chemistry, and other natural sciences.

The exams were obviously aimed at verifying the general preparation of candidates, to ascertain whether they possessed the basic skills on which to ground scientific research. However, besides testing the ability to understand English, solve a mathematical problem, and write in elegant Chinese, some of the test sections attempted to elicit from the students a personal rethinking of larger issues of historical change, contemporary politics, knowledge, and learning. The archives preserve the questions, not the answers, but the questions suffice to give us a sense of the examiners' goals. They did not prescribe univocal solutions but were open: what they presupposed was a critical attitude on the part of students vis-à-vis the school and its learning.

For example, exams focused on a series of issues at the center of the current intellectual debate concerning education and the meaning of the university. A question on the 1919 entrance exam asked applicants to write about the *daxue* (university) in the Eastern Han dynasty (25–220 CE) as the birthplace of political criticism by men of integrity. In 1918, applicants were asked to comment on the statement "general knowledge is the foundation of research." In 1920, the title for the *guowen* (national language, i.e., written Chinese) composition was "the advantages and disadvantages of the civil service examinations," a reference to the legacy of the imperial exam system. In 1921, the English text to be translated presented basic questions on the goals and means of school instruction: "Why do so many people go to school? What do they hope from their years of effort? What is it that we who try to teach them are trying to do for them?" Finally, in 1922 examinees were asked to put forth their opinions on the main event in students' recent life, in which many of them had probably participated as high schoolers: the title for the *guowen* exercise was "the lesson young people can draw from the May Fourth movement." In the same exam session, the Chinese-English translation passage touched directly on one of the most contested issues among students in general and at Beida in particular, the existence of exams and the possibility of alternative methods of selection and evaluation.

1. Exams are a competition, like a running race. 2. In a race only one gets the first place. Does it mean that all the others should not be willing to run? 3. 1500 people take the University entrance exams, and only 300 are accepted, why should all the others even try the exam? 4. There are people who said that exams are bad. What method do you think we should put in place instead of exams?[3]

Through historical comparison and contemporary examples, students were presented with a critique—or at least the possibility of a critique—of the role of the university, its methods, and its relation to the state and society. They were also asked to think about what the new university and its members ought to be, within that historical situation and particular configuration of knowledge. They were ultimately invited to imagine a different politics of education, in a different kind of educational setting. In effect, they were asked to imagine what Beida could be before even getting there.

## Living

The "average" student who passed the admission exams and headed to Beida was obviously male (no female students were admitted until 1920), well educated, and a resident of the more urbanized and richer area of the country.

He was also probably planning to study in the humanities or in law (comparatively few students chose the school of sciences).

Beida was the most expensive public school in the country: fees were set at about sixty yuan per year in 1917 and remained stable for the large part of the 1920s. However, life in Beijing was quite cheap, and a student could manage to live on 100–180 yuan per year. Altogether, students at Beida needed about three hundred yuan per year, barring incidents like hospital bills or exceptional book expenses. Not a huge sum but one that stands in marked contrast with, for example, the average monthly salary of a primary school teacher (between twenty-four and thirty-two yuan) or of an ordinary worker (4.5 to 6.5 yuan).[4] However, there were sharp differences among student themselves. A handful of students spent up to five thousand yuan per year, and many others disposed of one thousand yuan at least. They lived in luxurious accommodation outside the university and hired servants and cooks. In the majority of cases, however, families could provide two to three hundred yuan per year to a student, which was enough for survival but surely did not allow for any luxury. The average Beida student was therefore not rich, but clearly his financial status, albeit somewhat precarious, was well above the vast majority of Chinese peasants and the relatively better-off urban residents as well. Freshmen were then prepared to live a few years without much to spare, but they came to Beida from a relatively safe economic background.

The first problem that needed to be tackled was housing, but only one-third of Beida students were able to find room in the official university dorms. The remaining two thousand had to fend for themselves and found accommodation in more than one hundred *gongyu* (apartment houses) scattered in the neighborhood. These apartments were infamous for being small, overcrowded, and pricey. They were cold and prone to fires in the winter, hot in the summer, and noisy and unhealthy all year long. Concerned that such a poor living environment had a corrupting influence on student behavior and that the high rent constituted a financial liability for students, the school and the Ministry of Education tried to intervene several times in order to improve the *gongyu*—to no avail, apparently, as the problem lingered on in the following decades.

While the odds of getting a dorm room were not good, getting a decent one was extremely difficult. Yang Zhongxian, who was admitted as a preparatory science student in 1917, recalls his peregrinations around Beida, in search of better lodging accommodations.

> I entered the 5th dorm . . . and picked the middle room in a set of three, 2 students per room. We did not even have a proper window, and used a portion of

the door as a window. There was only one tiny table. After one year, I moved to the other dorm on Beichizi: it was not only better but also closer to classrooms. After yet another year, I moved to the Western Hall. There were three students per room, and I was placed in front of the door. It did not close well, so during the winter it was easy to catch a cold.[5]

There were notable differences among the three main dorms. Rooms at Sanyuan (Third Court), which was mainly devoted to freshmen, were originally classrooms, and the larger space would accommodate more than ten persons per room.[6] More typical were Xizhai (Western Hall) and Dongzhai (Eastern Hall), with sparsely furnished two- or three-person rooms. The rooms at Dongzhai were notorious for being extremely tiny: with two beds facing each other, bookshelves, and one table, there was barely enough room for one person to stand. A little stove provided a minimum of heat in the cold Beijing winters. Overall, hygienic conditions were not good. The buildings were in large part inherited from the old Imperial University: pipes were rusty and crumbling, and there was no hot water. "Whatever was lacking in material culture was compensated for by a generous supply of human labor. There was an abundance of servants hired by the university at the students' disposal, though hot water had to be boiled and carried in and out of the rooms."[7]

The lodging situations at Beida might have not been ideal, but there were characteristics that made this environment special (and, in many instances, seem to have endeared it to students.) First of all, life in the dorm was subject to few disciplinary regulations. Movement inside the dorms was extremely free, and few restrictions were imposed on students by "good-for-nothing managers." The disregard of general school regulations in the living quarters was reflected at the level of personal interaction by a certain degree of dissolution in the discipline of human relationship and by an asocial and anticommunitarian spirit students expressed in their daily lives.

In general, the student community at Beida was composite and divided in its interests and approaches to learning, culture, and politics. The intensifying of the "culture fever" in the May Fourth years made these differences sharper, and the dorm rooms became a wildly idiosyncratic space.

There were people under the light or the window with their nose deep into the *Wenxuan* reading the small-character annotations by Li Shan, while at the same time there were people outside the window loudly chanting Byron's poems. In one corner of one room, there was somebody who, wagging his head, was reading aloud in a cadence some old text of the Tongcheng school, while in another corner there were people discussing what kind of life Nora had after she left the "Doll's house." . . . Besides mocking each other in arguments, attacking each other in writing, in class or working they treated each other like enemies and it was clear that they were incompatible.[8]

The increasing division in attitude and intellectual leanings was reflected in the fragmentation of the physical space of the dorms. The large rooms of the Sanyuan dorms were split into tiny private individual spaces by hanging bedsheets on wires or rearranging bed and bookshelves. And if the need for privacy was understandable in the large, open space of Sanyuan, the situation in the much smaller rooms at Dongzhai and Xizhai was not different. Cramped rooms, where there was not enough space for the two occupants to stand at the same time, were reshaped into even narrower corridors with walls made out of shelves and tables. As a counterpart to this physical division, students started to develop the habit of not speaking to each other, not even when sitting side by side at a desk in the classrooms or even when sharing the same dorm room. Greetings to colleagues or mates entering or leaving seemed to have become a rarity.

## Bohemian Attitudes

This fragmentation both of physical space and the dissolution of rites of courtesy reflected the general attitude of laissez-faire at May Fourth Beida. In this period, the university was in fact affected by an incurable "unbridled freedom," aptly summarized by the refrain, "I don't care about you, you don't care about me, we don't mess with each other."[9] It was a place where "nobody would reject you when you arrived, but nobody would run after you when you decided to leave." Contemporaries described May Fourth Beida as "a place for weirdoes" or even a "multifarious, extremely variegated environment, in which everybody can do his own thing."[10]

There were almost no official occasions at Beida that created a sense of an ordered community. There was no commencement, no graduation ceremony, and no flag-raising in the morning. Rules in general were lax, and that allowed for the presence of a number of people who were at Beida but not of Beida: every day many unofficial student auditors entered the school gates, filled the classrooms and the library, used the athletic fields, and often even illegally sublet dorm rooms. These unsanctioned auditors were a recognized feature of Beijing University in the late 1910s, and the young freshman soon realized that it was practically impossible to know whether the person sitting next to him was a regular student or an "eavesdropper"—as the auditors were half mockingly called.

Contrary to other schools at the time, there was no "student uniform" at Beida, no regulated dress code that properly identified proper students. However, students, and especially Beida students (both official and auditors), were recognizable by their attire, which was a long blue gown, usually faded and patched. This was not a uniform imposed by school regulation but rather a choice of fashion with particular, possibly political, implications. The gown was an interesting sartorial choice, as it recycled a traditional form of attire—the silk gown of the imperial scholar-officer—but altered it for modern needs and shaped it into a modern symbol of identity. The student gown was not made of silk but of cotton; it was therefore cheap, durable, and convenient (layers could be placed underneath in the cold Beijing winter). It identified the wearer as a "student" without forcing him to accept the imposition of a uniform.

At Beida, the gown was widely common possibly also because it fitted so well with other characteristics of the school during the May Fourth period. Students at Beida were notorious among their fellow students because of their laggardness and general disregard for physical fitness: they did not excel in sports, nor had any inclination toward physical activity, and not much prowess is expected from someone wearing a gown. The gown then stood as a statement of the right to laziness, and maybe of undisciplined, independent movement. Moreover, students at Beida wore their gown as dirty and patched as possible: they wore it, in a sense, as a symbol of a bohemian statement of carelessness, of independence from rules, of autonomy. Far from constraining the students' bodies, the gown embodied their independent spirit and the disregard for regulations that was the hallmark of campus life.

The gown was also a form of sartorial free pass. Even when dirty and patched, it identified the wearer as belonging to a "respectable" group and allowed him unobstructed access to the commercial and modern areas of Beijing. This was especially convenient since Beida lacked a unified single campus, and classrooms and dorms were dispersed over central Beijing, north and east of the Forbidden City. The area, once strictly identified with the imperial government and the Manchu ruling class, had been subjected to rapid and radical transformation brought by capitalism, colonialism, and a modernizing state. The presence of the foreign legation quarter, established in 1861, brought trade in foreign goods, which found their place next to an increasing variety of local products in the markets of Wangfujing, the bustling commercial street close to Beida. The area just northwest of Tiananmen had been recently transformed into Beijing's first public park, Central Park, open to all but the more indigent. Beida students could access these areas with a few minutes' walk and find themselves a part of the strange spectacle of Beijing "modernity":

> With my countrymen I wandered along the quiet alleys and through the mad business streets of Peking—streets echoing with bells and shouting and a-gleam with golden signs. Streets where the penetrating noise of tambourines burst from the doors of smelly theaters; streets with stores dressed upon and lacquered like bride on their wedding day. . . . I wandered with my friends in Central Park. . . . We laughed importantly and joked in a business-like manner. We shot bold glances at passers-by—at the shy daughters of merchants, fat and rosy-cheeked, who wore blue trousers and gold bracelets; at the plain-looking, bobbed-haired girl students in short, foreign-style skirts, and at the prostitutes with their exquisite stone-like faces and perfect bangs. The latter went past us without looking. Neither our robes nor eye-glasses could hide from their experienced eye the thinness of our pocket-books.[11]

While reminiscent of the imperial tradition, the cotton gown allowed students to appear conspicuously in the landscape of urban modernity, to experience the strange mixture of new and old, and, in a sense, to find their positions in this landscape.

## Teaching and Learning

The attitude of independence and laissez-faire, a certain bohemian spirit, and the outspoken disregard for rituals and rules of belonging were all characteristics that marked the everyday in and around May Fourth Beida. They also were characteristic of the central feature of university life, the classrooms.

The reforms introduced since 1917 made classroom attendance voluntary, if not officially, then at least de facto. A large number of students took this idea a step further: they simply did not attend classes or attended only a small portion of them. As Feng Youlan, the famed philosopher who had been a student at Beida, recalled, "Nobody decided for you which classes you were or were not to attend; nobody decided for you whether you were to attend classes at all. As long as you went to take examination at the proper time, it was all right. If you didn't intend to get a diploma, you didn't even have to take the examinations: it was up to you."[12] Rather than in classrooms, students were more likely to be found in the library, or debating in dorm rooms and in study societies, and, in some cases, in theaters around the city.

Auditors and eavesdroppers were apparently more diligent than regular students in attending classes, and they often made up the large majority of the audience. The phenomenon became even more widespread during the

May Fourth years and into the early 1920s. When well-known philosopher Liang Shuming taught his course on "Confucian thought" in 1923, two hundred students came to attend, and he was forced to move the class to a larger room. However, only the ninety "real" undergraduates took the final exam.[13]

This somewhat haphazard attendance was both the product of and one of the factors behind the peculiar teaching and learning atmosphere at Beida. The reforms had given both the students and the faculty unprecedented freedom. This flexibility opened the way to a total reshaping of classroom teaching, which seems to have replicated the productive disorder of other aspects of the life in the school. Nobody rushed to classes, which started and finished well after the bell had rung. Some professors lectured for weeks without even getting to the real topic of the class. Classroom notes distributed at the beginning of the course were often ignored and then substituted with updated ones.

This "casual" approach to teaching did not translate into sloppiness or disregard for the learning process, however. Both regular students and the numerous auditors circulating around the school were attracted by the quality of the faculty and by the possibility to learn by frequent interaction with teachers famous for their scholarship. Both faculty members and students took the idea of "autonomous research" that was at the foundation of the 1917 reform seriously, and this shaped their attitude toward classroom teaching.

Despite their sometimes lackluster attendance record, students were respectful first and foremost of their teachers' intellectual excellence, even when it was accompanied (as was often the case) by oddities in personal character. Old-style, strict instructors, whose behavior was in many ways at odds with the laissez-faire attitude of Beida, also had a following of avid listeners. Gu Hongming, who taught English literature and Latin, was a very respected teacher, but he was also a Qing loyalist who still wore a queue; he came to class escorted by a servant, who filled his pipe and poured tea while Gu lectured, sitting back in his chair, smoking.[14] Huang Kan (Huang Jigang) was another classical scholar who was famous both for his severity and his erratic behavior. Once, while Qian Xuantong, one of the culturally progressive faculty members, was teaching, he heard Huang Kan lecturing in the adjacent room. The topic of Huang's talk was a critique of Qian's positions on literature; Qian then quickly switched the focus and started lecturing "against" Huang, and they went on in a sort of unscripted duet that lasted till the bell rang.[15] On the other hand, students were not tolerant of any lack of preparation: in one case, an incompetent adjunct professor was forced to resign when students challenged him by preparing twelve pages of critique and comments to his three-page lecture handout and by confronting him in class with in-depth questions.

The combination of a disregard for classroom attendance with a personal passion for research is a sign of the more general attitude toward learning and education among Beida students. In the late 1910s and early 1920s, students engaged in a debate on the process of teaching and learning, the goals and method of academic life. If the university was, as stated by Cai Yuanpei, a place where individual students and faculty members engaged in scientific research, many students argued that all the disciplinary rituals that still constrained intellectual independence should be abolished. First and foremost were exams. In March 1920, the debate over the abolition of exams reached its highest point with an article published in March 1920 in the *Beijing University Students' Weekly*. In that essay, Zhu Qianzhi, a philosophy student, described the practice of memorization that exams fostered as similar to the "force-feeding" of poultry by farmers, who funnel food down the chickens' throats with a pipe. Exams then correspond to the weighing of the chickens to see if they have reached the desired weight. The essay ended with a pledge:

> I, Zhu Qianzhi, after having achieved this kind of awareness, now declare I will not put myself though any other "chicken-weighing" exam. What about you, my self-aware friends? How can you be willing to be "weighed"? Why don't you show clearly your opposition? I thought you were all self-aware. Nobody should be willing to undergo this inhuman treatment! Let's oppose exams with one voice. My friends, let the exam brush fall![16]

Exams were indeed the main target of students' criticism, but every single rule that regulated the intellectual life at Beijing University came to be challenged, from roll calls to assigned seats, permission slips, and justifications for absences. The only reason compelling somebody to sit in a classroom, students argued, should be his subjective interest; everything else was simply an invitation to lie.

## Culture and Politics

It seems difficult to reconcile the picture of individualism, disregard and direct challenging of rules, atomization, and confusion of roles that we have just described with the ability for organized action that Beijing University students demonstrated in May and June 1919. The protests of May Fourth were hastily but carefully planned, and in the following weeks and months the students showed an amazing degree of coordination and preparation.

Beida students were, in a sense, *selectively disorganized*. There was logic to their actions. While they refused any ritualistic discipline, and they contested established regulations imposed by the school or by conventions (as youthful rebels tend to do), they had shown a penchant for organizing around issues, to establish groups in which participation was determined exclusively on the basis of personal interest. The organizational form they chose was called the Study Society (*xuehui*), dozens of which were formed at Beida just in 1917–1918. In those years, the school seemed to be at the center of a true organizational frenzy. The *Beijing University Daily* hosted a continuous flurry of announcements and proposals, but after a while the newspaper could not contain the inventiveness of students:

in dormitory screens and walls, and occasionally on playbills and reports, there was somebody publishing an appeal and there was always somebody responding; there was somebody calling a meeting, and there were always people showing up. As for the meeting place, for the larger meetings it was usually the canteen. When somebody wanted to speak, he would just stand on a stool and start speaking. Even in the bathrooms they started some "bathroom journals" in which they carried on debates.[17]

In the years 1917–1919, there was a multiplication of the formal and informal locations for encounter and discussion, in which some of the distinctions between students and faculty members, insiders and outsiders, seem to have been overcome. Luo Jialun vividly described the atmosphere at some of these meetings:

We also gathered in two other places: one was the faculty lounge on the second floor at the first institute of Hanhuayuan, . . . the other was the office of the librarian in the first floor. In those two places there was no barrier between the professors and the students, no standing on ceremony; whoever showed up, jumped into the debate, everybody raised points and everybody had to face criticism. Those two rooms filled with people everyday after three o'clock in the afternoon.[18]

Beida therefore presented a pattern of lively, almost frenetic organizational activity, a series of seemingly unlimited combinations of small groups of individuals, united around the discussion of issues and the attempt to find organizational forms capable of dealing with every kind of problem. Clearly not all these experiments succeeded; many of these associations, sometimes even the larger ones, were short lived. In some cases members convened only for a foundational meeting, drafted a statute, and went off to other enterprises.

Despite the limited scope of these organizations (few students and little space), most of them proposed goals and missions that were if not vague at least utopian. The Music Research Society aimed at "molding individual character"; the Eloquence Society wanted to "develop thought by renovating language"; while the Association for the Translation of New Knowledge stated that its goal was to "reform learning, propagate thinking, work together for the cultural movement, and plan for radical reform of the world."[19] One could dismiss all this as youthful idealism but for the fact that in each of these three cases, the lofty goals were followed by detailed regulations concerning the structure of the association, its working, and its administration. These young activists were obsessed with organizational details, fees, members' duties, methods, and structures; they were trying to give precise organizational forms to their ideals, aspirations, and challenges.

In a space that was porous and exciting, in which communal rituals were shunned and identity was dubious at best (who was a student? who was an auditor?); where the routines of teaching and learning were open to contention and established patterns of discipline (exams, memorization, attendance) were challenged in theory and in practice; and where individuals gave free expression to their bohemian personalities, the Study Societies were a true training ground for future political and cultural organizers. For students who were challenging established rules and practices, they presented the possibility to establish their own organizational rules and practices, and to meet with others on a basis of not disciplinary conditions but rather interest, passion, and militancy. It was the rebellious spirit but also the organizational practice and the disciplined participation, all trained at Beida, which were transferred in the streets of Beijing in 1919 and made students into full-fledged activists.

# Notes

1. The term "New Culture Movement" (Xin wenhua yundong) refers to the intellectual climate of the years 1915–1925 (although the chronology is flexible and debatable), a period that witnessed the foundations of hundreds of journals and groups, all searching for a cultural solutions for the future of China (the hopes for a political solution had foundered with the failure of the new Republic). The movement tackled crucial aspects such as the role of science, the need for a new language for art and literature, and the reevaluation of Chinese tradition, but also promoted radical social

criticism (against arranged marriages, traditional family structure, role of women, etc.).

2. Cai Yuanpei, "Beida Pingmin yexiao kaixue ri yanshuoci" [Speech at the Opening of the Beida Night School for Commoners], January 18, 1918, in *Cai Yuanpei Quanji* [Complete Works of Cai Yuanpei], ed. Gao Pingshu (Beijing: Zhonghua Shuju, 1984), 3:380.

3. The exam questions are collected in *Beijing Daxue yuke ruxue shiti 1917–1922* [Topics for the Admission Exams to Beijing University Preparatory Courses], Beijing University archives.

4. S. Gamble, *Peking: A Social Survey* (New York: George H. Doran Company, 1921), 133.

5. Yang Zhongxian, "Liunian Beida xuesheng shenghuo de huiyi" [Memories of Six Years as a Beida Student], in *Wo yu Beida: "Lao Beida" hua Beida*, ed. Wang Shiru and Wen Di (Beijing: Beijing Daxue chubanshe, 1998), 374.

6. Mao Dun, "Beijing daxue yuke diyilei de sannian" [Three Years in the First Class at Beida Preparatory Courses], in *Wo yu Beida: "Lao Beida" hua Beida*, ed. Wang Shiru and Wen Di (Beijing: Beijing Daxue chubanshe, 1998), 207.

7. Wen-hsin Yeh, *The Alienated Academy: Culture and Politics in Republican China, 1919–1937* (Cambridge, Mass.: Harvard University Press, 1990), 216.

8. Yang Zhensheng, "Huiyi 'Wusi'" [Remembering May Fourth], in *Beida jiushi*, ed. Chen Pingyuan and Xia Xiaohong (Beijing: Sanlian shudian, 1998), 61. Li Shan, Tang scholar (?–689), became famous for his expertise on the *Wenxuan*, on which he published six volumes of comments. Nora is the protagonist of Henrik Ibsen's *A Doll's House*, a play that was at the center of the debate of female emancipation in May Fourth's China. The Tongcheng school, named after Tongcheng county in Anhui, was one of the most influential literary schools of the Qing period.

9. Zhang Zhongxin, "Honglou diandi" [Bits and Pieces of the Honglou], in *Beida jiushi*, ed. Chen Pingyuan and Xia Xiaohong (Beijing: Sanlian shudian, 1998), 434.

10. "Introduction," in Chen Pingyuan, *Lao Beida de Gushi* [Stories of Old Beida] (Nanjing, China: Jiangsu wenyi chubanshe, 1998).

11. Sergei Mikhailovich Tretiakov, *A Chinese Testament: The Autobiography of Tan Shih-hua, as Told to S. Tretiakov* (New York: Simon and Schuster, 1934) 240–41.

12. Feng Youlan, *The Hall of Three Pines: An Account of My Life*, trans. Denis C. Mair (Honolulu: University of Hawaii Press, 2000), 328.

13. Liang Shuming, "Wusi yundong qianhou de Beijing daxue" [Beijing University at the Time of the May Fourth Movement], in *Beida jiushi*, ed. Chen Pingyuan and Xia Xiaohong (Beijing: Sanlian shudian, 1998), 214.

14. Luo Jialun, "Huiyi Gu Hongming xiansheng" [Remembering Gu Hongming], in *Beida gushi: Mingren yanzhong de lao Beida*, ed. Mu Zhou and Mu Xiao (Beijing: Zhongguo wujia chuanshe, 1998), 183.

15. Wang Kunlun, "Cai Yuanpei xiansheng er san shi" [Two or Three Things on Cai Yuanpei], *Guangming ribao*, March 4, 1980, reprinted in *Wo yu Beida: "Lao Beida"*

*hua Beida*, ed. Wang Shiru and Wen Di (Beijing: Beijing Daxue chubanshe, 1998), 360.

16. Zhu Qianzhi, "Fankang kaoshi de xuanyan" [Proclamation against the Exams], *Beijing Daxue Xuesheng Zhoukan* [Beijing University Students' Weekly], no. 13, March 28, 1920, 5–6.

17. Yang Hui, "Wusi yundong yu Beijing Daxue" [The May Fourth Movement and Beijing University], in *Beida jiushi*, ed. Chen Pingyuan and Xia Xiaohong (Beijing: Sanlian shudian, 1998), 51.

18. Luo Jialun, "Beijing Daxue yu Wusi yundong" [Beijing University and the May Fourth Movement], in *Wo yu Beida: "Lao Beida" hua Beida*, ed. Wang Shiru and Wen Di (Beijing: Beijing Daxue chubanshe, 1998), 306.

19. The three statutes have been reprinted in *Beijing Daxue shiliao: Dier juan, 1912–1937* [Historical Materials concerning Peking University: Volume 2, 1912–1937], ed. Wang Xuezhen and Guo Jianrong (Beijing: Beijing Daxue chubanshe, 2000), 2642, 2685, 2728.

∼

# CHAPTER EIGHT

# The Reluctant Mendicant
## Hugh Shapiro

### Fortune-Telling

When his food ran out in the winter of late 1935, Jin Daming gave in to beg-ging for alms on the street. Several years earlier, he had adopted the garb of a monk, heeding a spiritual call. Yet supplicating passersby proved demean-ing, and he shied away from holding out the monk's humble bowl. Hunger overpowered him, though, and after a stint of living in a cave near a Buddhist temple in the hills outside of Beijing, he "came down from the mountain," seeking anything that people would give. When begging failed, he turned to fortune-telling. Having consulted fortune-tellers in the past, he roughly grasped the idea of prognostication and began "reading people's numbers." But cold winter weather kept people on the move, and Jin had trouble scrap-ing together enough to survive. He then found refuge in the New World Gruel House, in the Tianqiao district of Beijing.[1] After twenty days of eating the charity's watery porridge, on January 11, 1936, he walked off the street into an elite hospital, complaining of dizziness, coughing, fever, aching bones, and malaise. The physician who examined the thirty-five-year-old man recorded these first impressions:

> In very dirty condition. Ragged clothing. Pupils reactive to light. Poorly nour-ished. Chest thin. Prominent ribs. Lung: impairment of pulmonary function.

Squeaking sounds heard on coughing. Heart sounds clear. Fever and sweating at night. General aching all over the body especially at wrists.

Date of birth: February 19, 1901 (27th year of the Guangxu reign).

Weight: 48.3 Kg (106.4 lbs.).

Temperature: 36.5°C (97.7°F).

Pulse: 96.

Dr. Wang, the attending physician, observed that Jin was "staying in a place where beggars are staying." By his third day in the hospital, however, it came to light that Jin hailed from an exceptionally influential family, in Sichuan province. His father, a wealthy man, was a powerful figure in politics. He had even worked together with the "father of the country," Dr. Sun Yatsen. What, then, happened to Jin, the scion of this prominent family? What drove his downward mobility, to the point of becoming an "indigent patient" subsisting only on hospital resources? Almost everything we discover about Jin is from the detailed medical case history generated during his five-month stay in the foreign-run hospital, the Peking Union Medical College (PUMC, *Xiehe Yiyuan*).[2]

## The Hopkins Paradigm

Founded in 1921 with Rockefeller Foundation support, the PUMC strictly modeled itself on the Johns Hopkins University School of Medicine. And the Hopkins paradigm dictated the totalistic mapping of patient experience. This meant uncovering as much as possible about the patient's preadmission background, while assiduously recording everything that transpired during his or her hospital stay. Quotidian details such as food consumed, medications prescribed, therapies administered, as well as less tangible aspects, such as the quality of patient sleep or even their random jottings with pen and paper, were all meticulously captured in the record. Word for word, moreover, the case histories record the structured interviews conducted by physicians.

Richly supplementing the medical record are the resourceful investigations of social workers who interviewed patients in the hospital and ventured out into the community to speak with employers, neighbors, and family members. Emerging as one of the country's most prestigious teaching hospitals, the PUMC trained its staff to observe patients tirelessly: probing, questioning, evaluating, and bringing to bear intricate physiological and psychological instruments.

A pioneering neuropsychiatric ward also operated within the PUMC. Patients with mysterious symptoms or compelling narratives were often transferred from the regular hospital to the neuropsychiatric ward for evaluation. Therapeutic interviews run by neuropsychiatrists sometimes deployed barbiturates such as sodium amytal to encourage the patient to talk uninhibitedly. By the late 1930s, after the eruption of full-scale war with Japan, sherry became the sedative of choice, replacing expensive or unavailable drugs. These interviews are also recorded verbatim.

Such scrupulously constructed histories witness a person in moments of stark vulnerability, divulging graphic details of the most personal sort. Dr. Wang observes, for example, that Jin "expectorated a large amount of foul sputum, greenish in color" of "fishy odor," containing "spongy masses." We learn, too, that the patient "admitted venereal exposure," having experienced "gonococcus infection." His wife, then age twenty-nine, suffered "menstrual disturbance and urethral discharge." Chest X-rays showed Jin with "chronic minimal pulmonary tuberculosis." He also endured a case of "relapsing fever," complicated by enteritis infection.

## An Unforgivable Crime

But a wholly different type of private detail is revealed by the patient himself, whose voice emerges as a distinct presence in the record. Ominously, Jin recounts that he enjoyed killing animals as a child. He offered no extenuations in the telling, only that he butchered rabbits and chickens until dissuaded from doing so by a missionary teacher encountered during elementary school. The teacher told him that animals should be cherished, not killed. From a social worker, we learn that Jin committed an unforgivable offense against his family. Menaced by debt, he stole his living grandfather's coffin, selling the expensive object for one-tenth of its value. The incident so infuriated the grandfather that he began telling people that he would prefer feeding the fish, by throwing his silver off a bridge into a river, than let any money touch his grandson's hand.

What happened to Jin Daming? How did this man, born in 1901 into genuine privilege, end up down-and-out in Beijing, more than one thousand miles from his native Sichuan, alienated from his family, and starving in a poorhouse? Part of the answer must be found in the profound turbulence of the times, known as the Republican era (1912–1949).

## Jazz and Epidemic Disease

A pivotal era of China's modern transformation, the Republican era (*Minguo*) exists between two momentous events of global significance: the collapse of the Qing dynasty (and the imperial system) in 1911 and the founding of the People's Republic in 1949. For this reason, *Minguo* is often characterized as an interregnum. While a useful rubric, such characterization risks cloaking the formative nature of those influential decades. We witness, for instance, the eruption of mass nationalism and the birth of a mercilessly self-scrutinizing intelligentsia that radically transforms cultural life, to name but two consequential phenomena.

A creative period of upheaval, the Republican era is sometimes likened to Germany's edgy Weimar. The radically contrastive nature of this period has engendered distinct points of analytical view, with some emphasizing its genius; others, its violence. Both visions are compelling. For the well connected or prosperous, it was a dynamic time of surging cosmopolitan urbanity, rich café life, stimulating jazz, film, and literature, and dynamic universities. For the unprotected, for the poor or the downwardly mobile, life was insecure. Precarious daily living occurred against a menacing backdrop of bitter internecine conflict, grotesque foreign invasion, economic dislocation, endemic violence, habitual want, and epidemic disease. Jin, who plummeted from wealth into poverty, personifies the unpredictable dislocations of this chaotic era.

## Beijing in Turmoil

In Beijing, the city in which Jin found himself penniless, a handful of factors exacerbated the pervasive insecurity of the era. First, in 1900 the city suffered the hysterical chaos of the Boxers, both the uprising and its suppression. Second, in 1912, Yuan Shikai's troops rioted, with the usual suspects joining in the mayhem. Third, during the 1920s, warlords fought brutally for control of the city, savaging its hinterland and driving uprooted farmers into the city, along with defeated soldiers and inflation. Fourth, despite the Qing collapse in 1911, many dependents of the empire had not been forced into the economy of the city until the 1920s. Fifth, the shift of the capital from Beijing to Nanjing by the new Nationalist government in 1928 decimated the city's service trades, causing losses in revenue and widespread unemployment. Sixth, the invasion of China's northeast in 1931 by Japan's Guandong army swelled Beijing with refugees, accelerating both the city's decline and the militarization of the region.

In David Strand's words, the typical Beijing resident had "ample images and experiences to draw on to construct a picture of imminent disaster whenever war appeared on the horizon."[3] Beijing in the 1930s also saw the advent of a dangerous secret police, which "disappeared" students and other politically suspect people at will, as Frederic Wakeman Jr. shows.[4] Inhabitants of the city learned to sort through rumors, ascertain hints from the movement of a crowd, interpret market fluctuations, or, for those caught on the street, read the facial expressions of approaching soldiers. Sensitivity to political change was an important urban skill, not just in Beijing but also in the country's other sites of turmoil, not just during the Republic, but throughout China's modern history as well.

By the mid-1930s, affluent families that had hitherto insulated themselves from the turmoil were showing signs of distress, as evidenced, for example, in appeals for aid. However, Jin Daming's family continued to thrive. His father, the influential political figure, sustained a posh style; his brother pursued studies at Qinghua, the famous university; and his cousin-in-law commanded esteem as director of Beijing's "China Foundation." Jin's family flourished; it held onto wealth, social connections, and status.

## Striking an Aunt

How, then, did Jin, the eldest son, end up destitute at the PUMC, with the Social Service Department providing ten cents per day so he could eat? According to Jin's own testimony, his troubles started early. His mother passed away when he was three. His first memories date to age four. At age five he began his studies, with his first teacher coming to his home. When Jin was six, his father remarried. His new stepmother and the boy remained indifferent toward each another. He recalls abuse meted out by a martinet father with "old ideas." At age seven, the boy struck an aunt (his father's cousin) with his fist, hitting her on the chest where he now has his own trouble. In Jin's telling, she later developed an abscess and died. At eight, the boy moved to his grandparents; his grandfather doted on him, and they got on well. At age ten, the boy spent time at his father's teacher's home and, together with the teacher's son, labored diligently at his studies. Outside school, he helped the farmers who worked the teacher's land. During this year, the Qing dynasty collapsed. At twelve, he attended a missionary school opened by a church and came to know the English teacher there.

## A Prestigious Middle School

Preparing for entrance examinations, he passed and gained entry to the competitive middle school attached to Qinghua University, in Beijing, where he spent five years. Jin describes his intellectual proclivities as leaning first toward literature and then to physics. He grew intrigued by electricity, then by the history of machines from the earliest times, delving into aerial navigation and its technology (he described the "Pitot tube," used on aircraft as speedometers), and finally, philosophy and poetry, especially the work of Longfellow.

We pick up the thread of Jin's narrative when he is seventeen, after being forced to leave Qinghua Middle School. Family members attribute his expulsion to "bad character" and poor academic performance. Jin states that he ran out of money. All interlocutors agree that he left Beijing and returned to his home in Sichuan, a densely populated inland province boasting rich soil that yields fine grain and "human talent." Back in Sichuan he enrolled in military school.

## Military Training and Opium

I believe a short interview like this with such a productive patient is far from sufficient. Would suggest admission and further psychological study.

—Dr. Zheng

Returning home to Sichuan province at age seventeen, Jin become a military cadet and began smoking opium. It happened one day in 1918, away from the academy, while he was making rounds on family property, collecting rent from the tenants. The tenants, who were relatives, invited him to stay for a smoke, and thereafter he smoked opium each day for the next fifteen years.

Some years later, he and a friend visited a third friend in prison, an addict, who was serving time for an unspecified crime. The inmate proposed sharing a round of opium, courteously inviting his two visitors to go first. They each took turns drawing on the pipe but to no avail, sucking only air. The prisoner then turned his head toward empty space and addressed the air: "Will you please smoke first?" Smoke then inexplicably wafted up from the lamp and thereupon they each took turns inhaling from the opium pipe. Jin shared this anecdote only when asked whether or not he believed in ghosts, during an interview at the hospital. Jin explained that he had never seen a ghost but that day in prison had seen the workings of one.

Compared to his generally animated discourse, Jin spoke about opium in a relatively lackluster way. The record is equally reticent about his military training at the academy. We know only that during this time, at age twenty or twenty-one, he married a girl six years his junior. There would be no children. In 1923, at age twenty-two, he graduated. Through the influence of his father who at the time was one of the highest officials in Sichuan, Jin landed a prominent position in the army. Thereupon, according to witnesses, he fell into social entertainments, went to prostitutes, and spent lavishly.

## Warlords with Modern Weapons

Face looks bright and speaks very intelligently.

—Miss Liu, social worker

Family connections, however, could not save the young officer from being sent up to the front lines, onto murderous battlefields, and into a tumultuous environment of killing, loosely described as the "warlord period" (1916–1928). Young Officer Jin's first combat experience took place sometime in 1923, shortly after his graduation from the academy in his home province of Sichuan. Fighting erupted between two generals, each sending thousands of troops into battle. The fresh graduate Jin was ordered to guard a certain post and was given command of one hundred men to do the job. Others said that the assignment required three hundred men; Jin succeeded with only one hundred. He attributed his success to the discipline he exerted over his men.

The warlord era witnessed upward of eight hundred wars waged by thousands of regional magnates vying for control of local satrapies. Historians generally bracket the warlord period between two events: (1) the eclipse of central authority that followed the death of militarist, strongman, and president Yuan Shikai in 1916 and (2) the establishment of the Nationalist government in 1928. Even after 1928, central authority, based in the new capital of Nanjing and in the Lower Yangzi River region, remained weak. Society at large, too, remained broadly militarized.

Confronting the monster of warlordism (and the idea of foreign imperialism), the Nationalist government came to exist in the wake of the "Northern Expedition" (beifa), a military-political campaign launched from Guangzhou in China's deep south. Deploying Leninist organizational techniques gleaned from a six-month sojourn in Moscow, Nationalist leader Chiang Kai-shek marched his party-army north under the banner of smashing warlord power and unifying the country. During the beifa, in addition to waging battle against warlord forces, Chiang Kai-shek negotiated the absorption of hundreds of warlord armies into the Nationalist (Guomindang, GMD) structure, after their pledge of fealty to the Nationalist cause. Sometimes this simply meant regional armies hoisting the Nationalist flag.

GMD leader Chiang Kai-shek also at this time decimated the emergent Chinese Communist Party (CCP). Yet in the late 1920s and 1930s, a resurgent CCP and powerful regional militarists, such as Yan Xishan and Feng Yuxiang, continued operating beyond Nationalist government control. Such military and political autonomy grew not least of all from the formidable weapons wielded by the warlords.

By the late 1910s, warlord arsenals contained such devastating weaponry from foreign suppliers as the Mannlicher magazine-fed rifle, the Maxim machine gun, and heavy artillery. Battlefield surgeons such as W. Graham Reynolds observed that the new weapons inflicted a different type of trauma on the body. Operating on wounded soldiers, he noted that the projectiles of the old-style matchlocks caused more internal tissue damage than the bullets of modern rifles. The asymmetrical projectiles of the older guns tended to break apart inside the body. If the combatant was not immediately killed by a modern bullet, if it did not strike a vital organ or an artery, chances of survival were somewhat better. Being of harder material and fired at a greater velocity with flatter trajectory, the new bullets often passed through the body.

## Organized Murder

Still, the viciousness of warlord conflicts stunned physicians working near or at the sites of battles. Medical reports in the *Chinese Medical Journal*, a respected forum of the era, describe horrible slaughter. Corroborated accounts by physicians depict looting soldiers entering hospitals to murder the wounded enemy as they lay in bed. The murder of captured prisoners was portrayed as ordinary, and retreating soldiers commonly sabotaged buildings that advancing troops would use as billets. Soldiers rampaged, terrorizing or killing civilians. The brutality of armed men during the Republican era stirred an early Nationalist leader to theorize on the "abnormal psychology" (*biantai xinli*) of warlord soldiers.[5]

Leaders who lived through these catastrophes, all along the political spectrum, were deeply marked by the experience. It was in this environment of militarized chaos that Mao Zedong formulated the famous dictum "political power grows from the barrel of a gun." But, and this is key to the sentiment, "the Party controls the gun." Civilian control of the military was essential to prevent society from lapsing into anarchy. Within this turmoil, Jin's father, despite his political influence, could only protect his officer son to a certain degree.

## Under Fire at the Front

Jin arrived to one of these killing fields in Sichuan, in 1924 he recalls, riding in a sedan chair supported by several men. As they neared the battle, a bullet struck the carrying rod of the chair, and he tumbled onto the ground. The enemy then unleashed a fusillade of bullets; the volley tore through the air above his head. He was already down and so escaped harm. Jin attributes his miraculous escape to "a virtuous deed which he had performed just two hours before." En route to the battle, Jin and the sedan carriers encountered a woman carrying a basket of potatoes. One of his accompanying soldiers, on horseback, seized the basket, feeding the potatoes to his horse. The woman broke down crying. Through tears she explained that she had planned to sell the tubers in order to buy medicine for her mother-in-law, who was stricken by illness. Moved by the woman's anguish, Jin paid her double the market price of the potatoes. Accepting his money, she went on her way.

## Shot in the Chest

An analogous karmic event saved the life of a friend at the front. In Jin's telling, the comrade, also a military officer, came upon an old woman carrying fuel and vegetables while traveling with his entourage. His soldiers confiscated the fuel, tossing her a dollar made of copper. Realizing the dollar was not made of silver, the woman despaired. With a pang of guilt, the officer proffered a silver dollar, accepting from the elderly lady the copper dollar in exchange. He slipped the copper piece into his chest pocket. Some time later a hostile soldier opened fire. The bullet slammed into his chest, striking the copper coin. Knocked from his feet by the impact, a storm of bullets passed over his prone body. In this way, the officer evaded death.

Jin related these two improbable events during an interview with a neuropsychiatrist. As a hospital patient, Jin was responding to this question: "Had he ever witnessed invisible forces, or invisible influences, at work?" The examiner also queried the patient on current events. Jin confided that he held little curiosity about the news and refrained from reading the newspaper. In military circles, he clarified, it is "experience and pull" that counted, not one's ability or how much one knew about political news. Yet, he added somewhat puzzlingly, if he returned to his military position, he would once again take up reading the paper. Jin also stated that he had originally joined the army due to his latent militaristic proclivities. For four years, from 1923 to 1927, he had served as a military officer and worked in "political circles." War, however, proved wearying, and Jin relinquished his officer's position. In the end, he did not much care for the military life. In China's interior, Jin reflected, "the life of a military officer is just like that of a bandit."

## National Weakness

Besides, he reasoned that he could pursue his "mission" in other ways, in other places. And what was Jin's mission? He aimed to ameliorate the appalling condition in which he found his country. Jin's aspiration was not an idle conceit. For several generations before his birth in 1901, a terrible quandary haunted people from all walks of life: how could China survive the devastating onslaught of Western power? Thinkers, workers, activists, writers, physicians, and students agonized over how to confront the brutal, apparently unstoppable foreign incursion. Aggressive countries such as Britain, France, Germany, Russia, and then the United States and Japan constituted a dangerous arena of rival nation-states. Measuring their relative power in terms of territory controlled (a distinctly nineteenth-century index), these recently industrialized nations encroached on fading empires across the globe, in Africa, India, the Americas, Asia Minor, the Mideast, and alas, East Asia.

## Global Power Shifts

For centuries, longer even, China had boasted a remarkable standard of living. From as far away as Europe, foreigners were inspired to hazard dangerous sea voyages or to work through elaborate land routes of middlemen, sometimes referred to as the "Silk Road," seeking tea, spice, silk, paintings, poetry, and pharmaceuticals. China, for long periods, enjoyed a quality of life higher than that of much of the world. Items taken for granted, such as books made of paper, items that could be had for a farthing in Chinese cities, were in Europe so expensive that they had to be chained to the reading tables. However, in the early modern age, European states grew into formidable powers while China, and other empires, grew vulnerable. And the new weakness of the old empires seemed discernable everywhere. Take, for example, medicine. For a millennium, physicians in China were sought after as efficacious healers. Genghis Khan himself, keenly attuned to useful talent, courted or kidnapped physicians from China, absorbing their skill into his empire-building machinery. Yet by Jin's lifetime, Westerners mocked medicine in China as superstitious quackery.

Explicating the forces driving these momentous shifts in global power is incredibly complex. Any analysis must be multifaceted and resist monocasual explanations. Consider, for example, the global cooling of the seventeenth century, which wrecked havoc on agriculture around the world. Both Europe and China suffered from this natural disaster. But the solutions to the ensuing crises worked out in Europe and China were quite different, setting the two regions on different trajectories as they entered the modern age.[6] Yet, this is but one example. To make sense of the rise of the West and the so-called decline of China, one must contemplate, at the very least, the following factors.

In Europe:
the endemic conflict of the Napoleonic Wars, inspiring military innovation;
the European Enlightenment;
the Industrial Revolution;
the conquest of the Americas, endowing Europe with astonishing wealth and new space; and
the internal exigencies of capitalism that required control of expanding markets, labor, and natural resources.

In China:
a burgeoning population (a demographic consequence of a flourishing society);
the scarcity of arable land; and
the Qing Empire's resistance to mobilizing resources at a national level, precisely at a time when Europeans were pioneering ways of centralizing raw material, energy sources, manpower, and money, and other assets key to nation building.

Further driving this global transformation was the contrasting views in China and in Europe of what it was that nations were supposed to do. Whichever way we understand these changes, Jin, growing up in the 1910s and 1920s, would have witnessed his homeland in weakness and pandemonium, appearing, perhaps, as irretrievably falling into an abyss.

## Amassing Firepower

What type of solutions to China's predicament did concerned people like Jin conceive? Leveling the battlefield was among the first ideas. This meant obtaining the devastating weapons wielded by foreign navies. The technology of the foreign militaries that began attacking China in the mid-1800s was shocking in its destructiveness. In what can be loosely called the Opium War era, beginning in 1838 and running to the late nineteenth century, foreign armies heaped sharp, relentless defeat on China. Each defeat brought exaggerated demands from the victors, impinging further on China's sovereignty. Memories of that humiliating period still rankle the popular imagination today. By the 1890s, China had constructed impressive arsenals and could bring to bear deadly firepower, from advanced warships and state-of-the-art shore batteries, such as the fifty-ton guns purchased from Krupp, in Germany.

However, 1895 witnessed a new type of military calamity for China: defeat by Japan, a smaller, island nation widely viewed in China as the junior of the two countries. In spite of fielding what in many battles were superior weapons, China lost. Japan's victory traumatized China's emerging national psyche, engendering the search for much deeper solutions. Amassing sophisticated weaponry would not suffice. Profounder change was needed. Not only did the country suffer ruinous interventions from outside, but also society seemed to be imploding from within. Something was wrong at the core, on the level of cultural praxis, and on the level of identity. This was the environment in which Jin grew up. His idea was to build a school. And after retiring from the army, this is what he attempted.

## A School and Model Factory

A man with his ideals and conduct will certainly cause people's suspicion that he is crazy.

—Dr. Cheng

In 1928, after four years of soldiering, at age twenty-seven, Jin opened a primary school. Of the students who enrolled, only the "dull-minded" could afford tuition, Jin lamented. Too many of the intelligent students were poor and unable to pay for their studies. The school failed. He then turned his efforts to industry, speculating in the mining business, gold mining. But the business collapsed "because I had no capital." At the critical moment, inexplicably, the person who had pledged to furnish the cash changed his mind. Jin then planned to open a factory, also with the goal of contributing to society.

By expanding China's industrial base he would "bring happiness to all citizens of China and prosperity to the whole nation." He "understands that most of his countrymen are without jobs, . . . so he would open factories to give employment." If he could "obtain ten-thousand dollars," then he would "establish a model factory in three years time." The model factory would function as a template, and in ten years it would be copied in every district throughout the country.

## Public Service and Graft

Indeed, acquiring the ten thousand dollars presented an obstacle but an easily surmountable one. All he needed to do was get a "prominent position" in his home province, Sichuan, where he enjoyed influential friends. With such well-placed confederates, gaining the "fat" position would be straightforward business. Once in the post, within one year he estimated, he could pilfer the needed funds. His vision of stealing money while in an official position gained through nepotism, and using that money to aid in national reconstruction, gave pause to his hospital examiners. The internal contradictions of this plan prompted one examiner to ask if the patient suffered mental illness. Jin denied strongly that he was mentally ill but admitted to sometimes being confused.

Nonetheless, against his inventive scheme for economic development, other visions paled. In his eyes, GMD leader Chiang Kai-shek was a very insignificant figure. But the factory enterprise, too, was not to prosper. For the next two years, at ages twenty-eight and twenty-nine, he idled at home, smoking opium, thinking many thoughts, spending much time brooding over his ups and downs, and wondering how he could make up for the failures.

Years later, reflecting on those and other perennial disappointments, he wished that he "could be a great General and save the country." If that proved impossible, he would like to be "the worst criminal and go out and kill people."

## Squandering the Family Fortune

> In all his life, the patient never earned a cent but his way of living was extravagant.
>
> —Dr. Zhang

Jin's hope of pulling together ten thousand dollars was not pure whimsy. In addition to receiving a sizable allowance from his father, the patient would borrow a total of seven thousand dollars from friends. Where the money went is not entirely clear. We do know that while idling in the family home, Jin smoked opium, racked up gambling debt, and visited prostitutes. He connected his time spent in brothels to a larger social good. In his own words, Jin frequented prostitutes because "he was interested in studying sociology." In brothels "he could meet all classes of people" and could thereupon "preach Buddhism to the morally fallen girls and unfortunate women."

Biding his time at home, Jin continued to squander his father's money, making abortive forays into business, smoking opium, gambling, and conducting social research. He stayed at home until 1933. Having exhausted part of the family fortune through profligate spending, his father asked his son to accompany the grandfather downriver to Shanghai, the cosmopolitan metropolis where the Yangzi River empties into the Pacific. For traveling expenses, the father provided eight hundred dollars, but the thirty-two-year-old disparaged the amount, saying it was not enough. The grandfather had brought one thousand dollars from his own home, so together the pair reached Shanghai with 1,800 dollars. Within four weeks, Jin reported home that the money was gone, although he had filched six hundred dollars of his grandfather's cash. His father sent another 250 dollars. Jin took the money and left his grandfather in Shanghai, proceeding to Beijing on his own.

## Death in Shanghai

It's unclear when Jin sold his grandfather's coffin. But because of this outrageous iniquity, the grandfather started experiencing dreadful nightmares. One night he dreamed a fierce scuffle with the grandson, falling out of bed. In another nightmare, the grandfather anxiously clutches a bag of silver coins, trying to prevent his avaricious grandson from making off with his money.

Something perfidious appears to have happened in Shanghai, but the record is silent on precisely what transpired. After the grandson left for Beijing, the grandfather would soon be dead. Jin's father then traveled from Sichuan to Shanghai, where he legally disowned his son. A Shanghai lawyer drew up the contract of disassociation and bore witness to its signing. The father then deposited with the lawyer an updated will, cutting out his son. Later, Jin claimed to have initiated the break in ties with his father, changing his surname to emphasize the point.

## Collecting Money for Tibetan Buddhism

Arriving to Beijing, Jin announced that he would raise money for the Yonghe Gong, a celebrated Tibetan Buddhist temple in the city. In a cryptic episode, Jin persuaded two policemen to accompany him on this mission. His stated intent: collect money from "decent people." He managed to gather three hundred dollars, immediately spending two hundred of it on his own pleasure in the red light district. Jin moved into a hotel, quickly burning through the rest of his cash.

He then located his cousin-in-law, Mr. Zhao, a "returned student" from the United States, and director of the "China Foundation." Jin asked him for a loan. Zhao agreed. When Jin arrived by automobile that afternoon to fetch the agreed-upon twenty dollars, a prostitute sat in the car next to him. In disgust, Zhao thought to himself: with such a flawed character, I cannot help this cousin anymore. (Years earlier, at age sixteen or seventeen, Jin made an equally harsh evaluation of Zhao, when the two were classmates at Qinghua Middle School. Jin's female cousin from Sichuan visited him in Beijing. In Jin's telling, she had "failed" to gain entry to any school. His classmate, Zhao, ended up helping her with algebra. The two "fell in love and had illicit relations." Although Jin believes in "modern ideas" he "condemned such practices." Jin's cousin went on to marry Zhao.) Regardless of Zhao's moral revulsion, he did continue to aid his onetime classmate, taking Jin into his home for a period of time, until Jin argued with this benefactor and stormed out. For a long time thereafter, Zhao and his wife (Jin's cousin) had no idea of Jin's whereabouts—until they heard that he was living in a Buddhist temple.

## A Buddhist Revolution

EXAMINER: Do you feel as yourself? "Am I really I?"

JIN: I often wonder about this, because it is a central question in Buddhism.

After leaving his cousin's home in anger, Jin stayed in Beijing for the next two years, from age thirty-two to thirty-four. He spent this time "wandering from temple to temple in search of real Buddhism." A capable teacher he came across trained him in Buddhist thought. At age thirty-four, Jin ran out of money and had to leave the city. He found a temple in the hills outside of Beijing where he could stay for free. Not having to worry about shelter, food, or clothing, he experienced great relief. For two years he lived at the temple, tending cows, pondering enigmas of mind and spirit, and, apparently, giving up opium.

EXAMINER: Have you heard the Buddha's voice?

JIN: Only superstitious monks say that they see or hear Buddha.

After all, Jin continued, Buddha was already "dead 3,000 years ago." Still, Jin described his "mission" as having been given to him "by Buddha himself." Jin described "his mission" as to perform a "religious revolution, like Martin Luther." The patient believed in the branch of Buddhism that advocated the "quiet sitting for hours" to discover the "secret between life and death." As Buddhism required a revolution, he was dedicated to be its "religious revolutionist." To foment a Buddhist revolution, he envisioned using two techniques. First, he would "propagandize for Buddhism through literary" means; second, he would "deploy force, law, and military action."

"Modern Buddhism is the lowest form," opined Jin, because its "principle is passive, living under very strict rules." His own formulation of Buddhism is "the highest active form," because he is "doing just what Buddha himself did 3,000 years ago." Jin admitted that people often criticized his conduct, saying that someone who is devoted to Buddhism should not live life the way he does. To be sure, he confessed to visiting prostitutes, drinking, gambling, and pursuing a rakish life of dissipation. However, justified Jin, these actions are but "his personal conduct (*si de*)." They "should not affect his mission" of carrying out a Buddhist "renaissance."

"At first," Jin explained, he became a "military officer," working to perform "my mission this way." Then he started a school. Thereafter he attempted to complete his "mission through a factory, a mining factory." But owing to lack of capital, the business collapsed. Then he found Buddhism. His father, Jin reflected, was a "Great Buddhist." As with many politicians, an attending physician noted, the father retired from politics late in life. He left political circles and studied Buddhism but did not become a monk. Despite father and son walking this same path, Jin's ideas about Buddhism, he explained, were too revolutionary. This is why his father would not help him in his quest.

In the winter of 1935, the head of the temple left. When the new head arrived, Jin did not get on with him. Leaving the temple, he returned to Beijing but not after first spending seven days living in a cave.

## In the Cave

Patient is dressed in monk's clothes but is not a regular monk.

—Social worker

Jin stayed in the cave for seven days, fasting for a good part of the week. Going without food for seven or eight days, taking only water, he claimed that he could still lift heavy objects and that his mind remained lucid. Even so, Jin explains, the "lowest form of Buddhism" involves "fasting." People observe that custom "only when material support fails to come."

In the cave, Jin experienced visions but only "blurred visions," he spelled out, "no exact things." In the mountains, Jin saw "houses upside down for 3 or 4 days consecutively." "What is your explanation for this?", queried the examiner. Summing it up in this way, Jin responded, "Due to nerves in my eyes."

EXAMINER: Are there other examples of such experiences?

JIN: Once, at the time when I saw the houses upside down, I felt that my whole body was shaking and felt that I was rising up in the air.

EXAMINER: Do you ever feel that a part of your body is not yours?

JIN: Often feel that my whole body is not mine, but that it is just a place where I stay; it is not strange to me; it is merely the difference between life and death; with life there is the body; with death there is no body.

Coming down out of the hills, before finding the gruel house, Jin begged and told fortunes. At this time he met an itinerant healer who could transfer the physical sensations of his patients onto a piece of wood. Mr. Liu had never experienced this personally. But once inside the wards of the PUMC, he claimed at times to feel pain when a doctor operated on another patient.

After entering the hospital, a social worker paid a visit to Jin's cousin-in-law's home, in an effort to learn more about the new patient's situation. Zhao, the cousin-in-law, divulged that, upon hearing of Jin's residence at the temple, he surreptitiously began sending money to the temple head, so that the temple would continue accommodating Jin. The financial arrangement was kept secret because the Zhao family was loath for their cousin to discover its involvement. As hospital social workers would come to grasp, the patient's entire family shared this sentiment, studiously eschewing contact with Jin.

## Crossing Burnt Bridges

Brother said that we would rather help a fellow countryman than his own brother.

—Social worker

However reluctant kin might be to get involved, the Social Service Department of the PUMC would not be thwarted. The department, in part, aimed exactly to uncover the full network of family members so that relatives might assist the hospital in patient management, by either providing sociopsychological background or paying bills, donating clothes, furnishing shelter, or, critically, offering a way out of the hospital once the medical work is done. To these ends, social workers showed exceptional ingenuity in locating Jin's estranged stepmother, his half brother, the father's concubine in Shanghai, and his cousin and her husband, Zhao, of the China Foundation. The main issue in play concerned what Jin would do next.

Where would he go? Of equal import, who would pay for him to get there? Jin's half brother, the son of his father and stepmother, was a twenty-year-old Qinghua University student who wore "a black shirt and gray trousers" and was "quite a stylish young man." The twenty-year-old utterly disapproved of Jin, yet did what he could, energetically ferrying messages between the social worker and the cousin-in-law, for example, and researching how much the trip from Beijing to Sichuan would cost. For Jin to reach his home in Sichuan, where his wife still lived, it would take $52.50, via train, boat, and bus. The itinerary would involve the following: Beijing to Hankou, $22.50, train; Hankou to Yichang, $4.00, boat; Yichang to Chongqing, $10.00, boat; Chongqing to Pixian, his home, $16.00, bus. Jin, the patient, wanted $70.00, so that he could take a military train instead of a regular train. Some people expressed concern that Jin would spend the money on the road and never make it home. The half brother's anxiety was that any money reaching his hands would be handed directly to prostitutes, "as it always was."

The social worker visited the stepmother's home at the moment when Jin had nearly exhausted the resources that the PUMC and allied institutions, such as a men's hostel for short-term tenants, were willing to expend. The social worker found a "very large house with red brick; foreign style in front, but a Chinese house inside," with the "family occupying one court." The social worker was shown by the "amah" to the "brother's study which was quite modernistic in decoration, with Qinghua College flag, movie star posters, and the brother's own photo, enlarged." The stepmother, a lady "over 50 wearing a pair of glasses in black frame," stated that there was no relationship between her family and Jin, that her own son was still a student, that Jin was much older and should be independent, and that the family has "no extra money to help him." Who, then, would help Jin?

## Charitable Institutions

Downward mobility brought Jin into contact with an impressive array of charitable organizations in 1930s Beijing. Granted, in the course of his decline, before availing himself of society's support, Jin first imposed on family and friends, borrowing, cajoling, and then stealing from his grandfather. After these resources were exhausted, or shut off, he turned to civic institutions, such as the New World Gruel House. Other institutions aiding Jin during this time included the poorhouse (Jiu Ji Yuan) and the Buddhist Society. He also found modest, temporary housing in Beijing, at two different places, for 11.5 cents per day, and 20 cents per day, respectively. Once inside the PUMC, he benefited from three separate services. First, the Medical Department supported him, then Neurology, and finally the Social Service Department, which provided a range of valuable services, including money to support his residence at the hospital hostel. What conclusions did the hospital reach regarding Jin's case?

## Diagnosis

The diagnosis of Jin's condition was indeterminate. Opinions from eight PUMC professionals included the following.

Physician: Psychopathic personality with asocial trends. Sinus of left chest wall, chronic, cause undetermined.

Social worker: His judgment with regard to single daily occurrences is fairly good. Interview the examinee to see if he is crazy. I think he is not.

Physician: Impressions, Psychopathic personality? Schizophrenic? Simple or paranoid?

Physician: Suffers social inadequacy. Looks actually ill, groaning all the time.

Physician: Quiet on the wards; patient is cooperative.

Physician: The patient is a schizophrenic case that should be admitted to neuropsychiatry for study.

Neuropsychiatrist: Of the opinion that patient is still in contact with reality and that patient did not show true paraegastic features.

Results of mental test, by psychologist: I.Q. 82. Borderline. M.A. (mental age): 13 years, 2 months. Neurotic score, 65. Emotionally mal-adjusted, seclusive, suspicious, many physical complaints, sensitive, discouraging and sad.

The patient had navigated the culture of this well-endowed hospital with notable nimble-mindedness. Yet after five months, everyone agreed that he must leave. Even the broad-minded head of the Buddhist Society informed a social worker that it could no longer help Jin. In the end, the hospital recommended "discharge." But to where should he be discharged? Jin's wife provided the last lifeline.

## Extracting the Final Resource

Just after being admitted to the PUMC, a social worker helped Jin write a letter to his wife, expressing his request to her for $120 of travel money, so that he could return home. The worker sent the letter by air. Near the end of Jin's stay at the hospital, physicians and social workers pressed him for his plan. According to Jin, if his wife sent the funds for travel, he would return home. Then he would sell the home, and the five acres of land worked by tenant farmers, whose rent payments had supported the wife during his several years' absence. Jin said that he would give something of the proceeds to his wife, letting her do as she pleased. As for him, he would either rejoin the military or become a monk. His vision of liquating the property and leaving his wife was not mentioned in the letter to her. After some time, his wife's response arrived, articulating poignant details of the struggle to make ends meet amid ubiquitous violence.

> Dear Husband,
>     Suddenly a letter arrived from you. The letter made me feel very sorry, both that you had left home several years ago, and that you have encountered such difficulties during this time. I received several letters from you the year before last, but no word from you since then. I do not know why. Where were you? What was your situation? I had no idea. Then I heard from some people that you had become a monk. I was so pleased to hear this news, for I too feel that society is hard to endure and for some years already I've harbored the same intention. As you know, our District Bi Xian continuously suffers attack from bandits and homes have been destroyed. All the creditors come for money, especially the Zeng family. Since I heard that you had become a monk, I asked people to mortgage the house, and I intend to become a nun in April. Then unexpectedly I received a letter from a stranger containing unfamiliar words and writing, saying that you want to come home and request money for travel expenses. Of course this is good news, but the letter is not in your handwriting, so how can I believe it? Now let me tell you in a simple way that if you really do intend to come home you must write me with your own hand, telling me the proper place to mail the money otherwise I will not do so, because it is a large sum of money and I must look to every possible way to pull it together. If not, I cannot wait for you. You and I are in different corners of the world and we cannot suffer for one another so please take good care of yourself. I have written much because I cannot finish in one word.
>
>                                                                         Jin Wang Yida

The patient's wife sent the needed seventy-five dollars for travel. The patient accepted the money from a social worker, who requested that Jin sign a receipt, which the worker sent via airmail to Mrs. Jin Wang, noting that her husband would arrive in twelve days' time. At the worker's request, the half brother had discreetly left a quilt for Jin. However, the patient refused it, explaining that he could do without it: it was summer, and the weather was warm. After a final "physiotherapy," which left an "ultraviolet burn over his right lower interscapular region," the hospital discharged the patient on June 3, 1936.

## On the Cusp

Following his discharge, we do not know what happened to Jin or to his wife, Jin Wang Yida. We do know that China was on the cusp of more tragedy, from which few would escape unchanged. Less than one year after Jin's discharge, a terrible era of carnage erupted. In 1937, full-scale war with Japan broke out. Millions would die. Following this horrific bloodletting, China endured another four years of destructive civil war, from 1945 to 1949. For people who lived through the mid-1930s, with its economic depression, internecine conflict, widespread banditry, and creeping foreign invasions, we can guess that many would have believed that the nadir of national life was behind them. But this was not to be. As bad as things had gotten by 1936, they were to get much worse.

## Further Reading

Bullock, Mary Brown. *An American Transplant: The Rockefeller Foundation and Peking Union Medical College.* Berkeley: University of California Press, 1980.

Dikotter, Frank. *Sex, Culture, and Modernity in China: Medical Science and the Construction of Sexual Identities in the Early Republican Period.* Honolulu: University of Hawaii Press, 1995.

Hershatter, Gail. *Dangerous Pleasures: Prostitution and Modernity in Twentieth-Century Shanghai.* Berkeley: University of California Press, 1997.

Lao She. *Teahouse* (Chaguan, 1954), trans. John Howard-Gibbon. Hong Kong: Chinese University Press, 2004.

Lary, Diana. *Warlord Soldiers: Chinese Common Soldiers, 1911–1937.* Cambridge, UK: Cambridge University Press, 1985.

Lee, Leo Ou-fan. *Shanghai Modern: The Flowering of New Urban Culture in China, 1930–1945.* Cambridge, Mass.: Harvard University Press, 1999.

Pomeranz, Kenneth. *The Great Divergence: China, Europe, and the Making of the Modern World Economy.* Princeton, N.J.: Princeton University Press, 2000.

Rogaski, Ruth. *Hygienic Modernity: Meanings of Health and Disease in Treaty-Port China.* Berkeley: University of California Press, 2004.

Strand, David. *Rickshaw Beijing: City People and Politics in the 1920s*. Berkeley: University of California Press, 1989.

Van Slyke, Lyman P. *Enemies and Friends: The United Front in Chinese Communist History*. Stanford, Calif.: Stanford University Press, 1967.

Wakeman, Frederic, Jr. *Spymaster: Dai Li and the Chinese Secret Service*. Berkeley: University of California Press, 2003.

Wakeman, Frederic, Jr., and Wen-Hsin Yeh, eds. *Shanghai Sojourners*. Berkeley: University of California, Institute of East Asian Studies, 1992.

# Notes

1. During the Republican period (1912–1949), the name for the city of Beijing (a.k.a. Peking) changed several times. "Beijing" ("northern capital") was the city's name during the late imperial era, during the last several hundred years, until 1928. In 1928, the Nationalist Party (Guomindang, GMD) established a government and moved the capital to Nanking, subsequently known as "Nanjing" ("southern capital"). No longer the capital, Beijing was renamed "Beiping" ("northern peace," and hence "Peiping" under a different romanization system). In 1949, the capital was reestablished in the northern city by the People's Republic of China (PRC) and the name was thus changed back to Beijing. In this chapter, the city will be referred to as "Beijing."

2. The material for this chapter draws on medical case histories held in the Records Division of the Peking Union Medical College (*Xiehe Yiyuan*), Beijing, China. The author is grateful for the expert assistance of the Records Division staff. Except for famous figures, such as Yan Xishan, pseudonyms are used for all people mentioned in this chapter.

3. David Strand, *Rickshaw Beijing: City People and Politics in the 1920s* (Berkeley: University of California Press, 1989), 198–200.

4. Frederic Wakeman Jr., *Spymaster: Dai Li and the Chinese Secret Service* (Berkeley: University of California Press, 2003).

5. Diana Lary, *Warlord Soldiers: Chinese Common Soldiers, 1911–1937* (Cambridge, UK: Cambridge University Press, 1985), 83–91.

6. See Kenneth Pomeranz, *The Great Divergence: China, Europe, and the Making of the Modern World Economy* (Princeton, N.J.: Princeton University Press, 2000); Frederic Wakeman Jr., *The Great Enterprise: The Manchu Reconstruction of Imperial Order in Seventeenth-Century China* (Berkeley: University of California Press, 1985).

~

# CHAPTER NINE

# Hu Lanqi: Rebellious Woman, Revolutionary Soldier, Discarded Heroine, and Triumphant Survivor

*Kristin Stapleton*

Hu Lanqi[1] lived during most of the twentieth century. She was born in Chengdu, the capital of inland Sichuan province, in 1901. She died in the same city in 1994. In between she had a remarkable and varied life of adventure. She abandoned her husband from an arranged marriage as well as one she had chosen herself. She taught at a famous progressive school in Sichuan in the early 1920s and was the inspiration for the heroine of a popular novel. She joined the Chinese Nationalist army in 1927 and the Chinese branch of the German Communist Party in 1930. She was jailed in Berlin for political activities in 1933 and published a memoir of this experience that got her an invitation to meet Russian writer Maxim Gorky (1868–1936) in Moscow. She organized and led a team of women who supported the Nationalist army's attempts to resist the Japanese invasion in 1937 and, during the civil war that followed victory over Japan, tried to persuade Nationalist generals to transfer their loyalties to the Communists. She discovered soon after Communist victory in 1949 that the new regime did not value her services very highly, and in 1957 she was declared politically suspect and labeled a "Rightist." She was forced to "reform herself through labor" and then beaten and verbally attacked by Red Guards during the Cultural Revolution in the late 1960s. She survived to see her "Rightist" label removed in 1978 and her Communist Party membership restored in 1987.

She spent the 1980s writing a detailed and moving memoir of her astonishing life.[2]

Given how famous she was in the 1930s, it is rather remarkable that, in the early twenty-first century, many more people in China and around the world are familiar with Mei, the heroine of the 1929 novel *Rainbow*, than have heard of Hu Lanqi. *Rainbow*'s author, Mao Dun (1896–1981), created the character of Mei after hearing about Hu Lanqi from a mutual friend. Mei's career closely follows the outlines of Hu Lanqi's life between 1920 and 1924. For various reasons, however, Hu Lanqi's identity as the model for Mei has never been widely known by readers of the novel.[3] Her own story has been ignored by most historians of China, despite the fact that, over the course of seven hundred very gripping pages, her memoir gives us a panoramic view of the most pressing issues and painful crises in twentieth-century Chinese history.

## Ideals for Women and Men in Early Twentieth-Century China

One of the striking aspects of Hu Lanqi's life in the 1920s and 1930s was how often and how far she traveled throughout China and the world. Until she reached the age of twenty, though, she rarely left her father's house. In her hometown Chengdu, people had long believed that good women should avoid being seen in public. Although many women did work in the fields throughout Chinese history, in cities they were supposed to stay indoors unless economic circumstances forced them into shameful occupations such as begging and prostitution. By the end of the Qing dynasty (1644–1911), when Hu Lanqi was born, the majority of women had their feet bound when they were very young. This discouraged mobility and was considered evidence that a family cared about the respectability of its girls.[4] If she had been born even five years earlier, Hu Lanqi probably would have had her feet bound. That she did not was perhaps the first sign that her life would be significantly shaped by a budding revolution in ideas about women's roles in China, extending to how they should be educated, what jobs they could take, and the nature of their social and sexual relationships.

Hu Lanqi writes that her father was a man of comfortable means, although it is not clear from her memoirs exactly how he came by his money. He was a descendent of a famous general in the Ming dynasty (1368–1644), she explains, and for that reason he (and presumably all of his forebears) refused to take up office under the Qing, who had defeated the Ming. He and his wife had nine children before she died in the late 1910s. When Hu Lanqi's father died in 1924, Hu Lanqi and her three surviving siblings inherited farmland and several pieces of Chengdu real estate, so it seems her family supported itself primarily from rent paid to them by tenant farmers and shopkeepers. They did not rank among the really wealthy. If they had, it is unlikely that Hu Lanqi's mother would have taken classes in the early 1910s to learn how to use a Singer sewing machine and then opened her own school in their family residence for other women seeking to supplement family income by sewing. They did have enough money, though, to send Hu Lanqi's older brother to law school a thousand miles away in the imperial capital, Beijing.

The education system was in the midst of great transformation when Hu Lanqi was a little girl.[5] The imperial civil service examinations had been abolished, and in their place a system of public schools was set up, including schools for girls. There were very few of these, however, until after the fall of the empire in 1911. Still, it became fashionable among some segments of elite society in Chengdu to send daughters to school. Hu Lanqi's parents placed her in a private school run by a young widow, a brickmason's daughter who had learned to read and write from a doctor who lived next door. The education Hu Lanqi received at this school was quite traditional: the students paid their respects to Confucius every morning by kneeling in front of his image. They memorized the "Three Character Classic," a time-honored way for children to learn simple characters, moral lessons such as respect for parents, and the outlines of Chinese history. "Teacher Cao was very skillful at using a bamboo stick to supervise us students as we recited our lessons; when the energy of the students in the class was low and our recitation was weak, she would whack the table with her stick. As soon as we heard that popping sound, we would all being reciting at the top of our lungs, as if she had broken open a hornet's nest."[6]

Although Hu Lanqi lived in relative isolation, surrounded mostly by women who could not travel about freely, she writes that she learned much about the outside world in conversation with them. Stories of women in unhappy arranged marriages made their way from courtyard to courtyard, and early in life Hu Lanqi learned the famous comment on a woman's lot in life: "Married to a chicken, follow a chicken; married to a dog, follow a dog." But this philosophy of resignation to fate was challenged by stories circulating in the modern newspapers that were beginning to appear in Chengdu in the first decade of the twentieth century. Hu Lanqi writes that when she was six or seven she heard her mother and teacher talking about Qiu Jin, a young woman from eastern China who left her husband and traveled to Japan to study. Qiu Jin (1875–1907) dressed in men's clothing and joined a plot to overthrow the Qing government. Her arrest and execution in 1907 were covered extensively in the newspapers and caused a great stir even as far away as Chengdu.

After the 1911 Revolution, revolutionary activists like Qiu Jin were declared martyrs and held up as models for the young. Hu Lanqi had begun attending one of Chengdu's public middle schools at this point, and she no doubt studied Qiu Jin's heroism there. But Chengdu's atmosphere was not very welcoming of heroic action by women. Hu Lanqi's parents made her live at the school because they were afraid of what might happen as she went back and forth along the mile of city streets between school and home. The collapse of the Qing dynasty and establishment of the Republic of China had been a chaotic process in Chengdu, and the streets were not safe, even for women carried by servants in closed sedan chairs. Local military leaders and bandits vied for control of the rich Chengdu plain throughout most of the period between 1911 and 1935; soldiers and ruffians were common sights in and around the city.

Hu Lanqi's mother fell ill and died sometime in the late 1910s. While ill, she engaged her daughter to the son of a friend named Yang. Hu Lanqi explains that her mother was anxious to find a good husband for her. Since the Hu family had helped the Yang family weather some tough economic times and become prosperous, Hu Lanqi's mother believed that they would treat her well. Hu Lanqi considered opposing the marriage, since she believed that she and her merchant fiancé had little in common. But after her mother and several siblings died in rapid succession, she went through with the wedding in the fall of 1920 to avoid paining her grieving father and grandmother. "On that day, I rode in a red sedan chair carried by eight men, crying my eyes out. What sort of wedding was this? It seemed just like going to a funeral."[7]

At this point, her story takes a very unusual turn.

Within a few months of her marriage, she and her husband moved to Chongqing, another large Sichuan city about ten days away from Chengdu by sedan chair, so that she could take a teaching job a friend had found for her there. She then hid out with the family of another friend until her husband gave up on her and returned to Chengdu. At the time, this was an extremely shocking story. Even more shocking, she was able to get away with it. Although the Chongqing school she had been working for declined to take her back because of her notoriety ("they looked at me as if I was a stranger"[8]), she soon found another teaching job. News of her bold action in abandoning her husband spread rapidly throughout Sichuan and actually won her a good deal of admiration among a group of young people who were struggling to change Chinese society. They helped her formally divorce Yang in 1923. Good timing and good connections saved Hu Lanqi from the disgrace and severe punishment that generally faced runaway wives in early twentieth-century China.

Just a year and a half before Hu Lanqi was married, young men and women in cities all over China had begun a series of demonstrations sparked by the decision at the Versailles conference ending World War I to transfer Germany's rights over territory in northern China to Japan, instead of restoring them to China. Many students at the new universities were outraged that the Chinese government had been unable to protect China's national interests. They launched the May Fourth Movement, as it was called after the date of the first large demonstration in 1919, which quickly broadened into a full-scale and wide-ranging attack on Chinese politics and culture. In Chengdu, hundreds of students demonstrated and gave speeches calling for patriotic action and cultural change. Hu Lanqi was very impressed to see a female student address a crowd of ten thousand people in a Chengdu park in the course of the movement.

Many May Fourth activists argued that China's national weakness was due to the lack of democracy and scientific thought in China. The custom of arranged marriage and the status of women had a bearing on both of these problems: if young people had to obey their parents in all such important matters, how could they develop the independence of thought necessary for the advancement of democracy and science? If women were slaves to their parents-in-law and husbands, how could they teach their children to be strong citizens of a Republic?

Hu Lanqi's decision to leave her husband came at the height of the debate over these matters. Most people who heard about her actions no doubt condemned her as a woman of no virtue. But among Sichuan's elite families, quite a few young men and women accepted the idea that marriage should be an agreement between two equal individuals. They also longed for romance. European novels in translation and many new Chinese novels had popularized the ideal of romantic love between men and women. Hu Lanqi's rejection of her husband gave these young people a romantic heroine to rally around. And some of her supporters were quite powerful. The unsettled conditions of politics in Sichuan during the early Republic had given rise to many competing regional leaders who tried to impose their rule on the province via their armies. Most of these militarists were relatively young themselves, graduates of the military academies set up in the last years of the Qing dynasty. Some of them shared the political views of the May Fourth activists, and most of them wanted to enlist the support of the sons and daughters of the elite in their efforts to control the province. One of them, Yang Sen (1884–1977), played a major role in Hu Lanqi's life.

Yang Sen had served in the Qing military in the last years of the dynasty. After the establishment of the Republic, he eventually became a regional commander with ambitions to become military governor of Sichuan. Hu Lanqi met him in 1921, when he controlled parts of southern Sichuan west of Chongqing. Through a friend's introduction, she went to work at the elementary school attached to South Sichuan Teachers College in Luzhou, Yang Sen's base. Because Yang Sen cultivated a reputation as a progressive military leader, he hired many recent college graduates as advisers and provided funds for schools, museums, parks, and sports facilities. Hui Daiying (1895–1931), an early advocate of Communism in China, was dean at the Teachers College during Hu Lanqi's time there and turned the school into a center of radical politics. In her memoir, Hu Lanqi writes that the teachers and students frequently discussed socialism and other ideologies and undertook physical labor together, a sharp departure from the old Chinese academic tradition.

Yang Sen's approach to the question of family reform was unique. He supported freedom of choice in marriage but believed that men, at any rate, should be free to marry as many people as they liked. He himself had five wives by the mid-1920s and encouraged all of them to educate themselves and become active outside of the house. Hu Lanqi taught two of them to read and was good friends with another, leading Yang to propose to her as well, she writes. When one of his younger wives made the offer on Yang's behalf, Hu Lanqi recalls angrily rejecting it: "I'm not as lacking in character as to do that. . . . I can't be a *taitai* (housewife)!" Yang Sen's wife gripped her hand and told her she was wise.[9]

Hu Lanqi didn't refuse Yang Sen because he was a military man. Although the Chinese press was beginning to call such men as Yang Sen "warlords" and blame them for the state of constant warfare that plagued much of China, many educated young people in the 1920s believed that China's weakness required that its male citizens receive military training and contribute to the military unification and defense of the country. So long as he shared her progressive politics, Hu Lanqi could look with favor on a soldier. So when a young officer she had just met gave her a copy of a short story collection by Lu Xun, China's most famous cultural critic, Hu Lanqi was touched. After a short courtship, she and Chen Mengyun married in spring 1925.

It was not the first marriage for Chen Mengyun, either, as Hu Lanqi quickly found out. His family had followed a custom that was relatively common in rural Sichuan in the early years of the twentieth century. When Chen Mengyun was a boy, they had engaged him to a girl they brought into their house to raise, thereby gaining a worker whom they could train to be a good daughter-in-law. In her memoir, Hu Lanqi observes that, in the cities, such girls raised by their parents-in-law were very pitiable. In the countryside, though, they could have a lot of clout in their families, since they provided essential labor power. When Chen Mengyun's first wife heard about his new marriage, she made her way with the help of relatives to Chongqing, where he and Hu Lanqi were living. "She was nine years older than Chen Mengyun and had raised him when he was a child. He didn't love her, but he feared her."[10] The first wife confronted Hu Lanqi and smashed up their room. A settlement was negotiated, and she returned to the Chen family home in the countryside.

Clearly, it was not just "modern" women like Hu Lanqi who could take the initiative to travel and manage their own affairs in the 1920s. Hu Lanqi's challenge to convention prompted this "traditional" wife to energetically protect her own claims in her husband's family. New technologies of communications and transportation and a decline in the stability of the social order were changing the life options available to all women, just as the new schools and the ideas they spread stirred a few to revolutionary action.

Shortly after her marriage to Chen Mengyun, Hu Lanqi decided to become a soldier herself.

## The Impact of War on Chinese Life

Mention has already been made of what might be called the cult of the military among Chinese youth in the 1920s. As the twentieth century progressed, more and more people were affected by the militarization of Chinese society. Both of the major political parties that ruled China after 1927—the Nationalists in the 1930s and 1940s and the Communists after that—sought to attract the most talented people into the armies they controlled. Military skills and habits of mind formed part of the curricula of public schools throughout the Republican period (1912–1949). And, even before the Japanese invasion of the 1930s, there were many opportunities for students to put their military training into action in the service of one of the dozens of regional commanders.

In 1923, advisers sent to China by the Third Communist International (Comintern) based in the Soviet Union brokered an agreement between the Nationalist and Communist parties under which the two pledged to cooperate to build a revolutionary government and army that could defeat all other regional powers and unite the nation. In 1926, under the command of Chiang Kai-shek (1887–1975), preparations were made to launch the "Northern Expedition" against all militarists who refused to recognize the legitimacy of the revolutionary government based in Guangzhou, a southern city near Hong Kong. Hu Lanqi and Chen Mengyun went to Guangzhou before the beginning of the Northern Expedition with the idea of joining the Nationalist Revolution. Hu Lanqi writes that the atmosphere was electric: she attended many rallies, heard rousing speeches by Communist leader Zhou Enlai (1898–1976) and other famous figures, and got to know some of the female revolutionaries, including Zhou Enlai's wife Deng Yingchao (1903–1992) and He Xiangning (1879–1972), the widow of Nationalist leader Liao Zhongkai (1877–1925). Chen Mengyun was admitted to the fifth class of the Whampoa Military Academy, which had been set up with Comintern help and was directed by Chiang Kai-shek and Zhou Enlai. He failed the physical examination, however. So, after they joined the crowds sending off the Northern Expedition troops in July 1926, Hu Lanqi and Chen Mengyun returned to Chongqing.

The Northern Expedition proceeded rapidly north to the Yangzi River, and the headquarters of the revolutionary government was moved to Wuhan, a major city in central China. The Whampoa academy relocated there also and began recruiting a new class of students. This time they invited women to apply. Hu Lanqi read the advertisement in a Chongqing newspaper and immediately decided to take the entrance exam. "In my school days, I had sung 'The Song of the Woman Soldier' . . . and read the 'Ballad of Mulan,' and they had stirred in me a desire to join the army and serve the nation, but up to then it had just been a fantasy. Now the central military academy was holding up a big flag to recruit women in Sichuan, promising to make my dream a reality. I can't describe how happy I was."[11] To prepare for the exam, she began studying middle school textbooks.

Chen Mengyun was not pleased when she was admitted, she writes. Nevertheless, at the end of 1926, she and thirty other young women from Sichuan went to Wuhan, where they joined several hundred women from other provinces in the first women's class of the Whampoa academy. Her classmate, Xie Bingying (1906–2000)[12] from Hunan province, claims in her own memoir that nine out of ten female recruits joined up to get out of arranged marriages and away from their families.[13]

Hu Lanqi and Xie Bingying agree that their military training and service was arduous, often frustrating, and occasionally petrifying. Both were powerfully moved by the camaraderie and sense of purpose they experienced in the army. They also learned to steel their hearts to violence and the sight of blood. Giggling girls were transformed into serious revolutionary soldiers. After a mere three months of training, the women's corps was sent on a "western expedition" to help repulse attacks on Nationalist positions by Yang

Sen's troops, among others. The women had been trained to do propaganda work—rallying local support for the Nationalists—and to nurse the wounded. Nevertheless, they carried guns and were ready to fight. Xie Bingying recounts how the group she was with captured three landlords whom the local farmers accused of rapacity and cruelty. After a short public trial, they were executed in front of the soldiers and farmers. "Waves of laughter and applause and shouting flooded the field where the three corpses lay."[14]

By the time their campaign ended, a month after it had begun, a political crisis in the Nationalist Party had erupted into the open and ended the women's military careers. Party leaders in Wuhan were outmaneuvered by Chiang Kai-shek, the leader of the "right wing" of the party, who had continued leading the Northern Expedition east of Wuhan toward Shanghai. Warning that the Communists were plotting a coup, Chiang demanded that they all be expelled from the Nationalist Party and that the government relocate from Wuhan to Nanjing, where he would dominate it. Given Chiang's military successes and the purge he had carried out against the Communist Party in Shanghai and other eastern cities, most of the "left wing" Nationalist leaders in Wuhan capitulated to Chiang. The military academy there was dissolved in July 1927, and Hu Lanqi, Xie Bingying, and all their comrades were released from the army. Xie writes that it was very difficult for the women to turn over their belts and guns, symbols of their status as revolutionary soldiers.[15]

Xie Bingying returned to her hometown in Hunan, where she was married to the man she had been engaged to since childhood (and, following Hu Lanqi's example, divorced him soon after). Hu Lanqi decided she did not want to return to Sichuan and the complicated family situation she would face there. Chen Mengyun's commitment to revolution was too weak, she decided, and she preferred to carry on the struggle without him. Between 1927 and 1937, she threw herself into politics, an aspect of her life to be examined in the next section. In 1937, though, she was in Shanghai and witnessed the Japanese attacks on that city, part of their all-out invasion of China. Once more military service called.

In the years between 1927 and 1937, the Nationalist government under Chiang Kai-shek had succeeded in overthrowing or gaining the allegiance of most of the major regional militarists. The Chinese army in 1937 consisted of central troops trained and commanded, for the most part, by Whampoa graduates. Many of the regional armies had been incorporated into the national army with their structures and leadership intact, however, so Chiang Kai-shek's control over them was never complete. And, since the split between the Nationalists and Communists in 1927, much of the attention of the Nationalist army had been devoted to trying to wipe out the Communists, whom they pursued across China during the Communist Long March of 1934–1935. The Japanese threat had produced a truce between the two parties late in 1936, and their forces were supposed to coordinate efforts to resist the Japanese in 1937. Nevertheless, hostility remained, and, even as Chinese fought against Japanese troops, the civil war never really ended.

Inspired by her service in 1927, Hu Lanqi organized her own women's support corps in the fall of 1937. With the help of the Shanghai YWCA, she recruited eighteen young women and trained them to work with the Nationalist Eighteenth Army stationed near Shanghai. Their responsibilities were the same as those she had been given ten years earlier: encourage local residents to support the Nationalists, raise troop morale, and nurse wounded soldiers. One of the corps's first acts was to organize teams of local women to help harvest rice at night in abandoned fields close to the front line. She acknowledged that she and her city recruits were useless in the fields themselves, but they gave moral support to the country women actually doing the harvesting and kept them from panicking when Japanese planes strafed the area.[16]

The Japanese quickly overran Chinese defenses and advanced west of Shanghai toward Chiang Kai-shek's capital, Nanjing. Along with hundreds of thousands of others, Hu Lanqi and her corps were forced inland. Eventually, after many grueling marches and sleepless nights, they made their way to Wuhan, which became the Nationalists' temporary capital for a time after Nanjing fell to the Japanese in December 1937. In Wuhan, Hu Lanqi gave accounts she had written of the work of her corps to the famous Chinese war correspondent, Fan Changjiang (1909–1970). These and her later reports were published and distributed widely in parts of China not occupied by the Japanese. Hu Lanqi's women soldiers became famous, and she herself was appointed China's first female major general by the Nationalists' Central Military Commission.

Hu Lanqi's reports and memoirs of the years of war against Japan provide a record of the devastation visited on China in the late 1930s. She didn't see some of the worst atrocities, such as those carried out on the people of Nanjing after its fall. Attacks from the air were frequent, however, and she saw the Hunan capital, Changsha, in ruins, torched by the Nationalist army to prevent the advancing Japanese army from taking advantage of stores of fuel and food there. Her corps encountered many dying and dead soldiers and civilians, and one of their male assistants blew out his own brains while cleaning his pistol. In 1942, after she had disbanded the corps, she was sent by the Nationalists' Ministry of Finance to reclaim abandoned farmland in Jiangxi province. Her mission was to set up a farm where children orphaned by the war could work to support themselves while receiving basic schooling. Just as things seemed to be going fairly well, a last-ditch Japanese action in July 1945 brought troops close to her farm. Once again, she took up her gun and rallied the local people to defend their community. A chilling anecdote from that period attests to the violence brought on by the terror and uncertainty people experienced throughout the war. As they prepared for the arrival of Japanese troops, Hu Lanqi's workers discovered a Chinese man lurking around her farm and became convinced he was a spy for the Japanese. After he refused to answer her questions, Hu Lanqi smashed him in the head with her pistol and told the workers to finish him off.

When Hu Lanqi was born at the turn of the twentieth century, no one could have imagined the bitter warfare that would one day lead her to kill this man. Civil war and Japanese invasion transformed China's social order, tearing apart communities, destroying many people's livelihood, and allowing energetic people who didn't flinch at danger and violence, like Hu Lanqi, to make new careers for themselves. Most women, of course, experienced war differently, many losing husbands and children and facing the terror of bombings, looting, rape, hunger, and dislocation. For Hu Lanqi, the tragedy of war dictated total commitment to the effort to bring about revolution and national liberation. All Chinese, male or female, rich or poor, should be willing to sacrifice everything and work together as equals.

## The Complications of Revolutionary Politics

Nationalism and revolution were the twin motivating forces in Hu Lanqi's life after she left her first husband, according to her memoirs. Her disappointment with the politics of her second husband, Chen Mengyun, was the first in a series of setbacks she encountered as she sought comrades in the struggle to save China. Deciding who was a true, and truly effective, revolutionary leader proved very difficult for Hu Lanqi. She allied herself with a wide range of political figures, and her "complicated" political history caused her serious problems after the establishment of the People's Republic of China (PRC) in 1949. In this, she was not at all unusual. Many, many people who were politically active in the decades before 1949 found themselves the targets of intense criticism and "struggle sessions" in the 1950s and 1960s. For Hu Lanqi, those years were more of a trial than the years of war with Japan had been. Even worse than the physical abuse she suffered was the Communist Party's 1957 judgment that she was a "Rightist" and a traitor to the revolution.

Over the course of the rivalry between the Nationalists and Communists in the 1920s and 1930s, each of those parties produced their own internal factions, and after many activists had lost patience with both in the 1930s and 1940s, independent "third" parties coalesced as well. People joined certain parties and factions within parties partly for ideological reasons but also because of personal connections. Hu Lanqi wanted to join a socialist youth group in Sichuan in 1924, but her application was vetoed because she was suspected of being Yang Sen's spy. She joined the Nationalist Party while in Guangzhou before the Northern Expedition in 1926. Then in 1927 while she was at the military academy, her old friend Chen Yi (1901–1972) visited her and persuaded her to apply to join the Communist Party. The leaders of the local Communist branch turned her down, she writes, because she refused to divorce Chen Mengyun, whom they considered to be too closely tied to warlords. By 1928, she had divorced Chen Mengyun and joined the Nationalist government of Jiangxi province, where she was in charge of women's work. Just before Chiang Kai-shek purged the leftist administration of that province in 1929, she was granted support by the provincial government to go to Europe to study social services there.

Hu Lanqi chose to go to Germany because, she writes, she wanted to learn how the German economy and social services had recovered so quickly after World War I. She soon made friends among the small Chinese community in Berlin. One of the students in Berlin, Liao Chengzhi (1908–1983), was the son of her old acquaintance from Guangzhou, He Xiangning, who had also helped find her a job after she was discharged from the army in Wuhan in 1927. Liao Chengzhi introduced Hu Lanqi into the Chinese-language branch of the German Communist Party in 1930 and helped her learn to read Marxist literature in German.

But her Communist credentials were called into question the following year. He Xiangning's good friend Song Qingling (1893–1981), widow of Sun Yatsen and sister of Madame Chiang Kai-shek, came to live in Berlin and befriended Hu Lanqi. When Song Qingling's mother died, she invited Hu Lanqi to accompany her as she returned to China for the funeral. Hu Lanqi stood with the family at the funeral in Nanjing in the fall of 1931, directly behind Chiang Kai-shek and Madame Chiang. When she returned to Berlin in 1932, she writes, the local Chinese Communists suspected her of sympathy with the Nationalists. They petitioned the German Communist Party and persuaded it to expel her. While she was appealing this decision, she began to organize and speak at rallies in Berlin to oppose the recent Japanese takeover of Manchuria, attracting the attention of the German authorities. After the Nazis seized power in Germany in 1933, she and many other Communists were thrown in jail. She claims that her party membership had been restored by the German Communists upon appeal, but the party was almost completely obliterated by the Nazi purges of 1933, and so it was difficult to prove her status.

When news of Hu Lanqi's arrest made it to China, Song Qingling and the writer Lu Xun (whose short stories Chen Mengyun had given Hu Lanqi ten years earlier) called on the German government to release her. She was expelled to France, where she immediately wrote an account of her experience. "In a German Women's Prison" was published in several languages and made Hu Lanqi famous. She was invited to attend a writers' conference in Moscow in the summer of 1934 and sat next to Maxim Gorky at a dinner at his residence. In Moscow she met several Chinese Communist leaders, including Li Lisan (1899–1967) and Kang Sheng (1898–1975). She writes that they asked her at that time to go to Hong Kong and act as a liaison between the Communists and disaffected Nationalist leaders. She accepted this assignment, even though her status in the Communist Party was still not entirely clear.

During her short stay in Hong Kong in the mid-1930s, she became acquainted with many political and military leaders who were unhappy with Chiang Kai-shek's government but then joined it again after the Japanese invasion. Between 1935 and 1949, she was associated most closely with Li Jishen (1886–1959), a commander in the Northern Expedition who led a failed rebellion against Chiang Kai-shek in 1933 and then served as a prominent Nationalist official during the war against Japan. Over the years, she served as Li's envoy during his frequent negotiations with other military officers. He probably provided financial support for her activities during the war against Japan, but her memoir is frustratingly vague on financial questions.[17]

Hu Lanqi was also in frequent contact with top Communist leaders throughout the war against Japan. This was fairly easy to do, since the Nationalists and Communists had agreed to work together in a United Front against the Japanese. But she writes that she was told by her main Communist contact, Wang Ming (1904–1974), to continue working for the Nationalist army and keep her Communist identity secret. Late in 1937, while she and her women's corps were in Nanchang, she had an emotional reunion with her friend Chen Yi, who by then was one of the top commanders in the Communist New Fourth Army stationed nearby and a prominent party leader. She told him that her corps would prefer to work for the New Fourth rather than the Nationalist army, but Chen's superior, Xiang Ying (1898–1941), rejected the idea, saying it might cause trouble with the Nationalist government. Nevertheless, according to Hu Lanqi, she and Chen Yi, who had fallen in love, became engaged.

During the Nationalist-Communist civil war that broke out shortly after the Japanese surrender, Hu Lanqi once again worked for Li Jishen, carrying messages from him to various Nationalist commanders advising them to abandon their support for Chiang Kai-shek. She herself urged Yang Sen, now serving as governor of Guizhou province, to go over to the Communist side. According to her account, he was pessimistic about the Nationalist cause but had no hope that the Communists would forgive and forget his own attacks on Communists in the past. He ended up accompanying Chiang Kai-shek to Taiwan in 1949, when the Communists took control over the Chinese mainland. Hu Lanqi, however, did not. In 1949, she was in Shanghai, hiding out with Communist friends. When the People's Liberation Army marched into the city, she celebrated. "I enthusiastically participated in the municipal committee United Front organization's study sessions, and longed for the organization to assign me work quickly, so that I could do even more for the Party and the people."[18]

She was disappointed. Her status as a member of the Communist Party was not recognized by the new regime. Communist leaders whom she had known for years did not want to meet with her. Chen Yi, whom she hadn't seen since getting engaged to him in 1937, was appointed Shanghai's first Communist mayor. When she asked for an appointment with him to discuss what work she could do for the party, she was told that he had already married and had children, so she should leave him alone. It is easy to imagine how insulted Hu Lanqi felt at that. As she recounts this incident in her memoir, she wonders how Chen Yi and his staff could have so misjudged her. Since the party had no use for her, she busied herself in other ways. After helping some Buddhist friends in Shanghai set up a vegetarian restaurant called "The Great Masses" (Dazhong fandian), she ended up taking a job as an accountant at an industrial college in the new capital, Beijing. A friend she had met in Europe in the 1930s helped her secure this position.

At first the years passed fairly quietly in Beijing. During the "Three Antis" movement of 1952, launched by the Communist Party in the name of rooting out bureaucratic corruption and inefficiency, Hu Lanqi had to report in detail on her accounting work. When her report failed to satisfy the party committee at her school, which suspected her of embezzling funds, she was questioned and criticized. Her soap and toothpaste were taken away. When she tried making a false confession, her supervisors became even angrier and locked her up for a month, during which time she contracted an infection of the joints. In her memoir, she writes that at the time she had two thoughts: first, she regretted not having been a little corrupt, so that she would have had something to report; second, she found it not at all surprising that she was suspected, since she handled a lot of money and had frequent dealings with workers and shopkeepers. And, besides, "people all over the world throughout history have been subjected to rough treatment, so what does it matter if I suffer a little?"[19] She ultimately was transferred out of the accounting office to a clerical job at the college library.

In 1954, the party started a campaign to criticize the writer Hu Feng, whom Hu Lanqi had known during the war against Japan. Her acquaintance with him hurt her reputation, and although she didn't lose her job, she was forbidden to work. She spent the time studying acupuncture. In 1957 she was caught up once more in a political campaign. The Anti-Rightist Movement was launched after Chairman Mao Zedong's calls for public criticism of the party had resulted in an outpouring of suggestions and complaints. Although Hu Lanqi herself hadn't made any public statements critical of the party or government, she did defend some friends who had in 1957. As a result, she found herself on the list of Rightists at her school. Already in her late fifties, she was sent to a foundry to reform herself through labor—pushing carts piled with coal. While laboring north of Beijing near the Great Wall, she learned that her younger brother had also been declared a Rightist for writing a "big character poster" critical of local leaders. He was assigned to a state prison farm and, during the Great Leap Forward famine of 1960–1961, starved to death.

While in the countryside in the late 1950s and early 1960s, Hu Lanqi practiced acupuncture, which she says was highly appreciated by the farmers she treated. Even in the regions surrounding Beijing, the state of health care at that period was very bad. After she was transferred from the foundry to a state farm and assigned the job of butchering animals, she claims that her acupuncture skills improved markedly. She was allowed to return to Beijing in 1962, but farmers continued to seek her out for treatment.

In 1966, the Cultural Revolution began, and once more Hu Lanqi became a target of attacks. Red Guards—high school and college students whom party leaders had called on to lead the new phase of the revolution—beat her until her hearing was damaged. They also burned the manuscript of a Chinese translation of Grimm's fairy tales that she had been working on since her return to Beijing.[20] The Red Guards had been instructed by Mao to lead the search for counterrevolutionaries, and so they subjected people like Hu Lanqi who had "complicated backgrounds" to interrogation. Work teams investigating her acquaintances from the days before 1949 demanded that she tell all she knew about their conduct and denounce old friends as Nationalist spies. When she refused, they threatened her with a death sentence. "I took seriously these threats intended to frighten me. My mind became confused and I began sometimes to talk to myself, as if I were speaking out loud in a dream. Then they accused me of pretending to be insane. It wasn't until several years later that I gradually recovered."[21]

Hu Lanqi's Rightist label was removed in 1974 as the Cultural Revolution wound down. She does not explain how that came to happen; presumably, some of her prominent friends had survived the purges and spoke up on her behalf. In 1975 her college told her it was time to retire, and she decided to return to Chengdu, her hometown. In the decades since she left it for the first time in 1921, she had made a few brief visits, but her younger sister still lived there. Some time before, Hu Lanqi had adopted one of this sister's sons as her own child. In the 1970s, he was working in a small town in northwest Sichuan near Tibet, and he invited Hu Lanqi to live with him. She tried it for awhile but decided she preferred life in Chengdu. In 1978, authorities in Beijing notified her that she had been cleared of all political accusations. In 1987, she was allowed to reenter the Communist Party.

In her memoirs, Hu Lanqi writes that she was ecstatic that the party had finally recognized her loyalty and contributions to the revolution. But she also recounts many stories of other patriotic people who, like her, suffered political persecution simply because they had associated with the wrong people and causes in the years before 1949. One such story helped to inspire her to become an activist once more when she was in her eighties. Huang Jilu (1899–1985), a well-known Nationalist official and scholar from Sichuan, fled to Taiwan in 1949, leaving his first wife and their children behind. The children blamed their mother for the abuse they endured because of their bad political status and class background. She was living in squalor and misery when Hu Lanqi met her and decided to spearhead a movement to improve the lives of the elderly. Hu Lanqi persuaded the West China Medical University to start a geriatric health center, helped raise funds for an eighty-bed retirement home, and organized an "Old People's Association" that quickly attracted one thousand members.

Hu Lanqi's restless energy, not dampened even by decades of political persecution, is remarkable. How did she avoid becoming bitter and disillusioned in the years after 1949? Certainly, she learned resilience from her experience of struggle before 1949. Her determination to defy social convention about women's roles, her army training, her service in the war against Japan—all of these strengthened her self-confidence and taught her to endure hard times in the hope for a better future. Although she mentions him very rarely in her memoir, it is possible that she was also influenced by Mao Zedong's writings, which emphasize the difficulties China would face in the task of building a better society and call on revolutionaries to prove themselves through self-sacrifice. On the other hand, she was experienced enough in the political struggles of the first half of the twentieth century to be cautious in the second. She admits in her memoirs that in the early 1940s she had considered joining the Communists at their base at Yan'an but had decided against it when she heard that an outspoken friend of hers had been "struggled against" during the Yan'an Rectification Movement of 1942–1943.[22]

Ultimately, her assessment of her own politics is rather harsh: she considered herself "immature" (youzhi). "In my actions, I relied on enthusiasm rather than analysis," she writes.[23] Enthusiasm pushed her to join whatever cause struck her as just and to work with anyone who seemed to be trying to help China. Her assessment of the Red Guards who had beaten her so viciously is the same. They were immature: committed to revolution but not thoughtful enough to figure out whether they were promoting it or only being manipulated. Hu Lanqi remained an optimist and an activist all of her life, and perhaps that was possible in part because she did resist analyzing the problems that tore China apart over her lifetime. She preferred to accept circumstances as they presented themselves to her and then forge ahead, fighting and surviving.

## Memory, History, and the
## Individual in the People's Republic of China

Hu Lanqi's memoir is a fascinating text, not only because it describes the life and times of an interesting woman. As a result of her experiences during the political campaigns of the early PRC period, she wrote and dictated her memoir with an intense consciousness of the political importance of each and every incident in her life. Her self-confessions of the 1950s and 1960s gave her practice in interpreting her life as a revolutionary, teaching her what to emphasize, what she could leave out, and what she needed to explain. Her memoir is a careful document that helps reveal the state of Chinese politics and historical understanding in the post-Mao decades of the 1980s and 1990s.

One example of this is how she describes top Communist leaders. As noted above, Hu Lanqi hardly mentions Mao Zedong, who dominated the Chinese Communist Party after 1935 until his death in 1976. References to Zhou Enlai, on the other hand, are frequent and laudatory. Like many others in the years after the Cultural Revolution, Hu Lanqi probably intended to imply a clear contrast between a cold, distant, manipulative Mao and a humane, moderate, caring Zhou. Her description of how Chen Yi treated her in 1949 is a more explicit criticism of the morality of a prominent Communist leader—so much so that her editorial assistant felt compelled to state that he only agreed to work with her because a friend of Chen Yi's family asked him to, assuring him that they did not object to Hu Lanqi's account of her relations with Chen.[24]

Hu Lanqi is very reticent in discussing her emotions and private life, except when describing her frustration at China's plight and the Communist Party's failure to recognize her revolutionary spirit. Her reticence is no doubt a reflection of the pressure put on all Chinese, first by the Nationalists and then much more vigorously by the Communists, to suppress individual feelings that might interfere with the needs of the nation. Several decades after Hu Lanqi wrote the story of her life, Chinese writers are now shifting their attention toward individuals' personal viewpoints and needs, and a new literature is emerging. Memoirists describe their love affairs and express confusion about how to behave in a rapidly changing world.[25] The certainties of the revolution have vanished. Those writers and readers of this new postrevolutionary age have a lot in common with the young Hu Lanqi, who left her husband to seek her own personal fulfillment. The young Hu Lanqi, disguised as Mei, is described in poignant detail in Mao Dun's novel *Rainbow*. Perhaps it is not too surprising that people these days are more familiar with her than with the Hu Lanqi who was a disgraced former Nationalist soldier, thwarted revolutionary, and activist for the elderly.

## Further Reading

Hu Lanqi's memoir was the main source for this essay, supplemented with some of her publications from the 1930s (see publication information in the notes). Mao Dun's novel *Rainbow* is available in a translation by Madeleine Zelin (Berkeley: University of California Press, 1992). Xie Bingying's memoir has been published in two quite different English editions: Hsieh Ping-ying, *Autobiography of a Chinese Girl*, Tsui Chi, trans. (London: Pandora, 1986) and Xie Bingying, *A Woman Soldier's Own Story: The Autobiography of Xie Bingying*, Lily Chia Brissman and Barry Brissman, trans. (New York: Columbia University Press, 2001). The earlier translation ends the account in 1928; the later one, by Xie's daughter and son-in-law, continues through the war with Japan.

Jon L. Saari's *Legacies of Childhood: Growing up Chinese in a Time of Crisis, 1890–1920* (Cambridge: Council on East Asian Studies, Harvard University, 1990) focuses on the lives of young boys at the time of Hu Lanqi's youth, but is a useful resource. On the May Fourth Movement, see Vera Schwarcz, *The Chinese Enlightenment: Intellectuals and the Legacy of the May Fourth Movement of 1919* (Berkeley: University of California Press, 1986). Debates over women's roles in the 1920s and 1930s are captured in the document collection *Women in Republican China: A Sourcebook*, edited by Hua R. Lan and

Vanessa L. Fong (Armonk, NY: M.E. Sharpe, 1999). An excellent study of the women's liberation movement, along with biographies of several women from Shanghai, may be found in Wang Zheng, *Women in the Chinese Enlightenment: Oral and Textual Histories* (Berkeley: University of California Press, 1999). On women who joined the Communist army before 1949, see Helen Praeger Young's *Choosing Revolution: Chinese Women Soldiers on the Long March* (Urbana: University of Illinois Press, 2001).

On Hu Lanqi's hometown, see Kristin Stapleton, *Civilizing Chengdu: Chinese Urban Reform, 1895–1937* (Cambridge: Harvard Asia Center, 2000). The Nationalist government and military is analyzed in Lloyd E. Eastman's *The Abortive Revolution: China under Nationalist Rule, 1927–1937* (Cambridge: Harvard University Press, 1974). Marilyn Levine writes about the experiences of Chinese studying in Europe in *The Found Generation: Chinese Communists in Europe during the Twenties* (Seattle: University of Washington Press, 1993). The campaigns of the PRC period are covered in Maurice Meisner's *Mao's China and After* (third edition, New York: The Free Press, 1999).

## Notes

1. Hu Lanqi is pronounced Hoo Lan-chee.

2. Hu Lanqi's memoir of her life up to 1949 was published in 1985. After her death, Sichuan People's Publishing House published a new edition that includes her recollections of post-1949 events, as well as a preface by Qin Yuqin, who compiled the post-1949 section from Hu Lanqi's oral narration, and a postscript by Fan Qilong, the writer who helped her edit the pre-1949 section. It also reprints "In a German Women's Prison," which she wrote in 1933. See Hu Lanqi, *Hu Lanqi huiyi lu, 1901–1994* (Chengdu, China: Sichuan renmin chubanshe, 1995).

3. Henry Yiheng Zhao discusses the complex relationship between Hu Lanqi's life, Mao Dun's novel, and Hu Lanqi's memoir in a stimulating essay entitled "'Hong' hou zhi 'Xia': zai xiaoshuo yu zhuanji chonghe chu" [The "Ruddy Glow" after the "Rainbow": The Place Where Novel and Biography Meet], in his book *Duian de youhuo* [The Lure of the Other Shore] (Beijing: Zhishi chubanshe, 2003), 35–44. The book has also been published in Taiwan, under the title *Shuang danxing dao* [Two One-Way Roads] (Taipei, Taiwan: Jiuge chubanshe, 2004). In that volume, the essay is on pages 40–49.

4. On the history of the practice of foot binding in China, see Dorothy Ko, *Every Step a Lotus: Shoes for Bound Feet* (Berkeley: University of California Press, 2001).

5. See Joshua Howard's biography of Li Chenggan in this volume for more on the late-Qing educational reforms.

6. Hu Lanqi, *Hu Lanqi huiyi lu*, 6.

7. Hu Lanqi, *Hu Lanqi huiyi lu*, 22.

8. Hu Lanqi, *Hu Lanqi huiyi lu*, 29.

9. Hu Lanqi, *Hu Lanqi huiyi lu*, 59.

10. Hu Lanqi, *Hu Lanqi huiyi lu*, 86.

11. Hu Lanqi, *Hu Lanqi huiyi lu*, 123.

12. Xie is pronounced She-eh. In the first English edition of her memoir, her name is spelled Hsieh Ping-ying.

13. Xie Bingying, *A Woman Soldier's Own Story: The Autobiography of Xie Bingying*, trans. Lily Chia Brissman and Barry Brissman (New York: Columbia University Press, 2001), 52.

14. Xie Bingying, *A Woman Soldier's Own Story*, 82. Hu Lanqi tells similar stories in her account of this action (see *Hu Lanqi huiyi lu*, 161–73).

15. Xie Bingying, *A Woman Soldier's Own Story*, 88–89.

16. Hu Lanqi et al., *Dongxian de chetui* [Retreat from the Eastern Front] (Wuhan, China: Shenghuo shudian, 1938), 15–25. War reports by Hu Lanqi and the members of her women's corps are also included in Hu Lanqi et al., *Zhandi yinian* [One Year on the Battlefield] (Chongqing, China: Shenghu shudian, 1939), as well as several other compilations. At the same time that Hu Lanqi organized her women's corps, Xie Bingying organized one as well, and took it from Changsha in Hunan to the Shanghai area. See Xie Bingying, *A Woman Soldier's Own Story*, 270.

17. Hu Lanqi rarely mentions encountering financial difficulties. In 1940 she returned to Chengdu briefly and bought some land on which she raised fruit trees, which suggests that she had considerable savings (see Hu Lanqi, *Hu Lanqi huiyi lu*, 483). She did complain that the Nationalist government did not fulfill its promises to fund her orphanage-farm in Jiangxi in 1944–1945 (526).

18. Hu Lanqi, *Hu Lanqi huiyi lu*, 609.

19. Hu Lanqi, *Hu Lanqi huiyi lu*, 631.

20. The story of the burning of her manuscript is not in the memoir itself but rather in her editorial assistant Fan Qilong's postscript (Hu Lanqi, *Hu Lanqi huiyi lu*, 694). Fan Qilong mentions this as one example of many significant incidents in Hu Lanqi's life that she described to him after the memoir was finished.

21. Hu Lanqi, *Hu Lanqi huiyi lu*, 659.

22. The friend whose experience in Yan'an had convinced her not to go there, Yu Bingran, committed suicide during the "Three-Antis" movement, but Hu Lanqi never learned why he was in trouble then. They had met in Germany in the 1930s (Hu Lanqi, *Hu Lanqi huiyi lu*, 620).

23. Hu Lanqi, *Hu Lanqi huiyi lu*, 665.

24. Fan Qilong, in the postscript to Hu Lanqi, *Hu Lanqi huiyi lu*, 688. Hu Lanqi states that she supported Chen Yi's family during the years of the civil war, after false reports of Chen Yi's death were circulated. They treated her as a member of the family, according to her (*Hu Lanqi huiyi lu*, 561).

25. On the cultural transformations of post-Mao China, see Geremie Barmé, *In the Red: On Contemporary Chinese Culture* (New York: Columbia University Press, 1999).

~

# CHAPTER TEN

# Zhao Ruiqin: A Peasant Woman in Gansu and Domestic Worker in Beijing

*Yihong Pan*

The festive atmosphere of the Chinese New Year was still in the air in Beijing in early February 1997, but the city felt cold and strange to Zhao Ruiqin (read Chow Ray-chin) with its dry wind and gray skies. Having just arrived along with two other women from a poor, mountainous village in the northwestern province of Gansu to look for work, she felt lost: "I was so scared and confused that I really don't remember much about the city."[1] At the age of twenty-nine, married with two children, a ten-year-old daughter and a five-year-old son, this was the first journey she had ever taken in her life farther from her rural village than her own county and the first time she'd ridden on a train. The journey had been long and exhausting, a five-hour ride on a bus winding along a bumpy, mountain road to the railway station at Tianshui, Gansu, and more than twenty hours on the hard seat of a stopping train with a change of train in between. There was a fast, direct train with soft seats and sleepers, but they could not afford such a luxury.

A fellow villager who met them at the railway station had already found them a job in a restaurant. Taken on the subway, a bus and another bus, and into the restaurant, Ruiqin began to work early next morning, having hardly recovered from train sickness. Her job was cleaning the windows and doors during the day and preparing food at night for the next day. A day's work lasted over ten hours. This kind of hard, low-paid job was easy to find in Beijing, a city in the throes of rapid expansion. "I never had to work so hard

177

before. But worse still, I was terribly homesick. Looking at the city kids on their way to school, I thought of my daughter. Will her father send her to school? I wanted her to go, but Yuge might not do it." Zhao Yuge (read Chow-Yu-ge) was her husband.

Yuge had not wanted Ruiqin to leave home in the first place. Ruiqin had made the decision on her own. It was just around the Chinese New Year when a fellow villager who worked as a migrant worker in Beijing came back for a family visit. She told Ruiqin what Beijing was like and how her job brought a much higher income than that of a farmer working in the country. Ruiqin was interested. Their mountainous location was poor, but Ruiqin's family had been especially poor. In 1995, Yuge had been diagnosed as having a tumor in his body and could not do much work in the field. They needed money for his medical bills, and they needed money to repay the debt of three thousand yuan for building a new house. Yet, Ruiqin could not make up her mind at first. Her children were still young. Although Mother-in-Law agreed to help take care of them, Yuge and Ruiqin's mother both strongly opposed this crazy idea: how could she, a simple illiterate countrywoman, survive in the big city? To them a city was a strange, dangerous, and hostile place. An aunt, however, encouraged her: "Go to see the outside world." Aunt lent her three hundred yuan as travel expenses. Ruiqin made the decision: "I had to; we needed the money." Three days after the Chinese New Year's Day, she and a girlfriend together with the returning woman embarked on the journey. When she left early that morning, Yuge was still in bed, not believing that she would actually go. She said good-bye. He got up and saw her off. Her daughter cried.

Home felt so much dearer and warmer now that she was in this dirty, shabby restaurant in Beijing. Overwhelmed by homesickness and the exhausting work, she and her friend quit the job and went back home after having worked for barely two days. Yuge was thrilled to see her back even though she had made not a single cent (they were not paid, as they had breached the contract) and had incurred more debt to pay for the trip. He told her that while she was in Beijing the villagers had seen on TV the news of Deng Xiaoping's death, and the TV showed the Tiananmen Square, the center of Beijing. Their daughter had looked for her mother on the TV; she had no idea how big Beijing was. The death of Deng, the dominant leader of China, was the first major political event that left a deep impression on Ruiqin. "Grandpa Deng was kind to us peasants," the elderly people told the young. They did not know much about the 1989 massacre, in which students and workers in Beijing mobilized prodemocracy demonstrations and Deng's leadership sent tanks in a bloody crackdown. The peasants knew that Deng Xiaoping launched reforms in 1978, which benefited them.

The first adventure failed, but while the villagers were still laughing at the two countrywomen, Ruiqin made her second journey to Beijing in the fall of the same year, this time with over ten other women of the village. She left Yuge with stronger determination: "This time I will stay there for three years without returning home. I will make money! If other people don't believe me and laugh at me, you should not!" Indeed, she would fulfill her promise, and she would make a change in her life and for her family, a change that she could never have imagined while growing up.

Born on September 1, 1968, the day of the Moon Festival, a time for family reunion, Ruiqin seemed to be fated to be away from home. The fifth in the family with three older brothers and one older sister, she was not a welcome blessing. Her mother was so disappointed at having given birth to another girl that she even thought of starving her to death, but the father intervened with the warning that this was illegal (although socially acceptable according to local custom). When she was only two years old, her father died of diabetes.

Ruiqin's village was several miles away from a small clinic in the nearest town, and poverty prevented many peasants from seeking medical care. Gansu province in northwest China is known as one the poorest regions in China. Located in the mountains, Ruiqin's county was no exception. For generations, peasants had cultivated land on the mountain slopes. By the early 1980s, the village still had no electricity. Only dirt roads linked it to the county seat. The biggest problem was shortage of water. You sowed seeds of wheat, corn, and potatoes, and if there was enough rain, there would be a harvest. If not, you would suffer famine. Daily, peasants of several villages had to walk up and down along narrow, winding paths to and from a spring, carrying water in two buckets on a shoulder pole. Even in 2004, they still relied on that one source of water, which they called the "Sacred Spring" (shen quan).

At the time when Ruiqin grew up, China was still in the Cultural Revolution (1966–1976). Mao Zedong and his radical central leaders implemented a series of policies that were supposed to promote the purest egalitarianism and socialism but that in effect impoverished further the Chinese peasants. They forbade peasants to engage in private economic activities, reduced the amount of private plots, limited livestock raising to only a few pigs and chickens, curtailed rural free markets, and discouraged sideline production such as orchards, market gardening, and handicraft industries. Although Ruiqin's mother was good at embroidery, she could not make any for sale to subsidize the family. Ruiqin's area is suitable for apple trees, but under Mao's decree that "grain is the key product" (yiliang weigang), peasants all over

China had to concentrate on grain production, regardless of the suitability of particular local conditions. As a result, the peasants worked day and night and still suffered poverty.

Having five young children, Mother had to remarry. A peasant woman alone could not earn enough to raise a family. Born in 1939, Mother had her feet bound as a little girl. When the People's Republic was founded in 1949, the Communist government's declaration of gender equality made her unbind her feet, "liberating" her from the old bondage. Gender equality, however, also meant that she must go to work in the fields since the party insisted that the most effective road to women's emancipation was to work outside the home. During the Great Leap Forward in 1958, peasants were organized into the people's communes. When the Leap led to the three years of great famine, peasants suffered starvation. Many died. In her village of about sixty households, only forty or fifty people survived and Mother was one of them.

Mother had two more children from her second marriage. The stepfather had been a widower from a nearby mountain village. He married into the house with the understanding that as soon as Ruiqin's eldest brother got married, he would take his wife and family back to his own village. This happened when Ruiqin was nine years old, but she refused to go with them. She disliked him. He did not feed the children enough and often beat them. Ruiqin cried and protested so vigorously that she was allowed to remain in the village with her second elder brother in their small house. Soon she learned to cook. Sometimes, Mother came for a short visit bringing food and handmade shoes. At night, Ruiqin went to share a room with a neighboring girl. It was a local practice for unmarried girls to share a room together, not only to keep each other company, but also as a practical solution to lack of rooms in their own house. Around the age of eleven, Ruiqin began to work outside the home, looking after oxen, carrying manure into the field, harvesting wheat, and doing whatever job she could in order to earn some work points in the people's commune. "What is the use for a girl to go to school?" her grandma remarked when her second elder brother was thinking of sending her to school. Only a couple of village girls of Ruiqin's age went to school in those days.

Generation after generation, girls grow up, marry, have a family, and deal with whatever hardships come along. Government might change; policy might vary, but the peasant life did not seem to change much. For peasant girls like her, Ruiqin believed that the future depended not on education but on marriage. Although the Communist Marriage Law of 1950 required free marriage, in rural China, arranged marriage at an early age was the norm. Relatives or neighbors helped the young find a spouse. After a couple of meetings, a wedding followed. Among the dozen girls of Ruiqin's age in the village, several had been engaged as early as the age of twelve. This was the time when the government was promoting late marriage. The legal marriage age in rural areas for women was twenty and, for men, twenty-two, but the locals simply ignored the regulation. People married around sixteen or seventeen without applying for a government marriage license. There would be a public wedding, and that was enough to ensure social acceptance for the newlyweds. It was unnecessary to have an official wedding certificate in this remote country. In fact, no peasants ever bothered with this even in the 1990s in Ruiqin's area.

At the age of sixteen going on seventeen, Ruiqin still had no marriage prospect. She had turned down two proposals. After all, a girl still had some say in such an important matter. One proposal had come from a man who lived much deeper in the mountains, where there were wolves around, and the other from a cripple, suffering from a disease caused by the lack of certain minerals in the local water. Her second elder brother became impatient: "If we don't get you married off I can't take a wife! You must agree whether you like it or not!" He needed money for his marriage. If Ruiqin agreed to marry, she would receive a bride price, which the brother could use to obtain a spouse for himself. This was the usual practice locally. Marriage was still a form of economic exchange.

A neighbor's wife introduced a third man. A year older than Ruiqin, his name was Zhao Yuge. Yuge means "rain brother." He was born in the rain when his mother was working in the fields. He is the fifth of the family with three brothers and a sister above him. The family was not well-to-do, and he had no education, but Ruiqin agreed. She was already an "old maid" in the village, and his village was in an attractive location. It was on the edge of a town, near a rural market and close to the local administration, with a post office, an elementary school, and a small clinic. To her this was a step upward from her isolated village. Besides, Yuge was not bad looking. She saw him once when going to the market. His clan belongs to the Northern Zhao and hers to the Southern Zhao, so there was no violation of the deep-rooted taboo against marrying someone with the same surname. She saw him again briefly when he came to pay a visit to the second brother. The bride price was the usual amount, 250 yuan and six sets of clothes. Second brother took all the money and three sets of clothes for his own marriage negotiation.

The wedding day was Chinese New Year's Eve in 1986. Ruiqin left her childhood village, accompanied by her future sister-in-law two days before. It was a special day for her: "I felt so sad and cried. Some women would cry a lot more. I did not think too much though. Doesn't every woman have to go through this?" Leaving home to marry into a stranger's house in a strange village was a frightening experience.

Ruiqin had a simple dowry—the three sets of new clothes given at the engagement, six pillowcases Mother had embroidered, a red blanket she bought with the money she made by gathering and selling medicinal herbs, and a red synthetic shirt, fashionable at the time, given by a close girlfriend. It also included a toothbrush and a tube of toothpaste given by her in-laws. Early on the wedding day, Mother-in-Law set up a pair of red candles at each corner of their small courtyard. An elderly lady was invited into their room to ceremonially "sweep" the *kang*, an earthen heated bed, typical in rural North China. She was invited to do this because she was a "good luck" lady, her husband and herself both being healthy and having both boys and girls. She swept the *kang* with a broom tied with red string, chanting auspicious words, and then spread walnuts and candies, all in even numbers, on the *kang*. Poor as they were, the wedding was celebrated with relatives, villagers, and a banquet of several tables each having eight dishes for the guests. The following day, Ruiqin began to do some light work in the house, and the third day according to tradition, she made noodles for another banquet. This was a test for the new bride to show her skills. She did well.

For several days after the wedding, the young couple was too shy to speak to each other, and when he took the initiative to talk, she was still too shy to reply. In her new life, Ruiqin soon made some women friends. It was much easier to talk to women. In the village, married women often gathered to do needlework, make shoes, and do knitting, especially during the winter season when there was not much work outside in the fields. Sitting on a heated *kang*, they chatted, laughed, and gossiped. Spring came; farmwork followed its rhythmic pattern. Ruiqin and Yuge gradually got to know each other. A year later, Ruiqin gave birth to a baby girl, Juan (meaning beautiful and graceful). The labor was at home, helped by a midwife. Following the local custom, she was not allowed to lie on the *kang* for fear of soiling it and had to sit on some sun-dried mud bricks on the floor. Fortunately, the labor went rather smoothly. Two years later she gave birth to a boy. The government's one-child-per-family policy was hardly imposed there. All peasants need male children to do the heavy manual labor in the fields and to take care of the parents in their old age. A banquet was held to celebrate his birth. A religious master was invited to choose a good name for him. When he was a year old, he got dysentery. For several days Ruiqin and Yuge waited at his side in the county hospital, but he died. Meanwhile in their village, married women with one or two children had been rounded up and put into trucks to be taken for a birth control operation. Village leaders left Ruiqin alone because all felt sorry for a young mother who had just lost her only son.

Ruiqin gave birth to another boy in 1992. This time, the labor was so difficult that she passed out. The fortune-teller named the son Jide (read Jeeda), meaning auspicious and virtuous. When Jide was seven months old, there was again birth control pressure in the village. Ruiqin agreed to have her fallopian tubes severed. She had a son, and in her words, "I did not want to have any more children. Looking around, women had to suffer so much just to give birth. We give our lives in exchange for the life of a child!" Yuge was unhappy about her decision, but Mother-in-Law supported her. She was a woman herself, having given birth to ten children, three of whom had died. Also too many children meant too much hardship, she knew.

The decade after Ruiqin's marriage was not just a time of a new stage in her life; it was a new stage for China as well. Mao Zedong died in 1976. Two years later, the Central Party Committee under Deng Xiaoping decided to launch economic reforms. The people's commune dissolved in Ruiqin's area in 1984. Farming was privatized. As the government has encouraged diversity in rural production, in Ruiqin's area, peasants have planted apple trees, bringing in much more profit than just grain production. Privatization of farming has stimulated production, leading to increased agricultural yields. About 1988, electricity came to Ruiqin's village. A couple of better-off families bought black-and-white television sets, and all the villagers went to their houses to watch it in the evenings. The TV brought a new world to Ruiqin and her fellow villagers. In Mao's time there was only a loudspeaker in the village that broadcast radio programs—news, propaganda items, and revolutionary songs and operas. Now with TV's more diverse programs and a relaxed political tone, Ruiqin saw a curious, strange, new, exciting, outside world, the cities of Beijing, Shanghai, and Hong Kong, even overseas, with names she could hardly pronounce. While the villagers were watching the TV, those with more knowledge of the outside world would volunteer explanations or comments, telling the others that their apples were sold all the way to these big cities.

A fundamental change was the "liberation" of peasants from the land. In the Mao era, the government implemented a tightly restrictive policy preventing peasants from changing their occupation. With the breakup of the commune system, what had been a massive disguised rural surplus of labor became obvious. One solution was to permit peasants to go to the cities to work at various jobs. These peasants have become known as peasant migrant workers. Many women peasants work as baomu ("nursemaid," "nanny," "housekeeper," or "domestic workers") in the cities. Rural areas have been suffering from overpopulation, whereas in the cities people are in need of help to look after babies, the sick, and the elderly. In 1984, the Beijing Municipal Women's Federation (an agency budgeted and administered by the government) established the March Eighth Domestic Services Company to help urban residents find domestic workers from various rural areas of China. In Mao's time young couples in the cities mostly had to rely on their own parents to take care of their newborn babies; some would hire nannies for a short period of time if they could afford to. When parents reached an advanced age, the younger generation was expected to take care of them. This traditional arrangement was proving increasingly inadequate. Lack of public facilities for child care and for other types of housework was becoming a common social issue, especially for women, most of whom were working outside the home. In 1988, Beijing had forty thousand rural women applying for domestic workers' jobs, and in 1989, three million rural women nationwide were working in the cities in this capacity. In addition, a great number of rural women have been working in other service industries, in restaurants, sewing, repairing various house appliances, hairdressing, and cleaning streets and buildings.[2]

To earn money, to see the outside world, and to gain self-autonomy has motivated increasing numbers of rural women to join the huge migrant peasant worker population in cities. Initially in Beijing, the majority of these domestic workers were unmarried, aged sixteen or seventeen, with little or no education. Most came from Anhui, an overcrowded province to the south, but gradually, married women from northern provinces began to arrive. In 1992, the first woman from Ruiqin's village left for Beijing. She was over forty years old and had a relative already working at Beijing as a migrant worker. She found a cleaning job in a hospital. Soon, she regularly sent back money and parcels of used clothes; she even sent a washing machine. It was rather useless, for there was no running water, but the machine was quite a show of modernity. Rumors went around about her: "Who knows how she has earned so much money!" "Women like her are waiting on other men, cleaning or something." Nonetheless, more women left for the city in spite of men's objections.

It was in such drastic changes nationwide that Ruiqin left home for the first time and again in the fall of 1997, when her county's Women's Federation and the Labor Bureau, in collaboration with the Beijing Women's Federation and the March Eighth Domestic Services Company, came to the village to hire women to take up jobs in Beijing. Ruiqin took this second chance. She did not want to continue to live a life like before, or like her mother's, working so hard and yet still suffering from poverty. She and over a dozen women in the village applied. Most of them were married, having at least one son, thus having fulfilled their duties to produce boys. The local women all would try to have at least a son. They would have to pay penalty fees for having more children. Sometimes when the birth control cadres came to the village, women went into hiding. All this was worthwhile as long as they could have sons.

After Ruiqin left, Mother-in-Law helped take care of some family chores. Juan, then ten years of age, was old enough to make simple meals, and Yuge worked on the small amount of land leased to them under the Agricultural Responsibility System. Like the first time, Ruiqin had only the clothes on her back and some pocket money, but she was more determined. Coming out of the railway station at Beijing, they sat on their chartered bus and passed Tiananmen Square. But she was not interested in sightseeing, only eager and anxious about her future.

A couple of days later, she got a job working in a paint factory. The miserable working conditions, crowded dormitory, and harsh forewoman were unbearable. She quit after about ten days. Then she got another job, through the March Eighth Domestic Services Company, as a domestic worker with a family. Again she quit because the employer's family did not treat her well. According to the contract there was a trial period, and after that whoever wanted to end the contract would have to pay a penalty. Ruiqin went back again to the Domestic Services Company. The next day, as she was sitting there with other women, a prospective employer came in and began to talk to her—this was the procedure of hiring. The job would be helping taking care of an elderly couple. Ruiqin agreed. She got to this new employer's home on November 11, 1997. The first thing she did was to make a long-distance phone call home. There was a telephone service in her local post office, which was close to her home. Yuge ran to the phone and was so happy to hear her voice. He had received no news about her for two months!

By November of 2004, Ruiqin has been working for that household for seven years. She might continue for some time more. Her employers, an elderly couple, are both retired government employees. Ruiqin's work is to do grocery shopping, prepare meals, clean the house, and do laundry with a washing machine. Aged ninety in 2004, the grandpa, as Ruiqin calls him, is in rather good health. The grandma, aged ninety-one, has injured hips but can walk and carry on with some basic activities on her own with a walking support device. Ruiqin shares a room with her and helps her when she needs it, for example, helping her when she takes a bath or pushing her wheelchair when she goes to the hospital. The hospital visit is not too often, about two or three times a year, so far, on average. The elderly couple has six children, three of whom live in Beijing. They often come to visit and help take care of some chores. When they come, Ruiqin cooks for them too. The average working hours are no more than seven or eight. Such a workload is comfortable compared with others. The starting wage back in November 1997 was 450 yuan in addition to free room and board. In May 2003, her wage increased to 600 yuan. Ruiqin regularly gets bonuses in cash or in things. When she is ill, the couple has a daughter take her to the hospital, and they help her with part of the bills. According to the contract, she should have one day off every week, and if she prefers not, she should be compensated with extra pay. After three years, she decided to take only three days off per year because the elderly couple does need help and because this would increase her income too. If she goes home for a visit, she will not be paid. Compared with other domestic workers from her area, Ruiqin believes that her situation is in the upper-middle range. She likes the sense of stability and familiarity with the same house. Some younger, educated peasant women might prefer to work in a restaurant, a hair salon, a small workshop, or as a domestic worker on an hourly basis, since all such jobs provide more freedom and flexibility and, in some cases, more pay.

The initial adjustment to the city life took some time. Ruiqin recalls, "At first, I was amused to find the bathtub in the washroom. What was this thing similar to a manger? Why did city people have to take a bath or shower often? This was not like home, where peasants got rained on, and that was their shower." Ruiqin is a bright woman, so it was not all that difficult learning to handle the natural-gas stove, to cook the food that the family liked that Ruiqin was not familiar with, and to do the regular household chores. It was hard having to bargain sometimes with the cunning male venders in the farmers' market or shopping in the supermarket with all the goods packed and labeled since she could not read and since many goods were unfamiliar. It was scary to go across the busy streets like other pedestrians who jaywalked easily and to have to take various routes by bus to visit her relatives. Especially frustrating was communication. To begin with, Ruiqin spoke only her own local dialect, unintelligible to her employers and people from other regions, and she had difficulties in understanding them as well.

After a couple of months the language barrier was over. Ruiqin learned to speak Mandarin, the standard speech, and even began learning to read and write with the encouragement of the elderly lady. She managed to write a few characters and the Arabic and Chinese numerals, but unfortunately, she did not persist. Yet, she is bright. As a little girl, she learned addition and subtraction. She has no problem handling money and daily purchases. She remembers all the telephone numbers of her relatives and friends, who have taken up various jobs as migrant workers in Beijing. While watching TV, she has learned a lot too. The TV programs show her a different world, with love stories, historical fictions, police and anticorruption dramas, or some series from Taiwan, Korea, Japan, Mexico, or the United States. "I am interested in all the TV series and I often explain to the grandma—she could not hear clearly. What I like the most is of course the TV series or films about rural life," she said.

Ruiqin sends almost all her pay back home every month. She has become the main provider of her family, and she has taken up a new identity, literally. Back at home she was called Shuiqing (read Shui-ching), but she had no idea how the name should be written. This wasn't important for a farmer's daughter or wife. Beginning in the mid-1980s, when the government implemented the personal ID system nationwide, under which everyone would have a picture ID, she did not bother to get one like many others in the village. When she left for Beijing, however, she needed to borrow her sister's ID. She was therefore known by her sister's name. When she got to her employers' family, she told them the false ID story. What was her own name then? She could only say it in her own dialect. Her literate friend was not exactly sure what the two characters should be; perhaps they were *shui* ("water") and *qing* ("clear"). Eventually, in the winter of 2000 when she obtained her official ID from her county's police station, the name became Ruiqin (*rui* = auspicious, and *qin* = a stringed musical instrument). At the age of thirty-two, she had an official name and officially recognized identity.

For the first three years, Ruiqin worked steadily without going back home. Other migrant peasants would go back annually. Ruiqin had her concerns. The trip cost money, and if she left, there would be no pay, and besides her employers would have to find someone else since they needed daily help. She would have to go through all the trouble of looking for another employer when she came back. She believes that for a Chinese peasant family, marriage is more for building and improving the financial security of the family than for romantic love, and for that reason, separation is acceptable. And she has a heavy responsibility since Yuge is in poor health. He might need another operation.

She missed her family all the time. Homesickness could be overwhelming. During the first three years at Beijing, she had no pictures of her family—taking pictures was a luxury. Later when she had some, she would look at them every day. In her words,

> At meal time, when I take up my own bowl to eat, I wonder what they are having for a meal. . . . When watching TV, my mind often wanders, thinking about

family matters a thousand miles away. . . . In dreams I go back to my childhood, looking after oxen, or back to the small room in our old house, never dreaming about Beijing. . . . My happiest experience in Beijing? That would be when I have my day-off to get together with my relatives. I can't sleep the night before.

On such a day they would dress up a little and meet at Tiananmen Square, a convenient place from all corners of the city. From there they would go window-shopping in the nearby Qianmen shopping district, full of traditional shops and street peddlers, or to the upscale, modern-looking Wangfujing Street.

There is a network of support in Beijing from her sisters-in-law, cousins, and fellow villagers, who have come to work like her. In this huge city far away from home, they keep in close contact and lend each other emotional and financial support. Telephone is the single most important means of communication. Ruiqin has one or two phone calls on average daily, and they would chat about everything, telling each other the difficulties in their working lives and their worries and concerns about home and children. They also gossip. News from home soon spreads throughout their extended community.

Although illiterate, Ruiqin can count days according to the Chinese lunar calendar all in her head. Once she knows when the Chinese New Year's Day is, she knows every day afterward what day it is. This is an important emotional link to her home since the local rural markets and community festivals all follow the lunar calendar. "You know today is a market day. Our house is close to the market and all the relatives will come to the market and visit us," she would tell the grandma and grandpa. At mealtimes, sometimes Ruiqin tells the elderly couple about village life, her life story, her large extended family, or the local festivals when peasants pool their money to invite opera troupes to put on performances. "The operas are not for us humans but for gods and ghosts. If we don't perform for them, there would be bad harvests. We have ghosts back home. It is true. My husband saw some. But Beijing doesn't, perhaps because it is too much crowded with all these people, traffic and so many buildings." She can be very articulate when she talks about home.

In the winter of 2000–2001, Ruiqin went back home for a month's visit for the first time after three years in Beijing. Her employers hired a temporary helper meanwhile, keeping the position for her. "You haven't changed much, Ruiqin," her villagers observed. Some who work as domestic workers in Beijing have. A neighbor complained that his wife forgot how to speak the local dialect—perhaps this was just showing off—and that she had become urbanized, dressing in fashionable clothes. Another woman would shake hands with men when she returned to the village, much to their embarrassment or amusement; men and women were not supposed to touch each other! Ruiqin did not feel she had changed, but Jide, her son, saw her as a stranger; he did not want to call her mother until many days later. And she found it a bit hard to readjust to the rural life, having to gather firewood to heat the *kang*, to cook with firewood or coal, or to have to be careful about using water since it had to be carried by Yuge from some distance away.

After a short month visit, Ruiqin left again for Beijing. The second visit back home would be in late 2003, in another three years.

Seven years as a domestic worker in Beijing, from 1997 to 2004, have changed Ruiqin. She has become the main provider of the house. She has gained a sense of confidence and pride in what she has contributed to the family. Her earnings have covered her husband's expensive medical bills for his operation at the county hospital, bought chemical fertilizers and insecticides, and enabled the family to hire laborers during the busy seasons for harvest and planting. Also, her income helped the building of a new house in April 2002. With the help of all the villagers, the house is larger and more modern: seven rooms, glass windows, solid wood rafters, brick walls at the front and two sides, and stone foundations. The building materials cost about ten thousand yuan plus food and drink for the helpers. For peasants, a house is the most important property of their own; the land still belongs to the state, only leased to the peasants to work on, but the house belongs to them. Since her village is close to the local market, the location of the house became ideal for starting a business. In early 2003, Yuge rented out rooms respectively for a small pharmacy, a barber shop, and a vegetable shop. The income was pretty good.

In 1997 when she left, the local men talked: why wait on other men while your men had to take care of children at home? By 2004, it is estimated that in Ruiqin's village and the nearby three roughly 70 percent of the 140 households have a woman working either as a domestic worker or at another job in the cities. Ruiqin's daughter and other younger, unmarried women were hoping to leave to work in the cities too. These women all send their remittances back home, and most of the money is used for house building. A good house would mean that family has a woman working outside. Their contributions have led to a construction boom.

Ruiqin's concept of consumption has changed a bit too. She would not mind Yuge giving pocket money to the children or spending some on cigarettes. Gradually, she has begun to think that she too deserves something for herself, some new, inexpensive clothes, for instance. Being very nearsighted, she has had a pair of glasses made, with a fashionable frame given by a granddaughter of the elderly couple.

Having been exposed to a larger world, she has begun to observe the world with a different and critical mind. She begins to ask, why are there so many differences between city and country, and between peasants and city dwellers? Why do farmers work so hard but still make so little compared to city people? Why do city people have a better life, better education, and medical facilities? It is so sad, Ruiqin thinks, that her mother and mother-in-law have suffered so much; they have never enjoyed one day of good life such as the city people enjoy. And why do city people feel they are superior to peasants? The elderly couple and their children are kind to her, Ruiqin feels, but in general, city people look down upon peasant migrant workers, who are doing the low-paid, heavy, manual labor jobs the city people do not want to do. Some feel that a domestic worker is just a servant, getting paid to wait on them.

Moreover, why do women live so differently from men? She commented,

> Rural women live a miserable life. I wasn't aware of this before since we all lived the same way. Giving birth was a life and death experience, and all had to undergo it several times. Now in the city, I have realized that the life of the peasant women is so hard. We have to work during the day like men. Back home men can rest and women have to cook and do all the household chores. Not just that, men beat their women regularly.

Even women themselves abuse other women. Ruiqin's own mother often complains about her daughters-in-law and sometimes beats them. When Ruiqin tries to calm her down, Mother would get furious at her for helping "outsiders."

However, she considers herself lucky that Yuge is not so bad-tempered and has a good sense of humor. He treats her rather well. When they fight, Ruiqin often has the upper hand and has managed to scratch him in a few places whereas he has only dared to beat her with a sunflower stalk. The frustrations are now that Yuge gets money he wants to spend on himself, and thinking that he is in ill health and might not live too long, he spends more time visiting neighbors rather than working in the field. He likes to smoke and drink. Ruiqin feels, "I cannot count on him, but he is a nice man. I have never thought of leaving him. I am not that kind of person! a person who forgets who she is."

"Why do city people have an easier life than us peasants? It may be fate," she figures. Fate determines where one is born, city or village, the social status of the family one is born into, and the kind of life one can expect or what opportunities one will have. But you might fight fate a little, too, she thinks, and for her, life is not all about hopelessness. She has her plans and hopes: "I would like to open a small convenience store when I go back. I hope our son would get a middle school education and learn a trade, while our daughter would learn to be a seamstress."

Home in that rural village is the center of her life. She does not hope to move into the city with her husband as some other migrant peasants have managed or hoped to do. She wants to return to her roots eventually. For all these years, she and her employers' family get along well. Especially, she and the grandma tell each other their concerns and worries, and she is a good listener. The grandma is grateful for her care and hopes that Ruiqin will stay to help her through her last days, and she even feels apologetic that this job keeps Ruiqin away from home. Ruiqin, however, is clear: "Grandma, I work here for my family and for my children. If I stayed at home to grow crops we would not make much income. I will return home one day and settle down."

One day in November 2003, a telephone call came with disturbing news. Juan, her daughter then aged sixteen, was pregnant, and the man was ten years her senior, crippled with polio. Ruiqin felt so guilty: "This is the result of my working in the city! Had I been home, Juan would not have to go to share a room with the younger sister of that man, who would not have taken advantage of my daughter! She is too young to be a mother, and too good for that man!" Having hurried back home, she and Yuge tried all they could to separate Juan from that man, but Juan was in love; it was already too late for an abortion. After quarreling, fighting, persuasion, mediation, and lots of tears, Juan had insisted: "What is wrong with a crippled leg? He is talented, and he is kind to me. You married a man with two good legs, you still have to leave home and go so far away to work in the city. My man can support me!"

Ruiqin and Yuge gave in. The wedding took place on the New Year's Day—no need for government registration or marriage license. In March, Juan gave birth to a girl. At the age of thirty-six, Ruiqin became a grandma. The son-in-law is indeed more capable than average. He is handy with many things and is willing to look after the baby when he is not out working in the fields or running his own small business. He writes good calligraphy. Juan now stays at home, looking after the baby most of her time, but she hopes that one day she might go out to Beijing, too, to find a job, not just for money, but also for experiencing a different life in a larger world.

Ruiqin stayed at home through the spring to help the building of another house of five rooms. Although this incurred some debt, Ruiqin's future income would cover this. Further major news came in early June of 2004: Jide, their son, passed the difficult entrance examination to the local middle school. Ruiqin and Yuge are so proud: the first one in the family to go to middle school, where he could learn to use a computer, and could hope for a different life from that of his parents.

The time at home was joyful. She and Juan became much closer. While not working, Ruiqin would spend time with relatives and villagers, just chatting. She said,

> I enjoy myself a great deal, so free. I don't want to watch TV when I'm back home; I like more to visit friends. I watch TV a lot in Beijing because life is boring there. City life is not all that attractive. Back home, we have blue skies and fresh air; I can see bright stars at night. And the summer is cool unlike Beijing's smoggy heat, and the spring at home is so beautiful when the apple trees bloom, but I know we are still poor and I have to leave again for Beijing.

In early June, she returned to Beijing, still working for the elderly couple.

Life has its ups and downs. Ruiqin keeps on. Isn't this what life is about—working hard to build a family, bring improvement in life, and build a secure future as much as one can? The economic reforms in China since 1978 have brought so many changes, which might have different meanings to different people. The changes have caused problems, ecological damage, polarization of wealth, social unrest, and corruption. In Ruiqin's village, "When you hear the loudspeaker it is nothing but cadres asking for money," Ruiqin remarked. Fundamentally, however, to Ruiqin, the economic reforms have provided opportunities, the opportunity to struggle out of poverty and to struggle to gain self-identity and autonomy, and to give a better life to her children.

## Further Reading

Davin, Delia. "Migration, Women and Gender Issues in Contemporary China." In *Floating Population and Migration in China: The Impact of Economic Reforms*, ed. Thomas Scharping, 297–314. Hamburg, Germany: Institut für Asienkunde, 1997.

Gaetano, Arianne M., and Tamara Jacka. *On the Move: Women and Rural-to-Urban Migration in Contemporary China.* New York: Columbia University Press, 2004.

Solinger, Dorothy J. "China's Floating Population." In *The Paradox of China's Post-Mao Reforms*, ed. Merle Goldman and Roderick MacFarquhar, 220–40. Cambridge, Mass.: Harvard University Press, 1999.

———. *China's Transients and the State: A Form of Civil Society?* Hong Kong: Chinese University of Hong Kong Press, 1991.

———. *Contesting Citizenship in Urban China: Peasant Migrants, the State, and the Logic of the Market.* Berkeley: University of California Press, 1999.

## Notes

1. This biography was based on intensive interviews with Zhao Ruiqin in Beijing. In April 2004, I made a visit to her home village in Gansu, when she was there for a short stay. I talked to her husband, children, mother, mother-in-law, and other villagers. I am deeply grateful to all of them for sharing their stories, and to Zhao Ruiqin in particular.

2. Zheng Xiaoying, chief editor, *Zhongguo Nüxing Renkou Wenti yu Fazhan* [Population Issues and Development of Chinese Women] (Beijing: Peking University Press, 1995), 97–98.

# Index

~

# About the Editors

**Kenneth J. Hammond** is associate professor of history at New Mexico State University. He is a specialist in the cultural and political history of the Ming dynasty and early modern China. He is the author of *Pepper Mountain: The Life, Death and Posthumous Career of Yang Jisheng, 1516–1555* (2007).

**Kristin Stapleton** is director of the Asian Studies Program at the University of Buffalo. Her research interests include the history of Sichuan province, East Asian urban history, and the history of Chinese humor.

~

# About the Contributors

**Daria Berg** is associate professor in the School of Contemporary Chinese Studies, University of Nottingham. She is a specialist in the gender history of eighteenth-century China.

**John Carroll** teaches at Saint Louis University and the University of Hong Kong. He is the author of *Edge of Empires: Chinese Elites and British Colonials in Hong Kong* (2005) and *A Concise History of Hong Kong* (2007).

**Joshua H. Howard** is Croft Associate Professor of History and International Studies at the University of Mississippi. Author of *Workers at War: Labor in China's Arsenals, 1937–1953* (2004), his current research interests include a history of child labor in China and the life and music of the radical composer Nie Er.

**Fabio Lanza** teaches modern Chinese history in the Departments of History and East Asian Studies at the University of Arizona. He works on political activism and urban space, and is currently completing a monograph on the invention of the category of "students" in early twentieth-century Beijing.

**Oliver Moore** is lecturer in the art and material culture of China in the Department of Chinese Studies at Leiden University. His research focuses on early and late visual media, and he is currently engaged in completing a study of early photography in China.

Breinigsville, PA USA
13 January 2011
253288BV00002B/31/P

9 780742 554665